Security Challenges and Military Politics in East Asia

SECURITY CHALLENGES AND MILITARY POLITICS IN EAST ASIA

From State-Building to Post-Democratization

Jongseok Woo

continuum

2011

The Continuum International Publishing Group
80 Maiden Lane, New York, NY 10038
The Tower Building, 11 York Road, London SE1 7NX

www.continuumbooks.com

Copyright © 2011, Jongseok Woo

All rights reserved. No part of this book may be reproduced, stored in a retrieval system, or transmitted, in any form or by any means, electronic, mechanical, photocopying, recording, or otherwise, without the written permission of the publishers.

Library of Congress Cataloging-in-Publication Data
Security challenges and military politics in East Asia: from state building to post-democratization / Jongseok Woo.
   p. cm.
 Includes bibliographical references and index.
 ISBN-13: 978-1-4411-9140-3 (hardcover: alk. paper)
 ISBN-10: 1-4411-9140-2 (hardcover: alk. paper)
 ISBN-13: 978-1-4411-8433-7 (pbk.: alk. paper)
 ISBN-10: 1-4411-8433-3 (pbk.: alk. paper)
 1. Civil-military relations–East Asia–Case studies. 2. Democratization–East Asia–Case studies. 3. National security–East Asia–Case studies. 4. East Asia–Armed Forces–Political activity–Case studies. I. Title.

JQ1499.A38C58 2011
322'.5095–dc22

2010026376

ISBN: HB: 978-1-4411-9140-3
      PB: 978-1-4411-8433-7

Typeset by Newgen Imaging Systems Pvt Ltd, Chennai, India
Printed and bound in the United States of America

Contents

List of Figures and Tables   vi
Acknowledgments   vii

Chapter One
   Security Challenges and the Military in East Asia   1

Chapter Two
   State-Building and Army-Building   23

Chapter Three
   The Dynamics of Military Intervention   63

Chapter Four
   Democratization and Building Democratic Armies   103

Chapter Five
   The Military and Democratic Consolidation   151

Chapter Six
   Conclusion   183

Bibliography   199
Index   215

List of Figures and Tables

Figures

Figure 1.1 Spectrum of the Military's Political Influence 7
Figure 1.2 Summary of Causal Connections 11
Figure 1.3 Security Threats and Major Domestic Actors 14

Tables

Table 1.1 Security Threats and the Military's Political Influence 16
Table 2.1 Ethnic Composition of the Military in Taiwan, 1950–1987 35
Table 2.2 Growth of the Armed Forces of the Philippines, 1965–1986 45
Table 2.3 Security Threats and State-Building 56
Table 3.1 Modes of Military's Political Intervention 96
Table 4.1 Taiwan–PRC Economic Exchanges, 1990–1996
           (in US$ millions) 119
Table 4.2 Distribution of Popular Votes/Seats in Legislative Elections,
           1986–1995 120
Table 4.3 Major Coup Attempts during the Aquino Presidency,
           1986–1989 129
Table 5.1 Post-Democratization Civil–Military Relations
           in South Korea 155
Table 5.2 Post-Democratization Civil–Military Relations in Taiwan 162
Table 5.3 Post-Democratization Civil–Military Relations
           in the Philippines 167
Table 5.4 Post-Democratization Civil–Military Relations in Indonesia 172
Table 6.1 Security Threats and the Military's Domestic Influence,
           Summary of Results 185
Table 6.2 Specific Manifestations of the Military's Engagement,
           Summary of Results 185

Acknowledgments

This book would not have been possible without the support, encouragement, and assistance of my mentors, colleagues, friends, and family members. First, I wish to acknowledge Zoltan Barany, my dissertation supervisor and mentor, who introduced me to the field of military politics when I took his class during my first year of Ph.D. study at the University of Texas at Austin. He was also kind enough to serve as my dissertation supervisor and provided helpful guidance throughout my dissertation years. After I left Texas, Dr. Barany read the book manuscript several times and gave me invaluable and scrupulous critiques on my writing. He may never know how much he has influenced me, but I truly appreciate his support and guidance. I also wish to thank the other faculty members at the University of Texas, including Patricia Maclachlan, Wendy Hunter, Henry Dietz, Tse-min Lin, Patrick MacDonald, Peter Trubowitz, George Gavrilis, Bruce Buchanan, and Lester Kurtz. Their comments and suggestions helped in improving this product.

I wish to thank my colleagues at the University of West Florida, including Alfred Cuzan, Michelle Williams, Jocelyn Evans, and Bill Tankersley as well as David Alvis, who is now at Wofford College. My colleagues, Michelle and Jocelyn, helped me from the initial stages of my book proposal. I would also like to acknowledge my graduate assistants. Brian Garst, now at the Cato Institute, helped me with documenting information related to the book. Jean Agustin meticulously worked on the endnotes of individual chapters and the bibliography; without his help, my book would have contained many errors.

I also wish to express my appreciation to the institutions that have provided me with funding for field research for this book project. I received the POSCO Korean Studies Scholarship, McDonald Research Fellowship, and Professional Development Award from the University of Texas at Austin, which enabled me to conduct field research in Seoul, South Korea, and library research at the University of Michigan, the University of California-Berkeley, and Stanford University. From the University of West Florida, I received the Research and Scholarly Activity Grants in 2008 and 2009, which gave me opportunities to conduct library research at the University of Southern California and Library of Congress in Washington DC.

Finally, but most importantly, I wish to express my heartfelt gratitude to my family. I thank God for giving me a wonderful wife, Eunjung, who always has a loving and caring personality. I love her so much. She has given me invaluable advice and feedback on the book manuscript. I am also thankful for my family members, my mother, my brother and sisters, and my parents-in-law, who always support my wife and me in our careers. They live in South Korea, and I miss them very much.

Jongseok Woo

CHAPTER ONE

Security Challenges and the Military in East Asia

Introduction

For the past three decades, a so-called third wave of democratization has swept across several Asian countries and, in the process, political influence of the armed forces has declined significantly. However, although most observers generally consider civilian control over the military as a given reality in post-democratization Asia, recent political events indicate that new democracies are not quite free from armed forces' political domination. The Thai military has recently staged a coup and removed the civilian leadership, while the notorious military junta in Myanmar has shown startling resilience to pressure from the international community. Less noticeably, Philippine politics have suffered from constant rumors and actual attempts of coups, while the Indonesian armed forces still enjoy political clout in the post-democratization period. Even relatively successful democratizers such as South Korea and Taiwan have struggled with depoliticizing praetorian soldiers during and after democratization. Despite different sociopolitical settings, armed forces in most Asian countries have played crucial roles in every stage of their political development—from state-building in the post-World War II era to the period of democratic consolidation.

Contemporary Asia features a variety of civil–military relations,[1] ranging from (1) decades-long democratic control of the military in Japan, (2) recent democratizers with relatively stable civilian control of the armed forces in South Korea and Taiwan, (3) democratizers with weak and unstable control over the top brass in the Philippines and Indonesia, (4) control of the military by a one-party authoritarian state in China, Vietnam, and North Korea, and all the way to (5) the military's political domination in Thailand and Myanmar. Except for Japan, most other East and Southeast Asian countries have experienced some type of military involvement in politics, either via a coup d'état and military dictatorship or junior partner of authoritarian civilian leadership. In these countries, the military as an institution has played significant roles in every stage of political development and decay, from the early state-building in the postwar period up to the current post-democratization era. One of the most crucial indicators of democratic consolidation in these countries is newly elected civilian leaders' ability to claim constitutional authority over the armed forces and military officers' political neutrality.

This book conducts a comparative analysis of the armed forces' political roles in four Asian countries: South Korea, Taiwan, the Philippines, and Indonesia. This book addresses important questions about the military's political role in Asian contexts from the early years of the republics (1940s–1950s) to contemporary post-democratization settings: What determines the armed forces' political influence and how does it affect overall political development? How do democratically elected leaders depoliticize the armed forces and establish firm civilian control over them? Finally, what is the most desirable model of civilian oversight of the military in post-democratization Asian politics? These questions have attracted much scholarly attention in other regions, such as Southern Europe,[2] Latin America,[3] and post-communist Eastern Europe,[4] and research on civil–military dynamics in these regions is already voluminous. Yet despite their prominent roles for decades, studies on Asian militaries have not produced theoretically rigorous and empirically rich products, as most have been confined to single case studies with little theoretical advancement.[5]

Previous work on Asian militaries suffers from a lack of rigorous factual analysis with multiple cross-country comparisons. Even multiple case works have been a mere collection of individual countries by different authors and, thus, are devoid of systemic comparison.[6] Therefore, this book intends to take the study of Asian military's political role one step further through a comparative analysis of four Asian countries: two countries in East Asia (i.e., South Korea and Taiwan) and two in Southeast Asia (i.e., the Philippines and Indonesia). Throughout the comparative analysis, the discussion focuses on how domestic and international security threats shape the military's organizational character, doctrine, and domestic political roles at different stages of political development, suggesting that the presence of significant security threats increases the military's overall power and role in domestic politics while a low level of threats hinders its intervention in politics.

Each of the chapters in this book shows that high threats in either the domestic or international arena—or both—bring about the expansion of the armed forces' organization and role expansion, creating favorable conditions for army officers to expand their political influence. At the same time, civilian leaders are tempted to mobilize top brass in the military into civilian politics because, when security threats are high, they have to rely on increasingly coercive means to secure both state security and regime security.

Consequently, high security threats as a structural cause shape overall domestic political patterns in specific ways—namely, the weakening of democratic norms and practices and the outgrowth of authoritarian and oppressive state apparatus maintained by the support of the armed forces. By the same token, changes in security environments provide major domestic political actors with opportunities to reevaluate the military's expansive political roles. The absence of imminent security threats strengthens the voice of pro-democracy groups vis-à-vis the authoritarian regime and the military, which explains why countries with benign security conditions experience more stable and thorough democratic regime transition with the military's complete withdrawal from politics. The presence of high threats provides the military with political clout and hinders stable democratic transition.

Given the condition of security threats as a primary structural cause, dynamic interactions of major domestic actors—civilian leadership, the military, and civil society—sculpt more complex and nuanced aspects of civil–military relations, ranging from the military's political domination to subordination to civilian leadership. In general, the presence of a strong civilian leadership prevents the military from dominating politics. A cohesive and unified army results in the professionalization and depoliticization of military officers, while a factionalized military becomes highly politicized and prone to intervening in civilian politics. Finally, strong and ideologically moderate civil society groups strengthen democratic norms and practices and work against the military's political intervention. The theory section of this chapter will discuss specific theoretical reasoning why this is the case.

Comparing Four Asian Countries

This book carries out a structured-focused analysis of four Asian cases from their state-building period in the 1940s–1950s through contemporary post-democratization politics. The method of structured-focused analysis has the advantage of sorting out, from numerous causal variables, key factors that have major influence on the dependent variable. At the same time, the structured-focused analysis makes it possible to apply the same set of research questions, variables, and measurements to the four cases under study. This method allows for the rigorous empirical testing of the presented theory.[7]

Paths of political developments in the four countries show interesting similarities and differences throughout different historical stages. Initially, the four countries embarked on the task of establishing sovereign statehood at the end of World War II. During the process, they had to cope with severe internal and external security threats with the onset of Cold War confrontations and the expansion of communism throughout the Asian continent. Furthermore, the four countries reveal startling similarities in terms of the rise and fall of the military's political roles. They all fought external and/or internal wars until they attained formal independence in the 1940s, during which the armed forces played roles as influential as their civilian counterparts. The countries also witnessed the armed forces' rise as politically influential bodies in the 1960s–1970s. Finally, they moved on to democratization and the military's depoliticization in the 1980s and 1990s (with Indonesia's democratization coming a little later, in 1998). In sum, the four countries' political developments reveal striking similarities throughout the second half of the twentieth century.

In addition to the similarities in terms of the military's political influence at different stages of political development, each case also demonstrates several noticeable distinctions at different historical stages. First, in terms of the security threats, South Korea and Taiwan mobilized enormous numbers of military forces to deal with both internal and external threats, while the Philippines and Indonesia had a relatively small number of military personnel during the state-building period (1940s–1950s). In the former cases, security challenges came from both domestic and international arenas whereas the latter cases dealt primarily with violence at home and insurgency movements. Second, South Korea (in 1961) and Indonesia (in 1965) experienced military coups and the installation of military dictatorial regimes. In contrast, the armed forces in Taiwan and the Philippines did not go through military dictatorship, but the top brass nevertheless participated in civilian political affairs under the guidance of authoritarian rulers. Third, the four countries pursued different paths of democratic regime transition. South Korea and Taiwan were successful democratizers, maintaining stable civilian control of the military, whereas democratization in the other two countries suffered from highly unstable regime transitions and politicized officers were unwilling to relinquish their political prerogatives. All in all, such similarities and differences present interesting questions. Exploring these civil–military interactions should deepen our understanding of political development and decay as well as the military's role in this process.

Throughout the comparative analyses of the four countries, explicit questions will be addressed. First, how did the armed forces in the four Asian countries come to acquire the ability to become dominant organizations and how did they evolve into highly politicized institutions? What factors contributed to the military's organizational and role expansion during the early years of the state-building? Certainly not every military had the capacity to overwhelm a civilian administration from the beginning; rather, many countries that achieved sovereign statehood had a small, poorly organized army in the early years of nation-building but later witnessed a vast increase in the manpower and organizational strength under specific circumstances. What brought about this dramatic change in many Asian militaries? The first empirical analysis of the book details the processes in which small and politically neutral armies turned into principal institutions that could overpower other sectors in societies.

Second, once the armed forces rose to become predominant organizations that possessed the capacity to overwhelm civilian politics, why did some militaries overthrow civilian governments via coups d'état and establish military dictatorial rules while other militaries subordinated themselves under the guidance of authoritarian civilian leadership? To be more specific, what made officers in South Korea and Indonesia stage coups and install military dictatorships in the 1960s while the top brass in Taiwan and the Philippines remained under civilian authoritarian guidance during the same period? Although the military's political influence was prevalent throughout the 1960s and 1970s across the four cases, notable differences also existed in the ways in which the army officers intervened in politics and authoritarian leaders exerted control mechanisms over the officers. The second part of the empirical work in this volume addresses the crescendo of the military's political power via different routes.

Third, what explains different modes of the military's disengagement from politics during the democratic regime transitions of each of the four countries? Specifically, what factors encouraged or motivated the Korean and Taiwanese armies to willingly withdraw from politics and come under the firm control by newly elected democratic leaders without significant military repercussion? Conversely, politicized army officers in the Philippines and Indonesia were unwilling to withdraw from politics, thereby making the democratization highly unstable and incomplete. What determined army officers' political orientation and behavior during democratization and how does this factor shape the post-democratization domestic politics? The third part of the empirical analysis in this book details the militaries' political roles during democratization.

The final set of questions deals with civil–military dynamics in the post-democratization era. What are the major obstacles and opportunities each state faces in institutionalizing civilian authority over the military? How will the armed forces' influence shape the road to democratic consolidation? What will represent the most desirable model of civil–military relations in post-democratization Asian societies?

Conceptualizing the Military's Political Influence

The military's role in domestic politics can take the form of numerous dimensions within civil–military interactions, ranging from the military's political domination to its subordination to the civilian leadership. The classical and most widely used scheme has been the study of military coup d'état, military dictatorship, and the praetorian state. However, as numerous scholars have already pointed out, coup/no-coup scheme is too simple and narrow to encompass a wider spectrum and more nuanced aspects of whole civil–military dynamics. Zoltan Barany notes that "the armed forces' political activism can take much more nuanced forms than coups d'état or the lack thereof and ought to be viewed as taking place along a continuum of multiple factors such as scale, means, and organizational prerogatives."[8]

A more recent and widely accepted dimension of the military's political influence involves examining civilian leaders' abilities to impose their will on their armed servants[9]; its core indicator is "who prevails when civilian and military preferences diverge."[10] Civilian control over the armed forces is stable when the latter willingly follow civilian leaders' orders—especially in foreign and security policy areas. However, although it is sufficiently broad, this scheme does not provide a specific classification of the entire spectrum of civil–military relations as the scheme is also dichotomous. Furthermore, the scheme has very limited utilities when applied to cases in which army officers remove civilian leadership and replace it with a military dictatorial regime. A more useful classification should have both sufficient width of spectrum from military domination to civilian rule and more specific and measurable categories of civil–military interactions within the entire spectrum. Some scholars have identified specific indicators of the military's influence in political and policy areas. For example, Timothy Colton enumerates four policy domains of military officers' preferences (internal, institutional, intermediate, and societal) and four methods of exercising their influence (official prerogative, expert advice, political bargaining, and force).[11] However, a more widely used scheme has been Alfred Stepan's conception of "military prerogatives" in 11 different political-policy areas, categorizing the military's influence from low to high.[12]

First and foremost, the military's political influence should be treated as a continuum between two extremes: from army officers' political domination to their total subordination to civilian leadership. More specifically, it should cover a wide range of civil–military dynamics, from military coup and dictatorship, to a less significant but still important institutional role under authoritarian guidance, to an indirect but significant informal influence with a veto power in important political decisions, all the way to total subordination under democratic civilian leadership. By elaborating upon several scholars' classification schemes for the civil–military spectrum,[13] this book classifies the wide spectrum of civil–military dynamics into four distinct categories: *control, participation, influence,* and *subordination*. *Control* signifies the military's political domination while *subordination* denotes civilian domination; *participation* and *influence* are located between the other two to denote more subtle and nuanced aspects of civil–military dynamics (see Figure 1.1).

More specifically, *control* refers to a situation in which army officers stage a coup d'état, overthrow civilian leadership, and establish military dictatorship. *Control* also includes cases whereby military officers execute what Finer termed "quasi-civilianization," in which coup leaders retire from the military and run for (in)direct/(non)competitive elections.[14] The cases of South Korea (in 1961 and 1979) and Indonesia (in 1965) are illustrative examples of this category. Meanwhile, *subordination* signifies a situation in which the armed forces are a politically neutral institution controlled by a democratically elected civilian leadership, which is the case in post-democratization South Korea and Taiwan. The military's subordination to civilian leadership is possible when the democratically elected civilian leaders exercise institutional—not personal—control over the armed forces in important political and policy issues.[15] *Participation* and *influence* are located between these two extremes. The armed forces may cross beyond their traditional role of defending the country against external threats and play an active and explicit political role as a junior partner or a guardian of authoritarian leadership, especially within administrative and law-enforcing areas (i.e., *participation*). Alternatively, army officers may stay outside the civilian political arena publicly, but exert significant informal influence over

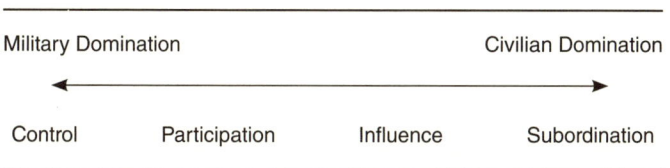

Figure 1.1 Spectrum of the Military's Political Influence

important political decision-making behind the scene (i.e., *influence*). *Participation* includes officers' involvement in politics in the Philippines (1970s–1980s) and Taiwan (1950s–1980s) whereas *influence* signifies civil–military dynamics in contemporary post-democratization Indonesia and the Philippines.

In measuring the armed forces' domestic political influence, this book relies on two major dimensions of the military's functions: "*scope*" and "*jurisdiction*."[16] *Scope* refers to the extent to which active or retired officers occupy important positions in the executive and legislative branches of the government. *Jurisdiction* refers to the military's decision-making powers in important political and security issues. The military's political influence is prevalent when its political presence is wide-ranging and when it possesses broad decision-making authority over not only the military and security areas, but also areas normally recognized as the civilian area of concern. Meanwhile, the military's political influence is inconsequential when limited within its own institutional matters (i.e., protecting the country from outside predators).

Multiple factors serve as specific indicators of the scope and jurisdiction, including (1) the number of active or retired military officers in key governmental positions (especially executive and legislative branches); (2) civilian leaders' decision-making authority in important government policies, especially in foreign and security affairs; (3) the military's compliance with civilian leaders' decisions on key security policy implementations, including military deployment; and (4) the armed forces' self-definition of primary missions, whether externally or internally oriented and whether security-related missions or nonsecurity/nonmilitary missions. Furthermore, civilian control of the military involves not only an objective control mechanism by the executive head, but also supervision and scrutiny by the legislative body. Therefore, oversight of the legislative branch in important security and military-related policy-making is also a critical indicator of democratic control of the military.[17]

Security Threats and the Military: A Theoretical Argument

Much of the existing literature on civil–military relations has focused on the problem of praetorianism, coup d'état, and military dictatorial rule in developing areas. Moreover, when dealing with the problem of armed forces' intervention in politics, scholars tend to rely on narrowly conceived institutionalist perspectives.[18] This institutionalist body of literature can be grouped into three major theoretical clusters emanating from the 1960s and 1970s literature: the "developmental" approach, the "military-centric" approach, and the "synthetic" approach.[19] These different strands examine military factors (personal ambitions, factional struggles, organizational character, corporate interests),[20] civilian factors (civilian leadership failure and sociopolitical crisis),[21] or both (concurrence of "disposition" and "opportunity," or "push factors" and "pull factors") to explain army officers' involvement in politics.[22] Despite notable differences in their theoretical arguments, each of the institutionalist perspectives shares one theoretical premise in common: explaining the military's political influence as a function of domestic political dynamics without seriously considering broader contexts of security threats. This point is more prominent in the study of Asian militaries than of any other region as Asian military specialists have focused on Huntington's notion of subjective and objective civilian control.[23]

Such an omission is problematic because the military is first and foremost a security institution that directly responds to domestic and international security challenges. Consequently, changes in security conditions should also bring about changes in the military's organizational character, doctrine, and domestic political roles. Yet institutionalist theories of civil–military relations simply assume as given the presence of well-organized military forces that can easily overwhelm civilian political power whenever they are willing. This dominant idea is well expressed in what Peter Feaver called the "civil–military problematique," which is a simple paradox: "the very institution created to protect the polity is given sufficient power to become a threat to the polity."[24] In other words, institutional theories begin from an assumption that any society has strong and well-organized armed forces, which raises the problem of the military's political domination when certain domestic conditions are met. However, historically speaking, not all military organizations have been strong enough to dominate society from the early years of state-building. South Korea and the Philippines, for instance, used to have very small militaries in the 1940s, but subsequently experienced vast organizational and role expansion through the experiences of internal and external security challenges, including interstate war and domestic insurgency movements. Thus, in many developing countries, a predominant military institution should not be assumed as a given, but one that expands in size and strength under the condition of high security threats.

In this respect, Michael Desch's approach to the military's political roles in changing security environments provides a fresh approach to the topic.[25] Desch encapsulates long-established arguments about security threats and civil–military relations, suggesting that a state with low internal and high external threats has the most desirable civilian control over the military.

According to Desch, when external threats are high, civilian leadership may become more experienced and knowledgeable about security issues. Moreover, high security threats will bring about a "rally around the flag" effect among the general public so that civilian leadership becomes stronger. Conversely, he predicts that a state with high internal and low external threats will have the weakest civilian control of the armed forces. In this situation, civilian leadership will be weak, divided, and inexperienced in national security affairs—a structural condition that can easily lead to military intervention in politics as the armed forces focus on internal security and nonmilitary missions.[26] Alfred Stepan concurs with Desch, presenting a similar argument in his discussion of the military's "new professionalism," in which army officers consider the internal security role to be their primary mission.[27] The major concern for both Stepan and Desch is the presence of internal security threats and their influence on the military's role expansion into nonmilitary areas.

However, the aforementioned causal mechanism—especially high external/low internal threats and firm civilian control—is not convincing enough and thus requires additional critical assessment. One should be critical about Desch's causal mechanism for several reasons. The first direct outcome of the presence of high external threats is the expansion of the military organization. When a state faces outside threats, the military consumes a large portion of its domestic resources at the expense of other sectors, making the armed forces the best organized and trained group in society. As Harold Lasswell points out, continuing external threats and war conditions create "garrison states" in which militaries specialized in violence become the most powerful groups in society.[28] Furthermore, high threats are detrimental to democratic norms and practices, as initially democratically elected civilian leaders rely on more coercive tactics to govern society. In turn, people are willing to suffer under a Leviathan-like oppressive regime when their survival is in grave danger. Consequently, high security threats bring about an expansion of a coercive military organization, more authoritarian civilian leadership, and an invitation of army officers to join the political realm by civilian leaders for state and regime security. On the contrary, an absence of serious security threats empowers civil society and pro-democracy groups vis-à-vis the authoritarian regime and politicized military, thereby putting the authoritarian regime into a defensive position. In sum, this causal logic is at odds with Desch's arguments, suggesting that high threats lead to the presence of a politically influential military whereas low threats lead to a politically inconsequential army.

Security Threats and the Military

This section develops a structural theory of civil–military relations that has a two-stage causal argument. First, security threats as a structural cause shape political opportunities, incentives, and relative power positions of major domestic actors—namely, civilian leadership, the military, and civil society. Second, dynamic interactions among the domestic actors serve as structural modifiers that determine a more specific and nuanced aspect of civil–military dynamics (see Figure 1.2).

The primary independent variable in this book is security threats, which can be either external or internal in origin and either high or low in severity. However, the term *security threats* is highly elusive and difficult to measure as it consists of not only a tangible threatening actor (both state and nonstate actors in both domestic and international arenas), but also civilian leaders' or high-ranking officers' perceptions of a threat. At the same time, civilian leaders or the top brass in the military can manipulate or exaggerate the threat perception for their domestic political purposes. Therefore, to measure security threats, the discussion herein examines individual countries' historical records of international war, small-scale conflicts, and domestic insurgents and guerrilla warfare. Furthermore, the investigation examines more specific historical contexts and the qualitative severity of security threats that each state faced. The perception of key political actors—whether civilian or military leaders—is also considered. However, the empirical chapters of this book will focus more on the factual information about the existence of threats in both domestic and international arenas.

High security threats, either in the domestic or international arena, may generate a structural condition for the military to be politically influential whereas low threats work against its political influence. As Samuel Finer has suggested, internal or external war conditions are "among the circumstances that may provide the military with opportunities for intervention"[29] and

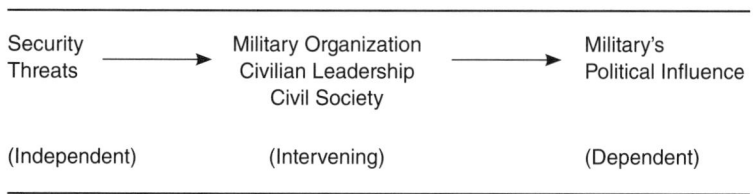

Figure 1.2 Summary of Causal Connections

dominance of domestic politics because the military is first and foremost a security institution that exists primarily "to protect the interest of one political group against the predation of others."[30] As the armed forces are a security institution created to protect the country from external attack, mounting security challenges will inevitably bring about the military's organizational and role expansion.

More specifically, high security threats produce politically influential militaries for several reasons. The first immediate effect of severe threats is the expansion of the military organization. As previously mentioned, existing literature on civil–military relations simply assumes the presence of a military institution that has the organizational capacity to overwhelm civilian politics. However, historical experiences suggest that not all newborn countries possessed strong armed forces that could dominate society from the beginning of the state-building process. Rather, most of these states witnessed the vast expansion of military organizations in the face of extreme threat conditions and the experience of war—or at least the constant threat of war and domestic insurgency. Thus, the presence of predominant army organizations cannot be a given condition for all societies, but rather an outcome subsequently shaped by security environments in the context of Cold War confrontations.

In addition to organizational expansion, high threats—especially the experience of interstate conflict or domestic counterinsurgencies—sculpt army officers' political beliefs that the military is the only institution that truly represents and defends the interest of the people. Such a belief is reinforced when civilian leadership fails to provide political order or undergoes factional-partisan infighting. The political voice of the military's top brass is strongest in countries in which the armed forces are deeply engaged in the state-building process. The political role of the *Angkatan Bersenjata Republik Indonesia* (ABRI; Republic of Indonesia Armed Forces) clearly illustrates this point. The ABRI developed into a strong organization during the independence war with Dutch forces (1945–1949) and assumed key administrative roles because the civilian government was barely functioning. The ABRI's role during state-building led the army leadership to declare the *dwifungsi* (dual function) doctrine in the 1960s, which codified the military's role not only in defense and security areas, but also in the executive, legislative, and judicial branches of government as an equal partner of civilian leadership.[31]

Furthermore, high security threats give civilian leaders structural incentives and opportunities to become more authoritarian and take coercive measures to rule society. Deteriorating national security conditions also serve as a threat to the regime security of civilian leadership. In this condition, civilian leaders consider the armed forces to be the most attractive strategic partner in securing both regime security and state security. Civilian leaders find it easier to mobilize officers into politics in order to expand their political power when society faces severe threats, whether domestically or internationally. This is particularly conceivable as the military's popularity among the general public rises when it is engaged in armed conflicts with either domestic insurgencies or foreign aggressors. Therefore, the direct outcome of rising security threats is installation of authoritarian regime and politicization of the military at the civilian leaders' invitation.

Finally, in this situation, civil society's influence in domestic politics becomes inconsequential. As previously discussed, one of the most prominent outcomes of unfavorable security conditions is the expansion and strengthening of the state apparatus that monopolizes the means of physical violence. High threats shift the power balance to favor the state apparatus over civil society. Worse yet, active or sometimes physically violent civil movements can aggravate domestic security conditions further, thereby providing authoritarian leaders with justification to bring the armed forces into the domestic politics in order to restore order. This vicious cycle of interaction is highly probable because civil society groups often adopt radical and physically violent tactics in response to civilian leaders' oppressive rule. Thus, domestic disturbances with violent interactions between the government and civil society provide the military with the opportunity and justification to intervene and install a military dictatorial regime.

On the other hand, the decline of security threats provides structural circumstances for a state to reevaluate the military's role in politics and security policymaking. More specifically, a low level of external and internal security threats creates few structural imperatives and incentives for military officers to intervene in politics. In addition, any civilian leader's attempt to mobilize the army into politics under these circumstances would be extremely difficult to justify and would generally face harsh resistance from domestic audiences. Meanwhile, the power balance between the state and society favors the civil society when no serious security challenge exists. Furthermore, civil society groups' pressure against authoritarian civilian leadership continues to be more influential. In sum, high security threats in both domestic and international arenas cause the military to be a politically influential organization whereas low threats render politicized army officers less influential, leading to a stronger civilian control of the military. Security threats' influence on three major domestic actors is summarized in Figure 1.3.

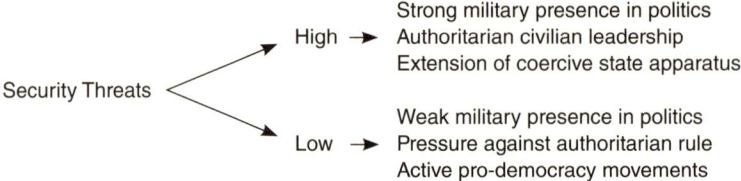

Figure 1.3 Security Threats and Major Domestic Actors

Structural Modifiers

Although the previous discussion illustrates a generalized pattern of the rise and fall of the military's political influence, it does not account for specific manifestations of its political engagement and withdrawal. That is to say, these structural conditions themselves cannot explain or predict different types of military involvement in politics—namely, *subordination, influence, participation,* or *domination.* For a structural theory to have explanatory power, other domestic variables as structural modifiers should also be considered. More specifically, three intervening variables at the domestic level—namely, the strength of civilian leadership, military cohesiveness, and civil society—explain the different modes of military involvement in and withdrawal from politics. Dynamic interactions among the major political actors shape specific manifestations of the military's political role in different stages of political development.

The first intervening variable at the domestic level is the strength of civilian leadership. The pattern of civilian leadership is the most crucial intervening variable, determining the ways in which the military both becomes involved in and withdraws from civilian politics. The structural condition of high threats renders the military the most effectively organized and trained organ in society, and civilian leaders mobilize officers into politics to deal with both state and regime security. Once army officers enter the political arena via civilian leaders' mobilization, it is the strength of civilian leadership that determines the modes of the military's engagement in politics. In other words, the military is likely to stage a coup d'état and dominate politics if civilian leadership loses its legitimacy or fails to maintain domestic security and political order. Given the presence of politically active officers, the existence of crisis situations or a power-vacuum in the ruling circle makes a military coup highly probable. On the other hand, politicized officers will remain under civilian guidance if civilian leaders exert strong leadership.

The strength of civilian leadership also accompanies different modes of the military's withdrawal from politics during democratization. The process of military withdrawal is highly unstable and incomplete when newly elected civilian leaders suffer from weak and divided leadership, fail to maintain political and security order, or simply lack support from pro-democracy groups in civil society. When civilian leadership is divided, weak, or perceived as illegitimate, military officers are unwilling to withdraw from politics and instead try to exert significant political influence—even after formally disengaging from politics. On the other hand, unified and strong civilian leadership that garners support from civil society encourages the military's complete disengagement from politics, resulting in more stable and complete democratization as well as the military's depoliticization.

The second intervening variable is the military's organizational cohesiveness through which structural influences are modified. A unified and cohesive army is conducive to stable civilian control and promotes military professionalism and its institutional autonomy.[32] Civilian leaders find it easier to monitor and control the armed forces when the military retains organizational unity with an effective hierarchical command structure.[33] However, a factionalized military creates two primary problems for civilian leaders: monitoring/sanctioning problems and factional groups' aspiration for political hegemony.[34] In a factionalized army, officers' allegiance is directed not toward their civilian masters, but toward their own factional leaders. Furthermore, interorganizational/interservice struggles, hometown/school loyalties, and interethnic rivalries can all create competitions within the military and promote its political intervention.[35] Consequently, civilian leaders find it hard to control army officers when army leadership is engaged in such factional competition.

The final intervening variable is the strength of civil society. Generally speaking, a strong and vibrant civil society functions as a deterrent to a military role in domestic politics. However, civil society may encourage a stronger presence of the military in politics, depending on the security threats and the strategy and ideology that civil society groups adopt. In times of high threats, the existence of a strong civil society itself may invite the armed forces into politics, especially when civil groups advocate for a radical ideology or adopt a strategy of physical violence, engendering sociopolitical chaos. Meanwhile, in times of low threats, civil society deters the military's political engagement when the former is ideologically moderate and adopts a nonviolent strategy for democratic reforms. At the same time, it is vital for newly elected civilian leaders during democratization to align with—and garner support from—pro-democracy civil groups.

Expected Outcomes

As presented, the structural theory has a two-stage causal connection. In the first stage, security threats determine the military's relative influence in domestic politics, as noted in Table 1.1. Civilian control is strongest and the military's political influence is minimal under the structural condition of low internal and external threats (Q4). Meanwhile, high internal and external threats bring about the worst civilian control of the military (Q1). To a lesser extent, a high level of security threats either in the domestic or international arena also stimulates a stronger political influence of the military (Q2 and Q3). These expected outcomes are exactly opposite of Michael Desch's hypotheses.

Although security threats in the domestic and international arenas determine the military's relative influence in domestic politics, the dynamic interactions among major domestic actors—namely, civilian leadership, the military, and civil society—are responsible for more detailed and nuanced manifestations of the military's domestic political role. A combination of strong civilian leadership (backed by strong civil society) and unified military organization leads to firm civilian control of the military. However, weak civilian leadership combined with a factionalized military breeds a potential coup d'état and a military domination of politics, especially when society faces grave security threats. The same domestic condition can lead to weak civilian control of the military, but a low probability of a military coup when threats are low.

Table 1.1 Security Threats and the Military's Political Influence

	High External Threats	Low External Threats
High Internal Threats	Worst Civilian Control (Q1)	High Military Influence (Q2)
Low Internal Threats	High Military Influence (Q3)	Firm Civilian Control (Q4)

A Roadmap to This Volume

The organization of this book is unique in that it differs from other edited volumes on Asian civil–military relations that simply catalog individual cases in different chapters. Each chapter of this volume is organized to compare all four cases at four different historical junctures, from the state-building through current post-democratization era. In this way, this book carries out a more rigorous comparative analysis across the countries under study.

The following chapters consist of a comparative analysis of four countries at four historical stages of civil–military relations. The four empirical chapters represent four distinct historical stages in terms of the military's political (dis)engagement: (1) the armed forces' role during the state-building period (1940s–1950s); (2) dynamics of the military's intervention in politics (1960s–1970s); (3) democratization and depoliticization of the armed forces (1980s–1990s); and (4) the building of democratic armies in post-democratization political settings (current).

Chapter Two explores how domestic and international security challenges during the state-building period shaped the armed forces' organizational structures and doctrines. All of the cases, apart from the Philippines, were forced to deal with overwhelming security challenges in light of the Cold War's military and ideological confrontations in the early years of state-building. For example, South Korea fought the Korean War (1950–1953) and faced subsequent North Korean threats. The Republic of China on Taiwan (ROC, or Taiwan) lost its civil war (1945–1949) with the Chinese Communist Party (CCP) and, after moving to Taiwan, faced even more daunting threats from the mainland Communists. Indonesia fought independence war with Dutch forces (1945–1949) and subsequently struggled with constant threats of national disintegration due to Islamist groups' rebellions throughout the archipelago. In all three cases, the first direct outcome of the security challenges was the expansion of the military organization. And these emergent democratic regimes did not last long as they degenerated into authoritarianism. In this process, authoritarian civilian leaders mobilized the armed forces into the civilian political arena to strengthen both national security and regime security. Meanwhile, the Philippines enjoyed favorable security environments during the state-building years, largely due to its geographic isolation from the Asian continent as well as an American security commitment. Until Ferdinand Marcos declared martial law in 1972, the Filipino political system was one of the most democratic among Asian countries, and the Armed Forces of the Philippines (AFP) remained small in size, politically neutral, and under civilian control.

Chapter Three explains how, once invited into politics by authoritarian leaders, the armed forces intervened in politics—either via coup d'état and military dictatorship (*domination*) or as the junior partner of authoritarian civilian leadership (*participation*) during the 1960s and 1970s. This chapter explicates how dynamic interactions among major domestic actors (i.e., civilian leadership, the military, and civil society) produced different modes of military intervention in politics. The politically active officers staged coups and dominated the political arena when three major conditions concurred in South Korea and Indonesia: extremely high security threats, failed civilian leadership, and factionalized armed forces. Meanwhile, Taiwanese and Filipino officers did not stage coups; rather, they participated in politics under civilian guidance when they had strong civilian leadership and unified military institutions. Empirical evidence from this chapter demonstrates that the strength of civilian leadership is the most important factor for preventing military coup d'état. Furthermore, military organizations that suffer from factional struggles breed officers' political ambitions whereas unified armies promote military professionalism and do not attempt to dominate the civilian political arena.

Chapter Four focuses on the dynamics of the military's withdrawal from politics during democratization (1980s–1990s). This chapter illustrates how changing security threats in the 1980s reshaped the relative power positions and political incentives of major domestic political actors (i.e., civilian leadership, the military, and civil society) to determine democratization and the army's depoliticization processes. Decreasing security threats as a structural cause initially enabled domestic political actors to reevaluate the armed forces' political roles, precipitating democratization movements such as those in South Korea and Taiwan. In these two cases, a combination of strong civilian leadership and unified armed forces brought stable and far-reaching democratization. However, the other two cases under study suffered from mounting domestic security challenges—namely, communist revolts and Muslim separatist movements in the Philippines as well as Muslim independence movements and communal violence in Indonesia. Worsening internal security conditions provided the armed forces with justification for their political influence, thereby making democratization and the military's depoliticization highly unstable and incomplete. In addition, two domestic factors—a weak/divided civilian leadership and factionalized armies—made military officers unwilling to withdraw from politics even after democratization.

Chapter Five illustrates civil–military dynamics in four cases in the post-democratization era. This chapter explains how South Korea and Taiwan have been more successful in establishing firm civilian control of the military and consolidating democracy than Indonesia and the Philippines. In the latter two cases, continuing domestic security challenges have posed barriers to establishing democratic control of the military. This chapter also illustrates that reorganizing the armed forces into a unified and cohesive institution is vital for making the armed forces professional and politically neutral. Finally, this chapter considers how the armed forces' political influence in these Asian countries will shape the road to democratic consolidation in the near future.

The conclusion brings together analytical findings from the four empirical chapters to provide support for and elaboration upon the theoretical arguments. The empirical findings demonstrate that a predominant body of institutionalist literature has limited theoretical utility in explaining the entire spectrum of civil–military interactions, from the military's political domination to stable civilian control. In addition, the empirical evidence effectively invalidates the conventional wisdom purporting to claim that high threats produce stable civilian control of the military. Instead, this book concludes that high threats bring about the expansion of the military organization, an increasingly authoritarian civilian leadership, and the politicization of the armed forces. Based on these theoretical insights and empirical evidence, the book concludes with relevant empirical and policy implications for the future of civil–military relations in these Asian countries.

Notes

1 For a recent comprehensive overview of civil–military relations in Asian context, see Muthiah Alagappa, ed., *Coercion and Governance: The Declining Political Role of the Military in Asia* (Stanford: Stanford University Press, 2001).
2 Hans Born, et al., *Civil–Military Relations in Europe: Learning from Crisis and Institutional Change* (New York: Routledge, 2009); Jurgen Kuhlmann and Jean Callaghan, eds, *Military and Society in 21st Century Europe: A Comparative Analysis* (New Brunswick: Transaction Publishers, 2001); Thanos Veremis, *The Military in Greek Politics* (London: Hurst & Company, 1997); Guillermo O'Donnell, Philippe C. Schmitter, and Laurence Whitehead, eds, *Transitions from Authoritarian Rule: Southern Europe, Vol. 1* (Baltimore: Johns Hopkins University Press, 1986); Geoffrey Pridham, ed., *The New Mediterranean Democracies: Regime Transition in Spain, Greece, and Portugal* (London: Frank Cass Ltd., 1984).
3 Alfred Stepan, *Rethinking Military Politics: Brazil and the Southern Cone* (Princeton: Princeton University Press, 1988); Louis W. Goodman, Johanna S. R. Mendelson, and Juan Rial, eds, *The Military and Democracy: The Future of Civil–Military Relations in Latin America* (Lexington: Lexington Books, 1990); Wendy Hunter, *Eroding Military Influence in Brazil: Politicians against Soldiers* (Chapel Hill: University of North Carolina Press, 1997).

4 Zoltan D. Barany, "De-mocratic Consolidation and the Military: The Eastern European Experience," *Comparative Politics* 30 (1997); David J. Betz, *Civil–Military Relations in Russia and Eastern Europe* (New York: RoutledgeCurzon, 2004); Timothy Colton, *Commissars, Commanders and Civilian Authority: The Structure of Soviet Military Politics* (Cambridge: Harvard University Press, 1979); David Betz, *Civil–Military Relations in Russia and Eastern Europe* (New York: RoutledgeCurzon, 2004); Timothy Edmonds, Andrew Cottey, Anthony Forester, eds, *Civil–Military Relations in Post-Communist Europe: Reviewing the Transition* (New York: Routledge, 2005).

5 Some of single case studies on Asian military include, Se-jin Kim, *The Politics of Military Revolution in Korea* (Chapel Hill: University of North Carolina Press, 1971); Ulf Sundhaussen, *The Road to Power: Indonesian Military Politics, 1945–1967* (New York: Oxford University Press, 1982); Monte R. Bullard, *The Soldiers and the Citizen: The Role of the Military in Taiwan's Development* (New York: M.E. Sharpe, 1997); Damien Kingsbury, *Power Politics and the Indonesian Military* (New York: Routledge, 2003).

6 Some of the edited volumes on multiple Asian cases include, Alagappa, ed., *Coercion and Governance*; Muthiah Alagappa, ed., Military *Professionalism in Asia: Conceptual and Empirical Perspectives* (Honolulu: East-West Center, 2001); Ronald James May and Viberto Selochan, eds, *The Military and Democracy in Asia and the Pacific* (New South Wales: ANU Press).

7 Alexander George and Andrew Bennett, *Case Studies and Theory Development in the Social Sciences* (Cambridge: MIT Press, 2005); Timothy J. McKeown, "Case Studies and the Limits of the Quantitative Worldview," in *Rethinking Social Inquiry: Diverse Tools, Shared Standards*, ed. Henry Brady and David Collier (Lanham: Rowman & Littlefield, 2004).

8 Zoltan D. Barany, *Democratic Breakdown and the Decline of the Russian Military* (Princeton: Princeton University Press, 2007), 10.

9 Peter Feaver, *Armed Servants: Agency, Oversight, and Civil–Military Relations* (Cambridge: Harvard University Press, 2003).

10 Michael C. Desch, *Civilian Control of the Military: The Changing Security Environment* (Baltimore: Johns Hopkins University Press, 1999), 4.

11 Timothy J. Colton, *Commissars, Commanders, and Civilian Authority: The Structure of Soviet Military Politics* (Cambridge: Harvard University Press, 1979), 234.

12 Stepan, *Rethinking Military Politics*, 92–7.

13 Samuel E. Finer, *The Man on Horseback: The Role of the Military in Politics* (New York: Frederick A. Praeger, 1962), 86; Eric A. Nordlinger,

Soldiers in Politics: Military Coups and Governments (Englewood Cliffs: Prentice-Hall Inc., 1977), 22–7; Claude Welch Jr. and Arthur Smith, *Military Role and Military Rule: Perspectives on Civil–Military Relations* (North Scituate: Dexbury Press, 1974), x.

14 According to Finer, the transition from direct military rule to "quasi-civilianization" is a recurring phenomenon in many developing nations. See, Finer, *The Man on Horseback*, 176–90.

15 Firm civilian control over the military is also possible in nondemocratic regimes. Authoritarian leaders' control, however, is possible only by politicizing the top brass in the military. Huntington's notion of "subjective control" clearly characterizes civilian control over the military in an authoritarian political setting. In subjective control, civilian leadership controls army officers by politicizing them. Samuel P. Huntington, *The Soldier and the State: The Theory and Politics of Civil–Military Relations* (Cambridge: Harvard University Press, 1957); also see Huntington, "Reforming Civil–Military Relations," in *Civil–Military Relations and Democracy*, ed. Larry Diamond and Marc Plattner (Baltimore: The Johns Hopkins University Press, 1996).

16 Alagappa, ed., *Coercion and Governance*, 32.

17 Andrew Cottey, Timothy Edmunds, and Anthony Forester, "The Second Generation Problematic: Rethinking Democracy and Civil–Military Relations," *Armed Forces and Society* 29 (2002): 31–56.

18 Ibid., 40.

19 More recently, some works on civil–military relations adopted the rational choice institutionalist perspectives. Some of the prominent examples include, Feaver, *Armed Servants*; Wendy Hunter, *Eroding Military Influence in Brazil: Politicians against Soldiers* (Chapel Hill: University of North Carolina Press, 1997); Deborah D. Avant, *Political Institutions and Military Change: Lessons from Peripheral Wars* (Ithaca: Cornell University Press, 1994).

20 Morris Janowitz, *The Professional Soldier* (New York: Free Press, 1960); Bengt Abrahamsson, *Military Professionalization and Political Power* (Beverly Hills: Sage Publications, 1972); Alfred Stepan, *Authoritarian Brazil: Origins, Policies and Future* (New Haven: Yale University Press, 1973).

21 Samuel P. Huntington, *Political Order in Changing Societies* (New Haven: Yale University Press, 1968); Leonard Binder, et al., *Crises and Sequences in Political Development* (Princeton: Princeton University Press, 1971); Claude E. Welch, Jr., ed., *Civilian Control of the Military: Theories and*

Cases from Developing Countries (Albany: State University of New York Press, 1976).
22 Finer, *The Man on Horseback*; Gary W. Wynia, *The Politics of Latin American Development* (Cambridge: Cambridge University Press, 1978).
23 Huntington, *The Soldier and the State*, 80–6.
24 Feaver, *Armed Servants*, 4.
25 See Desch, 1999; Michael C. Desch, "Threat Environments and Military Missions," in *Civil–Military Relations and Democracy*, ed. Larry Diamond and Marc F. Plattner (Baltimore: The Johns Hopkins University Press, 1996).
26 Ibid, 11–16.
27 Stepan, *Authoritarian Brazil*, 18.
28 Harold Lasswell, "The Garrison State," *American Journal of Sociology* 46 (1941), 457.
29 Finer, *The Man on Horseback*, 72.
30 Feaver, *Armed Servants*, 4.
31 J. Soedjati Djiwandono, "The Military and National Development in Indonesia," in *Soldiers and Stability in Southeast Asia*, ed. Soedjati Djiwandono and Yong Mun Cheong (Singapore: Institute of Southeast Asian Studies, 1988), 77.
32 Barany, 1997; also see Jongseok Woo, "Crafting Democratic Control of the Military in South Korea and the Philippines: The Problem of Factions," (paper presented at the annual meeting of the *Southwest Political Science Association*, Denver, CO, April 8–11, 2009).
33 Some scholars present an opposite argument, suggesting that a cohesive army is more likely to dominate civilian politics. See, for example, Morris Janowitz, The Military in the Political Development of New Nations: An Essay in Comparative Analysis (Chicago: University of Chicago Press, 1964); Stanislav Andreski, *Military Organization and Society* (London: Routledge, 1968); Finer, *The Man on Horseback*.
34 The rational choice institutional logic of civil–military relations clearly illustrates this point. See, Feaver *Armed Servants*; Avant, *Political Institutions and Military Change*.
35 Kposowa, Augustine J., and J. Craig Jenkins, "The Structural Source of Military Coups in Post-Colonial Africa, 1957–1984," *American Journal of Sociology* 99 (1993), 130.

CHAPTER TWO

State-Building and Army-Building

At the conclusion of the Pacific War in 1945, several Asian nations gained independence and embarked on state-building missions. Both during and after the war, all four countries that this book compares—namely, South Korea, Taiwan, the Philippines, and Indonesia—experienced some type of war and conflict, as evidenced by Korea's independence war with Japan and the Korean War, civil war on the Chinese mainland, the Philippines' war with Japan, and Indonesia's independence war with the Dutch colonial forces. These newborn nations further became the focal points of military and ideological confrontations throughout the Cold War years. Such security challenges during state-building years had tremendous impacts on the nature of the power of civilian political leaders and the military's organizational and doctrinal characters. This chapter explores how domestic and international security threats encroached upon the nature of civil–military relations during the state-building period in the four Asian nations.

The structural theory of civil–military relations detailed in the previous chapter suggested that internal and external threats affect the military's relative influence vis-à-vis other sectors in the domestic political space. Security threats influence both the armed forces and civilian leadership. Specifically, the presence of high threats brings about the expansion of the military organization to the detriment of other domestic sectors, as a large portion of domestic resources are allocated to the armed forces. In the civilian political segment, high threats result in the centralization of political power within one or a small number of political leaders—usually the head of the executive branch. Meanwhile, civilian leaders reverse democratic norms and practices to become authoritarian rulers who take coercive measures to safeguard both the regime's security and the state's security. When security threats are high, political leaders find it expedient to mobilize the top brass in the army into civilian politics for their political purposes. Thus, the apparent outcome of the presence of high threats is the military's organizational and role expansion, authoritarian civilian leadership, and army officers' influence in civilian politics.

This chapter explores how security threats during the early years of state-building led to the expansion of the military organization and its role expansion in four Asian countries. These four countries faced mounting security challenges with the onset of the Cold War, although the origin and nature of the security threats differed from country to country. For example, South Korea and Taiwan suffered from severe threats both domestically and internationally due to the presence of the communist regimes in North Korea and mainland China, respectively. Meanwhile, Indonesia faced difficulties in establishing a centralized sovereign statehood due to sociopolitical cleavages along religious, ethnic, and geographic constellations. Only the Philippines benefited from favorable security environments during the time of independence up until the late 1960s, when Maoist communist insurgencies and Muslim separatist movements surged, posing threats to the central government. All in all, variations in the nature and origin of security threats resulted in somewhat different patterns of political development across the four cases.

This chapter is composed of four major sections. The following section examines the security threats and the rise of the Korean army as a politically powerful institution in South Korea from the late 1940s to the late 1950s, when the first civilian president, Rhee Syngman, was forced to step down. The second section explores the role of the armed forces of the Republic of China on Taiwan (hereafter, Taiwan) during the civil war on the mainland and after the retreat to Formosa Island in 1949. The third section discusses political roles of the Armed Forces of the Philippines (AFP) as it grew from a politically neutral institution in the 1940s and 1950s to a highly politicized body under the Marcos presidency in the late 1960s and 1970s. Finally, the fourth section examines Indonesian armed forces' political roles from the years of the independence war in the 1940s through Sukarno's Guided Democracy in the late 1950s.

I. State-Building and the Army in South Korea

Liberation of Korea

The conclusion of the Pacific War in 1945 resulted in the liberation of the Korean peninsula from 35 years of Japanese colonial rule. However, the newly independent territory soon became a focal point in a worldwide military and ideological confrontation between the United States and the Soviet Union in East Asia. The two superpowers divided the Korean peninsula for temporary military occupation along the 38th parallel. On September 12, 1945, the U.S. armed forces established the Army Military Government in the southern part of the peninsula to rule the territory until the newly elected South Korean government took over political authority. Ultimately, the allegedly temporary occupation by the two superpowers resulted in the establishment of two permanent sovereign entities in Korea. General elections for the National Assembly in 1948 founded the Republic of Korea (ROK) (hereafter, South Korea) in the southern part,[1] while the Democratic People's Republic of Korea (DPRK) (hereafter, North Korea) was declared in September of the same year.[2] In South Korea, the National Assembly elected the first president, Rhee Syngman, one of the prominent leaders of the independence movements during the Japanese occupation period. President Rhee represented the conservative elements in society and was the United States' favorite due to his position of staunch anticommunism.

South Korea's defense force was created during the American occupation period (1945–1948). During this time, the U.S. military opened the first military training school, offering courses in English language and basic military skills to help facilitate the operations of the military government in Korea. This Military English Language Institute was subsequently replaced by the South Korean National Defense Officers Training Academy in 1946, which in turn was reorganized into the Korean Military Academy in 1948.[3] Through this army-building process in South Korea, the United States significantly impacted the country's military organization, training, and overall political orientation. The Korean armed forces were small in size— approximately 50,000 men—in the first year of the Republic. Moreover, military officers were not openly involved in politics, but remained politically neutral, as the Constitution prohibited active military personnel from assuming the post of the prime minister or a minister in the government. However, the Korean army soon witnessed an unprecedented organizational expansion through the end of the Korean War in 1953.

Security Challenges and the Korean Army

The state-building period involved severe security threats for South Korea, both internally and externally. Only two months after the South Korean government was established, North Korean guerrilla forces and antigovernment insurgents adhering to communist ideology began to infiltrate into South Korea's territory, organizing and supporting pro-communist guerrillas and impoverished citizenry to engage in violent uprisings in major cities as well as peasants in the rural areas in the context of socioeconomic chaos.[4] One such incident occurred in October 1948, when a South Korean constabulary regiment, indoctrinated by communist ideology, revolted against the government and occupied the cities of Yosu, Sunchon, and several towns located in the southwestern part of the Korean peninsula. Although the Korean army put down the insurrection, hundreds of guerrilla forces escaped into the mountains to continue the guerrilla war. One month after the incident, another revolt by a constabulary force took place in Daegu City, in southeastern Korea. Although military units quickly suppressed these insurrections by the Korean constabulary forces, the incidents revealed that guerrilla forces were already posing serious threats to the newborn government in South Korea.

These guerrilla incidents forced the Rhee Syngman government to adopt strong anticommunist schemes. Immediately after these insurrections, the National Assembly acted swiftly to pass the National Security Law. Article 1 of this law called for defending "the national security and interests" from the enemy of the state, which the law defined as "any association, groups, or organizations" that plotted against the state.[5] The law was initially applied against the South Korean Labor Party and other pro-communist groups; however, the Rhee regime later used it to suppress any political opposition activities, including opposition political leaders, religious organizations, labor unions, student movements, and newspapers. In sum, domestic security threats that emerged from the beginning of the republic enabled the democratically elected Rhee government to become increasingly authoritarian and take coercive measures to govern the country.

In addition to the threats from the domestic insurgency movements, changes in external security environments gave rise to even more challenges to the newborn country, stemming from the expansion of communism throughout East Asia. In mainland China, Chiang Kai-shek's Kuomintang (KMT) government lost the civil war with the Chinese Communist Party (CCP) and retreated to Taiwan in 1949. Victorious Mao Tse-tung and the CCP proclaimed the People's Republic of China on the mainland, which created grave concerns for the Rhee government. To make matters worse, the United States National Security Council decided to withdraw U.S. troops from South Korea as early as April 1948. By June 1949, the United States had almost completely pulled its armed forces from South Korea, leaving only the Provisional Military Advisory Group to the Republic of Korea, with approximately 500 personnel.[6] The withdrawal of the American military forces, coupled with Chinese communization, served to deteriorate South Korea's security environment significantly.

Yet it was the Korean War that brought significant changes to the political topography in general as well as specific organizational and doctrinal characteristics of the armed forces and their domestic political roles. As early as 1949, both Koreas were launching military attacks and counterattacks along the borders. While the military confrontations were swelling, U.S. Secretary of State Dean Acheson gave a speech that signified the United States' defense perimeter in Asia.[7] The containment line excluded South Korea and Taiwan. As a result, after Acheson's defensive perimeter speech, Joseph Stalin gave permission to North Korean leader Kim Il-sung to attack South Korea. With the approval from both Stalin and Mao and with all American forces already withdrawn from South Korea, North Korean forces embarked on a massive attack upon South Korea on June 25, 1950. Although the South Korean armed forces already numbered slightly more than 100,000 at the outbreak of the war, they were so poorly trained and equipped that North Korean forces occupied Seoul—the capital city—within just three days of the initiation of the war.

Korean society made tremendous sacrifices during the war, which resulted in the deaths of three million people—roughly 10 percent of the total population of the two Koreas.[8] The Korean War ended with no clear victor, but rather an agreement of armistice, formally concluded between the United Nations Command (UNC) and the communists on July 27, 1953. Although the armistice agreement did bring a precarious peace to the peninsula, it also continued to aggravate the military and ideological confrontation between the two Koreas.

The first direct outcome of the Korean War was the expansion of the military organization and its political roles.[9] The war resulted in a massive expansion of military institutions in South Korea. During the state-building period of 1948, the South Korean defense forces numbered approximately 50,000 men. Even at the beginning of the war in 1950, this number amounted to a little more than 100,000 of poorly equipped and trained forces.[10] However, the war forced the country to move toward total mobilization of domestic resources for military buildup. At the conclusion of the war, South Korea had armed forces amounting to 700,000 of heavily armed and trained personnel. Consequently, the South Korean army had developed into the best-organized and funded state institution, consuming over a half of total governmental expenditures throughout the 1950s.[11] During this military buildup process, the United States became the army's most crucial supporter and builder. Immediately after the armistice agreement was signed on October 1, 1953, South Korea and the United States signed a Mutual Defense Treaty, culminating in American military assistance totaling nearly $6 billion from 1950 to 1979—the equivalent of almost 80 percent of South Korean defense spending and 10 percent of the country's gross national product (GNP) during this period.[12]

President Rhee Syngman and the Military

In addition to the organizational expansion of the armed forces, three years of war left the democratically elected President Rhee as an almost omnipotent figure in postwar Korean politics. During the war, Rhee strengthened his political position and centralized political power by revising the constitution and terrorizing opposition political forces. Through such efforts, the president mobilized the military for his political ambitions. The war and continuing threats from North Korea fostered the preoccupation of military officers as well as the general public with a strong conservative and anticommunist ideology.

In centralizing its political power, the Rhee regime actively exploited the communist threat from North Korea and anticommunist ideology, satisfying two important political purposes. First, in domestic politics, the threat perception and antagonism against communist North Korea bred a "rally around the flag" effect that unified the general public and the military under the Rhee leadership, which served to justify the centralization of political power in his hands. Due to continuing threats from North Korea, South Korean society showed little antipathy to Rhee's increasingly authoritarian rule. Second, in international political realms, Rhee's staunch anticommunist position helped ensure continuous American military and economic support throughout his rule. The United States needed a prominent and symbolic political leader who had experience in leading the independence war against Japanese colonial forces and therefore had a high regard among the general public. At the same time, the leader was supposed to have a strong anticommunist ideology in order to support the American grand strategy in East Asia. Rhee satisfied all these qualifications, thereby enabling him to gain continued support from the United States even when he became an authoritarian leader in South Korea.

The first momentum of strengthening Rhee's political power came during the 1952 presidential election, when the Rhee government attempted to revise the 1948 Constitution so that the president was elected through popular referendum, not by the National Assembly vote. Rhee wanted to revise the Constitution to include a popular election for two reasons. First, he did not have a broad support base within the National Assembly—even within his own political party. Second, he had developed a hostile relationship with the National Assembly from the beginning of the government formation in 1948 due to differences in the form of government. Most legislators favored a cabinet political system, whereas Rhee pursued a strong presidential system. Given this hostile relationship, Rhee was certain to fail in the presidential election. When the bill for constitutional amendment was proposed, it was overwhelmingly rejected in the National Assembly vote, as expected. Rhee subsequently pressured the National Assembly by organizing the general public into anti-National Assembly demonstrations and adopting various other tactics of physical terror to intimidate the opposition Assemblymen.

The Rhee government turned to more heavy-handed tactics against the opposition Assemblymen after the president failed to amend the constitution in his initial attempts. On May 15, 1952, Rhee declared martial law in the Busan area, the temporary capital during the war, claiming that communist guerrillas had penetrated the area and threatened to overthrow the government. He used the military police to arrest 50 Assemblymen for allegedly receiving political bribes from the communist groups. With the military forces and the police encircling the National Assembly building, Rhee successfully forced the National Assembly to pass the constitutional amendment for popular presidential election. Following a new constitution and electoral systems, Rhee was elected as president for the second time in the August 1952 presidential election, winning about five million votes (74 percent of the total votes). He kept hold of his presidency by using the military to suppress opposition political leaders, going so far as to move two army divisions to the Busan area even during a time of war. Worse yet, the constitutional amendment set a precedent for subsequent political leaders to revise the constitution based on their political expediency.

The forced constitutional amendment in 1952 created tensions between the president and the top brass in the army, as a number of high-ranking officers opposed mobilizing the armed forces for the president's political ambitions. Leadership in the Korean army was divided over the issue of active military officers' political participation. One group of officers led by General Lee Jong-chan wanted the armed forces to maintain strict political neutrality. They opposed the politicization of the officer corps and the president's use of them. Another group of officers that included Park Jung-hee yearned for deeper political involvement to overthrow the corrupt civilian government and establish a more efficient military dictatorial regime. Despite the differences between the two groups of the officer corps, these officers shared an important commonality: They began to openly express their own political attitudes. The growing political activism among younger officers eventually manifested as a coup d'état in 1961 when the civilian leadership lost political control.[13]

As the president witnessed military officers' growing political activism and influence, Rhee felt he needed to build a mechanism to control them. In doing so, he relied on two strategies: his personal charisma and his political skill in manipulating factional struggles in the military. Rhee earned respect from both the general public and the military for his leadership of the independence movement during the Japanese rule. Indeed, he spent

30 years in exile in the United States and became the first president of the Korean Provisional Government while in exile. He was the only man with enough personal charisma to control high-ranking officers. Rhee further strengthened his authority over the military by circulating key positions within the army to secure his personal control over the highest-ranking officers. He removed uncooperative officers from the army leadership, such as Generals Lee Jong-chan and Choi Kyong-rok, who opposed Rhee's mobilization of the armed forces for his political ambition. Moreover, Rhee created a new military police unit within the Department of Defense in order to oversee not only the entire armed forces, but also civilian politicians.[14] Throughout the 1950s, all the key positions within the military were determined by Rhee's political expediency.

Factional Struggles in the Armed Forces

Most importantly, Rhee astutely exploited the factional struggles within the armed forces. Since the inception of the Republic, the South Korean army was organized into several distinctive groups according to their prior experiences under the Japanese rule—namely, either joining the Japanese Imperial Army or organizing the guerrilla forces for national independence. The first group was made up of Chinese-origin officers who fought the Japanese army for national independence on mainland China and Manchuria. These officers were organized either as part of the Chinese Nationalist army under Chiang's KMT leadership or as independent guerrilla forces. The second group of officers included those of Japanese origin who joined the Japanese Imperial Army during the Pacific War. The third distinct group comprised Manchurian-origin officers who participated in the Manchurian Defense Force under Japanese influence. The final group included North Korean-origin officers who escaped from North Korea before and during the Korean War.[15]

In the earliest years of state-building, Rhee depended primarily on Chinese-origin officers, until they were overwhelmed by the Japanese- and Manchuria-origin soldiers. The Chinese faction had strong political ties with Kim Koo, a prominent political leader during the provisional government in China who had created and trained the Chinese-origin soldiers during the independence war against Japan. However, Kim Koo was assassinated during the early state-building period, and the Chinese faction subsequently lost its power base and influence in the Rhee government. The next factional group with which Rhee formed a political alliance was the officers with a Japanese military background. Rhee relied on the Japanese faction for two main reasons: to have a better image of a well-trained and equipped Korean army and to counterbalance the once-dominant Chinese faction. The Japanese faction impacted Korean politics tremendously, primarily because the officer group brought the Japanese Imperial Army's political activism during the Pacific War to Korean politics. The 1961 coup d'état was spearheaded by young army officers with a Japanese military background. The political crisis surrounding the 1952 constitutional amendment and ensuing martial law led Rhee to select the third military faction, the officers with Manchurian background. Along with the Japanese faction, the Manchurian officers brought values quite contrary to democracy and civilian supremacy over the military to Korean politics.

Downfall of the Rhee Syngman Regime

Rhee's personal skill of controlling and mobilizing military officers for his political purposes had been so successful that he did not lose control over the military leadership until the very last moment of his presidency. However, his increasingly authoritarian and coercive political tactics as well as the mobilization of the armed forces for his political expediency resulted in two significant political outcomes. First, the Rhee government isolated itself from the general public. In addition to the constitutional amendment in 1952, Rhee proposed another amendment bill to the National Assembly in September 1954 that aimed to abolish the two-term restriction on presidential tenure for the first president of South Korea. This amendment would, in effect, enable the president to remain in office for life. The National Assembly passed the bill on November 29, 1954. Yet such undemocratic practices eventually eroded Rhee's political support base in the general public. Furthermore, Rhee's mobilization of army officers into civilian politics ultimately made them politically active and—worse yet—aggravated factional struggles among them.

The Rhee government lost popular support largely because of its failure to ensure economic performance in addition to Rhee's undemocratic political practices. Following the end of the war, the South Korean economy showed no indication of significant improvement, especially compared to its Northern counterpart. North Korea's Kim Il-sung carried out two economic plans targeted to be accomplished by 1960. During the first Three-Year Plan (1954–1956), North Korea experienced a 220 percent increase in national income and 280 percent increase in gross industrial product. During the second Five-Year Plan period (1956–1960), national income in North Korea increased 210 percent and gross industrial product by 340 percent.[16]

Although it is difficult to accept North Korea's economic indicators at face value, North Korea undeniably far surpassed South Korea in terms of economic performance and military buildup throughout the 1950s and 1960s.

In contrast to its northern neighbor, the South Korean economy showed few signs of recovery. Even with significant economic and military assistance from the United States throughout the Rhee regime, South Korea lagged far behind primarily due to the lack of viable economic plans and rampant political corruption in the government and the ruling Liberal Party. South Korea's GNP growth rate achieved 5.2 percent in 1954, 4.0 percent in 1955, and 0.3 percent in 1956 whereas inflation was 26.4 percent, 51 percent, and 42.9 percent for the same years. Rhee's failure to implement a feasible economic recovery plan significantly weakened his political position among the general public, especially young officers in the military.

To make matters worse, Rhee's political base—the Liberal Party—split between hardliners and softliners during the late 1950s. The softliners in the ruling circle tried to recuperate the constitutional democracy and pursued more moderate measures in dealing with political opposition forces; meanwhile, the hardliners wanted to tighten political control and use more heavy-handed approaches to suppress the political opposition. However, the decisive factor that ousted Rhee from his presidency was the military's decision not to follow his order to put down student demonstrations. By this time, the armed forces had already risen as the veto power group against the civilian leadership in South Korean politics. The next chapter discusses the political dynamics from the fall of the Rhee regime to subsequent political turmoil in the short-lived Second Republic under Chang Myon and the military coup d'état in May 1961.

II. State-Building and the Army in Taiwan

Losing the Civil War on the Mainland

The Republic of China, the first modern government of mainland China, was established with the overthrow of the frail Qing Dynasty in 1912. However, the modern state-building process was not smooth as it had to deal with numerous domestic and international security challenges until it retreated to Formosa Island in 1949. Internally, the newborn republic was too weak to gain full control over its mainland territory, as influential warlords declared themselves to be emperors and ruled most of the provinces amidst the fall of the Dynasty. According to one estimate, more than 1,300 warlords existed and 140 regional military uprisings occurred during the early decades of the nationalist republic.[17] Furthermore, the nationalist KMT government had to fight Mao Tse-tung's Communist revolt throughout the 1930s and 1940s. To make matters worse, the Japanese invasion of mainland China in 1937 in effect placed the country under total anarchy. While facing these security threats, the army of the Republic of China played a decisive role in the political and nation-building processes—not only on the mainland, but more so after the KMT's retreat to Taiwan. Senior officers in the army became increasingly influential actors in domestic political, administrative, and economic areas as the country struggled with multiple threats during the modern state-building period.

Since the inception of the modern republic, the KMT government had to fight multifront military confrontations. The KMT's first task was to crush the flourishing provincial warlords in the 1920s and deter Japanese aggression in the 1930s and 1940s. However, the conclusion of World War II and Japan's withdrawal from the mainland gave rise to an even more bitter battle with the Chinese Communist Party (CCP) and its People's Liberation Army (PLA) on the mainland until the KMT retreated to Taiwan in 1949. When the KMT withdrew to Taiwan, nearly 600,000 soldiers and another 600,000 civilian refugees also moved to the island.

The end of the civil war between the nationalist KMT and Mao's CCP in 1949 did not resolve the internal battles between the two Chinese governments; rather, the battles became even more intense after two sovereign states were declared in Taipei and Beijing. The KMT in Taiwan had to struggle for its regime survival from constant internal and external threats. Internally, it had to deal with the uncooperative native Taiwanese, who did not welcome the mainlanders and the government, but rather preferred independence.[18] The native Taiwanese perceived the arrival of Chiang's KMT forces as another form of colonial rule by another external authority, just as Japan had ruled them for decades. The mainland Chinese, an ethnic minority, monopolized key positions in political, economic, and military areas while ethnic Taiwanese were systematically excluded from the ruling circle. Meanwhile, externally, the KMT had to cope with the increasing threats from the mainland's PLA forces as the latter pledged to liberate the island and truly end the civil war.

KMT in Taiwan

When Japan was defeated in the Pacific War in 1945, Taiwan came under the KMT's rule. Immediately after Japan retreated from the island, Chiang dispatched the KMT officials and the army to replace the Japanese occupation forces and establish the Chinese governmental authority. The KMT appointed General Chen Yi as the chief administrator of the Taiwan Provincial Executive Office; he simultaneously became Taiwan Garrison Commander.[19] General Chen was entrusted with extensive powers over the areas of civil administration, judicial authority, and military command. The Chen administration showed little respect for the native Taiwanese or their living conditions, which had seriously deteriorated under Japanese rule. Although General Chen permitted the islanders to have provincial and local elections, he did not entrust the Taiwanese locals with any decision-making power over important political issues. Rather, the mainland Chinese—an ethnic minority—monopolized all the important posts in the government.

The corrupt and incompetent Chen administration used heavily oppressive measures to control the islanders, which provoked violent demonstrations calling for self-government by the Taiwanese natives. On February 28, 1947, Taiwanese islanders revolted against Chen's rule. A series of violent clashes between ethnic Taiwanese and the KMT authority occurred when General Chen decided to nationalize businesses on the island. The uprisings escalated into even more violent riots against the KMT armed forces. Chen declared martial law and brutally suppressed the demonstrations. According to one official figure, it is estimated that more than 60,000 ethnic Taiwanese participated and more than 6,000 were killed by the KMT forces in the uprisings.[20]

Chiang initially defended General Chen's brutal repression, charging that the CCP forces and the Taiwanese natives trained by the Japanese army were behind the riots. However, shortly after the February 28th Uprising, General Chen stepped down as chief administrator, and civilian administrators replaced the position to placate the enraged Taiwanese. Yet the incident had crafted a deep schism between the native Taiwanese and the mainland Chinese that lasted for decades. The ethnic tension continued to become a major source of domestic instability as most of the key positions in the KMT party, government, and military continued to be monopolized by the ethnic mainlanders. For example, of 10 KMT Central Standing Committee (CSC) members, none was of Taiwanese origin throughout the 1950s and 1960s. There were only two Taiwanese out of 21 CSC memberships in 1970.[21] The situation in the legislative bodies was similar to the executive branch, as both the National Assembly and the Legislative Yuan—which had been originally elected in 1947 on the mainland—were monopolized by mainlanders.[22] After 1949, elections for both bodies were temporarily brought to a halt since they were assumed to represent not just the island of Taiwan, but also the entire territory of Chinese mainland. Indeed, Chiang and KMT elites never imagined that they would stay in Taiwan for long, but anticipated retaking the mainland territory by force in the near future by resuming the civil war.

The monopoly of key positions by ethnic Chinese was also as conspicuous in the KMT military as in other governmental bodies. As Table 2.1 indicates, ethnic Taiwanese constituted the majority at the private soldier level, yet the Chinese mainlanders—an ethnic minority—were dominant at higher-ranking positions. Mainlanders' monopoly of the leadership positions continued until the 1970s, when Chiang Ching-kuo assumed political leadership and embarked on the slow but steady Taiwanization of civilian politics and the military hierarchy.

Some Taiwanese activists who opposed KMT rule went abroad to form organizations supporting Taiwan's independence. However, their influence on the Taiwanese people was minimal due to the Chiang regime's harsh punishment of any discussion related to the issue of Taiwan's independence. One such example of punishments by the KMT was that of professor Peng Ming-min, a well-known political science professor at the National Taiwan University who advocated for Taiwanese independence. Peng was sentenced to eight years in prison, but was later released due to international pressure. He moved to the United States to continue Taiwan's independence movement. In 1993, he returned to Taiwan to become a candidate of the Democratic Progressive Party (DPP) for the 1996 presidential election.[23] Likewise, the February 28th Uprising and the ensuing ethnic tensions between Taiwanese islanders and Chinese mainlanders continued to be major sources of internal political instability and challenges for the legitimacy of KMT's rule throughout the 1950s.

Table 2.1 Ethnic Composition of the Military in Taiwan, 1950–1987

Year	Generals		Colonels		Lieutenants		Soldiers	
	M	T	M	T	M	T	M	T
1950–1965	97.7	1.3	90.4	9.6	86.2	13.8	47.2	52.8
1965–1978	92.6	7.4	81.2	18.8	65.3	34.7	31.6	68.4
1978–1987	84.2	15.8	67.4	32.6	51.7	48.3	21.3	78.7

M=Mainlanders; T=Taiwanese
Source: Hung-mao Tien, "Social Change and Political Development in Taiwan," in Harvey Feldman, Michael Y. M. Kau, and Ilpyong J. Kim, eds, *Taiwan in a Time of Transition* (New York: Paragon House, 1988), 14.

Security Threats from the Mainland

An even more imminent security challenge for the KMT regime in Taiwan was Mao's CCP and its PLA forces. On October 1, 1949, a victorious Mao Tse-tung proclaimed the People's Republic of China on the mainland as well as plans to finish the civil war and "liberate" the island. The KMT not only lost the entire mainland territory to the CCP, but also faced a looming attack by the PLA without the much-needed external support. U.S. intelligence estimated that the PLA had organized enough troops and vessels to launch an invasion across the Taiwan Straits. Chiang's KMT estimated the total number of PLA troops to be 585,000.[24] In fact, the PLA's Third Field Army numbered more than 300,000 and planned for an amphibious attack on the island. Mao's armed forces expected to completely liberate Taiwan by 1950.

In such a dire situation, the United States—a long-standing supporter of the KMT—showed no sign of a military support, but rather tried to distance itself from Chiang Kai-shek. From a strategic point of view, Washington was not concerned with whether Chiang or Mao would rule mainland China; it simply wanted a strong and stable government that could check Japanese military expansionism in Asia. When Chiang's KMT forces lost the mainland, the Truman administration modified its previous China policy to terminate its security commitment to the incompetent and corrupt nationalist government and accept the new political reality on the mainland. At the conclusion of the civil war in 1949, Truman was ready to develop a cooperative relationship with the CCP if the communists terminated their relationship with Stalin's Soviet Union.[25] Indeed, the Truman administration was naïve enough to think Mao "might well turn out to be the 'Asian Tito'."[26] Because of Truman's predisposed perception of mainland China, even the powerful pro-KMT China Lobby in Washington was not influential enough to improve Taiwan's security conditions. As a result, without support from the United States, the KMT government fully expected PLA forces to attack in spring 1950.

However, the Korean War changed Washington's security policy toward Taiwan as well as Chiang's military strategy for mainland China. The outbreak of the war in Korea in June 1950 dramatically changed the American perception of Chinese communists and their political aspirations. The PLA was engaged in the Korean War in October 1950 under the slogan of "Resist America and Aid Korea."[27] Thus, the war forced Washington to reevaluate the overall security policy of East Asia and the Pacific regions. The U.S. Joint Chiefs of Staff recommended resuming military assistance as well as installing an Advisory Group for the KMT government. In 1954, the United States and the nationalist Taiwanese regime signed the Mutual Defense Treaty, and Washington poured massive military and economic aid to the island. Under the Defense Treaty, the United States assisted Taiwan in modernizing its weapons, equipment, and training. As such, the war in Korea changed the American perception of Mao's communist forces and the strategic value of Taiwan.

The Korean War effectively diverted the Chinese communists' attention away from Taiwan for some time while also providing Chiang's KMT government with a window of opportunity to resume the civil war and retake the mainland. When the Korean War broke out and the United States resumed aid to Taiwan, Chiang planned a strategy of military counterattack against communist China to recover the mainland territory, which became the essential foreign policy goal of the KMT government throughout the Cold War years. Chiang always believed that the humiliating retreat to Taiwan was not a permanent outcome, but rather a temporary stay. Thus, the KMT deployed its forces closer to the southeastern part of the mainland and installed military bases with about 100,000 troops on the islands of Quemoy and Matsu just off the mainland. Furthermore, the KMT launched commando raids and reconnaissance flights over the Chinese territory. It carried out bombing campaigns in areas south of the Changjiang (Yangtze River), including Shanghai, the most populated city in the southeastern part of the mainland. During the military campaign period, the KMT forces dropped some 40,000 rounds of bombshells on Shanghai, killing approximately 1,400 people and damaging industrial facilities.[28]

The KMT also employed guerrilla forces on the mainland. The nationalist government on Taiwan estimated that, as of June 1950, approximately 400,000 anticommunist forces were continuing their civil war on the mainland. Two months later, that number had grown to 1.6 million, with more than 55 percent of them being under KMT command.[29] An estimated 1,800 battles occurred on the mainland, resulting in 300,000 CCP/PLA casualties.[30] However, Chiang's strategy of military counterattack failed to retake the mainland mainly because the United States did not want the two Chinese forces to enter into another full-blown war and because the guerrilla forces faded away with the violent crises in Quemoy.

After the Korean War ended, Mao redirected his military forces and adopted even more aggressive policies toward the KMT on Taiwan. During the 1954 and 1958 Taiwan Straits crises, the PLA bombed the islands of Quemoy and Matsu, where the KMT military bases had been installed. In the first Quemoy crisis in 1954, the PLA fired 17,243 rounds of bombshells on the island as a form of military demonstration against the signing of the Mutual Defense Treaty between the KMT and the United States.[31] The PLA forces launched an even heavier attack in the second Quemoy crisis that broke on August 23, 1958.[32] As a result, for both the KMT on Taiwan and CCP on the mainland, the 1950s were a decade of the most perilous security environments, with both entities on the verge of entering into full-scale warfare.

Generalissimo Chiang Kai-shek and the Taiwanese Army

The immediate impact of the CCP's threats to the nationalist Taiwan was twofold: the massive expansion of military organization and the centralization of political power of the charismatic leader Generalissimo Chiang Kai-shek. The KMT government stepped up its military buildup from 500,000 men to one million by 1958. Meanwhile, the overwhelming threats from the mainland rendered the concentration of political power in Chiang, who had strong control over the nationalist armed forces.

Chiang's political authority over the military became deeply entrenched even before the nationalist forces moved to Taiwan. Chiang took over KMT leadership three years after Sun Yat-sen, the founding father of the Republic of China and the KMT, died in 1925. Sun dispatched Chiang to Moscow to study the organization of the Soviet Army and the Bolshevik party organization. Under the guidance of the Soviet military advisors, the Whampoa Military Academy was established in Canton. Chiang assumed the role of the first superintendent of the military academy. During the period on the mainland, Chiang's political power within the party became firmly established through his control of the Whampoa Military Academy as his connection with the officers helped him during factional struggles within the KMT party following Sun's death.[33]

Chiang consolidated his political power within the KMT by manipulating cliques within the party: the C.C. Clique, the Whampoa Clique, the Blueshirts, and the Political Study Clique that had dominated the party throughout the 1920s. Among them, the Whampoa Clique served as Chiang's military power base, as it was made up of the graduates of the military academy. As such, Chiang's influence in the party and the army further increased as members of the Whampoa Clique moved up the ladders of the military and party hierarchies.[34]

As Chiang consolidated his leadership in the party, the military became his most important political asset as it had become increasingly influential in the governmental policy-making process, primarily due to internal and external threats. Senior army officers' influence in the KMT leadership had grown over the course of fighting the warlords, Mao's communist forces, and later the Japanese army. As early as 1929, the military presence in the KMT was overwhelming, accounting for 280,000 members while civilian membership totaled only 266,000.[35] The army's role in the KMT party spread further as Mao's communist forces embarked on armed struggles with the KMT and as the second Sino-Japanese war occurred in 1937.

The trend of the armed forces' political and social functions continued to increase after the retreat to Taiwan. The presence of serious domestic and international security threats forced Chiang to put key constitutional elements on hold with the declaration of martial law, which gave the military the right to intervene in social and political affairs. Furthermore, through the emergency legislation in 1950, the KMT government created the Taiwan Garrison Command (TGC) within the Ministry of National Defense to implement all aspects of martial law and maintain domestic security order. Under martial law, political activists critical of the KMT's rule over Taiwan and Chiang's leadership were tried and sentenced by military tribunals, along with those who committed criminal offenses. Between 1950 and 1986, approximately 10,000 criminal cases involving civilians were tried in Taiwanese military courts.[36] In addition, the martial law regime installed Military Training Offices in schools at all levels to build support for the KMT rule. The army also created its own network of newspapers, television, and radio studios as well as publishing companies.[37] After its retreat to Formosa Island, the KMT government mobilized virtually all of its people and available domestic resources for military buildup. As a result, the armed forces in Taiwan became the most influential and best organized institution in the country. The coercive state apparatus, which included the army and the police, participated in the governing process throughout the martial law regime.

In conclusion, the KMT government had to face extreme security threats during the early state-building years, fighting provincial warlords in the 1920s, the Chinese Communist insurgents, and Japanese troops that invaded mainland China. The security threats were even more intimidating after the KMT retreated to Taiwan. The presence of security threats brought two of the most prominent political outcomes to the Taiwanese society. The first direct effect of the threats was the expansion of the Taiwanese army and its political roles. Meanwhile, continuing threats resulted in the concentration of all political powers into one political leader, Generalissimo Chiang, who brought the top brass in the military into civilian political affairs. Section two of the next chapter explains how Chiang, and later his son and successor Chiang Ching-kuo, created a control mechanism over the politically influential officers in his government.

III. State-Building and the Army in the Philippines

State-Building under U.S. Influence

Centuries of colonial rule by Spain and later the United States ended with the establishment of the Philippine Commonwealth in November 1935 with a semi-independent status. After the Pacific War ended, the United States transferred sovereignty to the Philippine people so that the country became a fully independent republic on July 4, 1946. However, the Armed Forces of the Philippines (AFP) had been originally created in 1935 under the guidance of the then-Field Marshal General Douglas MacArthur. The AFP forces were incorporated into the U.S. army to fight the Japanese aggressors when they invaded the Philippines in December 1941. Given its military establishment and war experience under the American influence, the AFP borrowed heavily from the U.S. Army's organizational character, ideology, and political attitudes.[38] The AFP remained the least politically oriented military in the region and was placed under the control of the democratically elected civilian leaders. In fact, the 1935 Constitution prohibited active military personnel from being engaged in partisan political activities.[39] As a result, from its establishment up to the point of President Ferdinand Marcos' declaration of martial law in 1972, the Philippines remained one of the most democratic countries in Asia.

Due primarily to its geographic isolation from the Asian continent, the Philippines faced no major external threats for decades after independence. Moreover, the United States served as the guarantor of Philippine security from any external aggression. The country has long been one of America's major allies, cemented by two sets of military agreements: the Military Bases Agreement (MBA) of 1947 and the Mutual Defense Treaty in 1951. Through the MBA, American air and naval bases were stationed in the country; meanwhile, the defense treaty provided the Philippine government with various kinds of military assistance from the United States. As such, throughout the Cold War years, the United States essentially assumed responsibility for Philippine security.

Internal Threats: CPP and MNLF

Since the birth of the republic, the major source of security threats in the Philippines came from domestic fronts. The Hukbalahap (or Huk) rebellion resulted in an expansion of the AFP's role during the 1940s and 1950s. The Huks originally emerged as the People's Anti-Japanese Army, which sought to engage in guerrilla warfare against the Japanese aggression during the Pacific War. However, once the war ended, the Huks rebelled against the Manila government because they were not recognized as a legitimate political organization. The central government deprived the Huks of several congressional seats that the Huk leaders won during the 1946 elections. However, the Huk rebellion was not strong enough to pose a serious threat to the Ramon Magsaysay government, which was established in 1953. President Magsaysay effectively minimized the Huks' influence in the country by carrying out various strategies that combined a military counterinsurgency program with positive economic inducements to the insurgents.[40]

Yet the Huk rebellion did lead to a modest expansion of the AFP organization and its role in the 1950s. The original size of the AFP forces was 37,000 soldiers, with a $70.8 million military budget, in 1948; the number of soldiers swelled to 59,000 men, with a $572 million budget, by 1970.[41] In addition, the AFP forces assumed responsibilities beyond national security, including officers' participation in local governments and economic development programs.

The Philippines' internal security conditions significantly deteriorated during the 1960s and 1970s. The most serious threats came from the Communist Party of the Philippines (CPP), which was formed in December 1968, and its New People's Army (NPA) organized a year later. Although the CPP originated from the Huk movements, the CPP qualitatively differed from previous communist movements and was much better organized, adopting the strategy of Maoist guerrilla warfare in rural areas and pledging to overthrow the central government. The CPP was organized and led by highly educated elites and was able to build a nationwide organization. Jose Maria Sison, a professor at the University of the Philippines who organized the Labor Party as early as 1962 and the Nationalist (or Patriotic) Youth in 1964, became the leader of the CPP after losing his position at the university. He helped the CPP gain rapid popularity among the general public by advocating various socioeconomic reform programs, especially the land reform program. As a result, within five years of its establishment, the CPP became strong enough to open 20 guerrilla war fronts in seven different provinces outside Manila, including northern, central, and southern Luzon, Mindanao, and the eastern and western Visayas.[42] The number of armed clashes between the AFP and the NPA guerrillas continued to increase until Ferdinand Marcos declared martial law in 1972. The CPP and NPA further increased their strength and activities even after the martial law, peaking during the mid-1980s when the Marcos regime was overthrown and the democratic regime transition occurred.

Other domestic security challenges came from Muslim separatist movements in the southern provinces of the Philippines. The Muslim movements in the country had centuries-old historical legacies, but the direct cause of their reemergence was rooted in intercommunal clashes among various religious groups in the 1960s. At this time, an increasing number of Christian Filipinos migrated into traditional Muslim territories, raising religious, cultural, and economic confrontations between the two religious groups. Violent clashes between the two began to occur. The March 1968 Jabidah massacre in Corregidor, known as the "Corregidor Incident," provoked a Muslim separatist rebellion after about 28 Muslim trainees were executed without having access to the proper judicial process.[43] Violent clashes ensued in Cotabato in 1970 over the issue of landownership, and violence erupted again during the 1971 election campaign.[44] Both Christian and Muslim politicians mobilized their private armed bands for elections. In particular, grievances among the Muslim population increased as the central government sided with Christian immigrants, supporting their political and economic rights.

In 1968, the same year that the CPP was formed, Udtog Matalam—a prominent Muslim leader in the southern part of the archipelago—announced the formation of the Muslim Independent Movement (MIM), calling for the establishment of an independent Muslim state covering the provinces of Sulu, Palawan, and Mindanao.[45] While the NPA continued to increase its size and influence throughout the islands, the Muslim Moro National Liberation Front (MNLF) became a more serious security threat to the central government as early as the mid-1970s. By early 1972, the MNLF had emerged as a well-organized political and military organization and, with the declaration of martial law, engaged in full-fledged armed struggles with the AFP, gaining economic and diplomatic support from Muslim nations such as Malaysia, Libya, and other countries from the Islamic Conference. Violent conflicts spread throughout the southern part of the Philippines and resulted in deaths of thousands of Filipinos as well as more than 500,000 refugees.[46] The security challenges from both the NPA and the MNLF continued throughout the Marcos regime, reaching their peak during the final years of the Marcos rule.[47]

Marcos Resorts to Authoritarianism

The domestic security challenges from the communist and Muslim insurgents presented the Marcos circle with justifications for the extension of the president's tenure beyond the constitutional limitation and the further centralization of political power in his hands. Yet Marcos' attempt to strengthen his power dates back to his constitutional presidency of 1965, when he conducted extensive reforms in the AFP structure to strengthen his personal control over the armed forces. During his first 13 months in office, he concurrently served as Secretary of Defense. In addition, he conducted the largest-scale military reshuffling since the formation of the AFP, giving priority in promotions to officers from his hometown, Ilocos. The "Ilocanization" of the AFP officer corps was especially prominent in crucial positions for the Marcos regime security, such as the Presidential Guard Battalion (PGB), the National Intelligence and Security Authority (NISA), the Metropolitan Command of the Philippine Constabulary (METROCOM), and the Manila Unit of the Integrated National Police (MUINP). Officers from the Ilocos region received commandership positions in those units concentrated around metropolitan Manila, taking charge of the Marcos regime security. Marcos also mobilized AFP officers during the 1969 presidential elections, using them to mobilize and coerce voters. Through this process, military officers began to actively participate in domestic political processes even before martial law was declared in 1972.[48]

Marcos adroitly exploited the security threat perception among the general public to justify his increasingly authoritarian rule and the extension of his presidential term beyond the constitutional limit. As early as February 1970, Marcos himself mentioned several times the possibility of declaring martial law, and security conditions were worsening enough to justify it. The early months of 1970 witnessed violent student demonstrations, targeting both Marcos and the American-established facilities. Anti-Marcos and Anti-American demonstrations intensified the sense of a pervasive political crisis. Furthermore, the 1971 election was tainted by numerous incidents of physical violence, in which 223 people were killed and another 250 wounded.[49] In addition to the growing political turbulence, natural disasters such as volcanic eruptions, earthquakes, severe droughts, and typhoons further aggravated the socioeconomic conditions of the country. Kidnappings, robberies, and murders became increasingly rampant throughout the archipelago in the final years of the Marcos constitutional presidency.

In addition to these crises, two incidents of physical violence gave Marcos the final push to declare martial law. The first event was a bomb explosion during a Liberal Party rally at Plaza Miranda in the heart of Manila in August 1971, killing nine and injuring 90, including eight senatorial candidates.[50] Initially, the Marcos government charged the NPA for the terror, but the incident provided the president with an excuse to suspend the writ of habeas corpus. However, it was later speculated that the Marcos regime itself—along with a segment of the AFP—was responsible for the bombing. The second and final catalyst for Marcos was the attack on the car of Defense Secretary Juan Ponce Enrile, which Marcos later admitted had also been crafted.[51]

The day after the bombing incident—two years before his second and constitutionally final presidential term was set to end—Marcos declared martial law. He justified the installation of an oppressive martial law regime by citing the 1935 Constitution, which stated that presidents can declare martial law "in case of invasion, insurrection, or rebellion or imminent danger thereof." Marcos declared that "[W]e will eliminate the threat of a violent overthrow of our Republic. But at the same time we must now reform the social, economic, and political institutions of our country."[52] With the martial law regime, he proposed to build a "New Society" that included removing "the inequities of that society, the cleanup of government of its corrupt and sterile elements, the liquidation of the criminal syndicates, and the systematic development of our economy."[53]

Marcos used the declaration of martial law to entrench his authoritarian rule over the country, thereby significantly expanding his presidential power. Although it did not result in the installation of a military dictatorial rule, the presence and influence of the top brass in the AFP in domestic political process expanded enormously. Marcos simultaneously weakened or even nullified his political competitors' power bases by abolishing Congress and imprisoning key political opponents, including Senator Benigno Aquino, the most likely successor to the presidency. Marcos also closed several pro-opposition newspapers, radio, and television stations. Finally, he prohibited any type of street demonstration and political opposition movements. Consequently, within the first five years of martial law, approximately 70,000 people had been imprisoned by the military tribunals.

AFP in the Marcos Government

The declaration of martial law was possible due to AFP officers' support. Marcos himself revealed in 1974 that he closely consulted with 12 high-ranking officers five days before declaring martial law. Thus, it is not surprising that the first notable outcome of the martial law regime was the expansion of the number of military personnel and the size of the military's budget. As Table 2.2 indicates, the Philippines had relatively small armed forces until the late 1960s due to the lack of significant external threats and the security guarantee from the United States. The AFP had just around 50,000 personnel for the first six years of Marcos' constitutional presidency. However, during the first eight years of his authoritarian rule, the number almost tripled, reaching 150,000 by the end of the 1970s.

Table 2.2 Growth of the Armed Forces of the Philippines, 1965–1986

Year	Total	Year	Total*
1965	51,500	1977	139,000
1968	47,000	1980	156,300
1971	58,100	1983	150,300
1974	89,900	1986	165,000

Note: *Total number includes Army, Navy, Air, Constabulary (PC), Local Home Defense Forces (LHD), Marines, and Coast Guard.
Source: International Institute for Strategic Studies, *The Military Balance* (London: IISS, various years).

Defense spending also increased almost tenfold in the first four years of martial law, comprising more than 30 percent of total spending of the Marcos government. The defense budget consistently increased throughout the Marcos presidential years, culminating in 45.7 percent of governmental spending for the final year of the Marcos rule.[54] The president extended other benefits to the AFP as well to secure officers' allegiance to him. In 1972, he promoted all officers one grade, raised the officers' salaries by 150 percent, and increased other benefits. The so-called "twelve disciples" of high-ranking officers who supported Marcos' decision in 1972 were promoted to the highest positions of authority and responsibility in the military establishment. Some of the key officers in the Marcos circle included Defense Secretary Juan Ponce Enrile, AFP Chief of Staff General Romeo C. Espino, PC Chief General Fidel V. Ramos, and Presidential Security Command Chief General Fabian Ver.[55] Along with other disciples, these generals played key roles in buttressing not only the martial law regime, but also the overthrow of Marcos and the democratization process in the mid-1980s.

The AFP expanded its role into business management in state corporations, many of which had been confiscated from opposition elites. For example, the AFP took control of the steel and sugar industries and all major utility companies. To reward officers loyal to the president, Marcos built two defense-related businesses: the Philippine Expeditionary Forces to Korea-Investment and Development Corporation, a military investment company, and the Philippine Veterans Investment Development Company for retired officers.[56] In addition, numerous senior officers were allowed to stay in office beyond the compulsory retirement period of 30 years in service while many retired officers were appointed to key positions in central and local governments, such as ambassadors, Presidential Regional Officers for Development (PRODs), governors, and loan collectors for land banks.[57]

In return, the AFP served the Marcos government as the guarantor of the authoritarian rule until 1986, when a group of officers turned against him and sided with the pro-democracy civilian elites for a regime change. From the declaration of martial law in 1972 until 1978, when civilian courts replaced the military tribunals, the AFP arrested and prosecuted most political dissidents—many of whom were communists and their supporters. But those arrested also included opposition politicians, journalists, and college students. The martial law regime further militarized the Philippine society by organizing the Civilian Home Defense Force (CHDF) to train 36,000 people annually. In addition, the AFP integrated police forces into its command structure, which enabled the Marcos regime to mobilize them into local politics and elections in provincial cities and municipalities. Juan Ponce Enrile, the secretary of national defense, concurrently served as the chairman of the National Police Commission (NPC).

Marcos' mobilization of AFP officers for his political purposes resulted in the politicization of the armed forces and seriously harmed military professionalism. During the martial law regime, a small number of officers who graduated from the Philippine Military Academy (PMA) formed a secret factional group in the military—the so-called Reform the Armed Forces of the Philippines Movement (RAM). RAM officers aimed to restore professionalism in and the public's respect for the armed forces. As such, the RAM played a decisive role in the downfall of Marcos' regime and the establishment a democratic leadership in 1986.

The Philippine democracy turned into an oppressive authoritarian regime with Marcos' declaration of martial law, a process in which the AFP played key roles in order to maintain the regime. Growing security threats from the domestic front—especially insurgency movements by the communist CCP/NPA and the Muslim MNLF—throughout the 1970s and 1980s provided Marcos with opportunities to expand his power as well as the role of the AFP in civilian politics. Under the martial law regime, the AFP experienced unprecedented expansion of the organization and its roles beyond the responsibility of the national defense. Yet the honeymoon period between Marcos and the top brass in the AFP did not last long, as a segment in the military turned against him to overthrow the authoritarian regime and install a democratic one. The next chapter discusses Marcos' mechanism of controlling high-ranking officers and how it politicized the overall military organization as well as harmed the professionalism and institutional integrity of the AFP.

IV. State-Building and the Army in Indonesia

When World War II ended, Indonesia proclaimed independence from Japanese and Dutch colonial rule, although it had to fight another five-year "revolutionary" war with Dutch forces until it finally gained independence in 1949. The independence war and subsequent security challenges from the domestic front heavily influenced the Indonesian military's organizational character, doctrine, and officers' political orientation. From the state-building years up until 1998, when President Haji Mohammad Suharto was ousted from office and the country embarked on democratic governance, the armed forces in Indonesia dominated civilian politics.

This section examines the relationship between Indonesia's experience with internal and external conflicts and security threats during the early years of the state-building on the one hand and the organization, doctrine, and political orientation of the Republic of Indonesia Armed Forces (*Angkatan Bersenjata Republik Indonesia;* ABRI) on the other. From the time of independence in 1949 up to the formal installation of the Suharto presidency in 1968, Indonesia experienced three distinct phases of political development: parliamentary democracy in 1949–1956, increasingly authoritarian Guided Democracy in 1957–1965, and the 1965 coup d'état and power transition from President Achmad Sukarno's fall to the installation of the Suharto government with ABRI's political domination. This section discusses the first two periods, from the parliamentary democracy to the authoritarian Guided Democracy; the dynamics of the military coup and installation of the military dictatorial rule will be discussed in the next chapter.

Birth of the ABRI

The Indonesian armed forces began to form slowly and grew as a national independence force during Japanese occupation in the early 1940s. In 1943, the Japanese army created two main military institutions in Indonesia to mobilize the islanders to support Japanese forces waging warfare in Southeast Asia. First, the Japanese occupation forces formed *Heiho* in April 1943 to mobilize indigenous Indonesians; by the end of the war in 1945, about 40,000 islanders had received military training in military transportation, road building, and defense duties. Second, the Japanese also established the Army Defense of the Fatherland (*Pasukan Sukarela Tentara Pembela Tanash Air; Peta*) in late 1943 as territorial defense forces. By the conclusion of the war, approximately 38,000 *Peta* soldiers and 1,600 *Peta* officers had been trained by the Japanese army.⁵⁸ The ABRI was formed by integrating numerous paramilitary organizations such as the *Barisan Pelopor* (Vanguard Corps), *Hizbullah* (Army of Allah), and the *Seinendan* (Youth Corps), in addition to *Heiho* and *Peta*.⁵⁹ These groups voluntarily cooperated with the Japanese in the hopes that Japan would support Indonesia's independence from the Dutch, who had ruled Indonesia by establishing the Dutch East Indies Company in the 1600s—occupation that lasted until Japan replaced them.

The independence war began immediately after the Japanese withdrew from Indonesia when World War II ended and as the Dutch colonial authorities did not recognize the Indonesian declaration of independence. These multiple military organizations were subsequently unified as the ABRI to fight against the Dutch for independence from 1945 to 1949. Most ABRI officers, including General Sudirman, the commander-in-chief of the army, and General Suharto, came from *Peta*. After negotiations with the Indonesian revolutionary forces failed, the Dutch army began attacking the ABRI forces. The Dutch, with 150,000 soldiers, were dominant in major cities but had little influence in rural areas.⁶⁰ Their attempts to maintain control over Indonesia brought about violent uprisings in many parts of the archipelago.

During the independence war period, the ABRI actively participated in civilian political affairs since the newly established civilian government was not well organized and the ABRI was the only effective organization that could perform administrative functions in the islands. Not surprisingly, throughout the five years of the revolutionary war, the ABRI earned respect from the Indonesian people and a strong self-belief that it was the only institution that truly represented and defended the interests of the people. In December 1948, the Dutch forces attacked Jogjakarta, the capital city, and captured Sukarno and other civilian leaders. However, the ABRI—under General Sudirman's leadership—refused to surrender and continued the independence war until Indonesia finally gained formal independence in 1949.

The five-year war of independence set the basic organizational structure and political orientation of the Indonesian army. The ABRI was not originally organized by civilian politicians, but spontaneously sprang from the masses during the war. Consequently, officers in the ABRI did not consider themselves to be instruments of the civilian leaders, for whom enforcing their political will proved to be difficult from the beginning of national independence.⁶¹

Parliamentary Democracy in Indonesia, 1949–1956

After gaining formal independence in December 1949, Indonesia started as a parliamentary democracy, with multiple political parties competing for seats in the parliament. Until President Sukarno installed authoritarian rule with Guided Democracy in 1957, three major political parties dominated the parliamentary government: *Partai Nasional Indonesia* (PNI, the Indonesian Nationalist Party), supported by secular nationalists; *Masjumi*, backed by modernist Muslims from outside Java; and *Nahdlatul Ulama* (NU), representing traditionalist Muslims based in Java.[62] Indonesian politics in the early 1950s was quite democratic; elections were relatively free and fair, the courts were independent from other governmental branches, civil society was thriving, and freedom of press was guaranteed.[63] Most importantly, the ABRI formally disengaged itself from civilian politics and withdrew back to the barracks during the parliamentary democracy period.

However, the parliamentary democracy involving numerous political parties formed based on ethnic and religious cleavages turned out to be too weak to deal with problems emerging throughout the archipelago during the 1950s. Given the diversity in culture, religion, ideology, and ethnicity, the parliamentary system was unable to form a stable and workable long-term coalition government; rather, the democratic system itself became the main source of threats to the national integration and stable state-building. Before long, the political consensus of the early period of the republic fell apart as political parties became ideologically and ethnically polarized. In the seven years of the democratic trial, seven different coalition cabinets took turns running the country.

The flagging parliamentary democracy provoked ABRI officers' political interference, with the first such incident occurring in October 1952. A group of military officers in Jakarta incited the general public to demonstrate in front of the Presidential Palace while a delegation of senior ABRI officers was meeting with President Sukarno to call for the dissolution of the ill-functioning parliament.[64] The protest was organized to boycott the parliament's attempt to interfere with the ABRI's reorganization and demobilization plans. Some of the politically active officers insisted that they had the right to participate in important political decisions on the grounds that the independence and state-building had been achieved largely through the military's own efforts, not by civilian leadership.[65] Some observers speculated that General Abdul Haris Nasution and several other officers planned a military coup to abolish the parliamentary system and create a more powerful presidency.[66] Although this "October Affair" did not result in a significant political crisis, the incident demonstrated that the ABRI—although formally disengaged from civilian politics—was ready to exercise veto power in civilian politics from the early years of the state-building.

A source of political friction and national disintegration resided within the ABRI itself, which worsened domestic security conditions throughout the 1950s. The ABRI was originally composed of numerous paramilitary groups and personnel from different provinces who had diverse ethnic and religious backgrounds. Although traditional Muslims were dominant in numbers at the lower position within the army, secular Javanese officers were overrepresented at the higher ranks. The ABRI leadership perceived the fundamentalist Muslims in the army as the main threat to the security of the state. Thus, the first Constitution written in 1945 spelled out *Pancasila* (or Five Principles) as the official principle of national identity, not Islam. *Pancasila* was first devised by Sukarno to embrace five main principles: belief in God, humanitarianism, the unity of Indonesia, democracy, and social justice.[67] Fundamental Muslims in the army who refused to accept the *Pancasila* principle organized the Darul Islam rebellion in the areas of West Java and some parts of Central Java. These officers were strongly committed to creating an Islamic republic in Indonesia. The Darul Islam uprising began as early as 1948 when S. M. Kartosuwirjo, commander of the Hizbullah forces, declared the Islamic State of Indonesia.[68] The Islamic independence movement continued to spread to Aceh and South Sulawesi in the 1950s, when the parliamentary democracy suffered from a lack of strong leadership.

A more serious threat to national integrity came from the very institution of the ABRI. The Indonesian army had to deal with intra-military fragmentation as regional military commanders turned against the central command and joined local rebellions based on traditional Islam. Local rebellions received support from regional military officers around the islands of Sumatra, East Java, and Sulawesi and seriously challenged the authority of the central government. In most cases, these rebels allied with local Islamic leaders who wanted to make Islam the basic principle of the state. Another factor that harmed the ABRI's organizational unity came from tensions between the officers who had military training in the Dutch military and those trained by the Japanese occupation forces. Whereas the former were better educated and more professionally trained, the latter had experiences of independence guerrilla warfare and therefore a stronger sense of patriotism and national pride. In particular, Japanese-trained officers had close connections with local political elites and business owners.

Such military fragmentations made it extremely difficult for the central government to establish an effective and hierarchical command structure. To solve the problem of the ABRI's factionalization, Army Chief of Staff General Abdul Haris Nasution attempted to establish a system of officer rotation and strong central command authority. However, the attempt faced resistance from local commanders, leading to the loss of Nasution's leadership in the ABRI.[69] In sum, the early years of state-building in Indonesia faced multiple sources of domestic security threats throughout the archipelago. The most serious threats during the early 1950s were religious conflicts, while the late 1950s were overshadowed by ethnic and regional conflicts—both within and outside the ABRI.

Guided Democracy and ABRI's Role Expansion

Indonesia's parliamentary democracy in the early years of state-building was not effective enough to control emergent domestic security challenges, which forced President Sukarno to declare Guided Democracy in 1957.[70] Guided Democracy effectively abolished the parliamentary system and returned to a presidential one codified in the original 1945 Constitution. Under the newly established authoritarian system, Sukarno declared martial law, bringing ABRI officers into politics who took extensive political, economic, and administrative roles. Guided Democracy originally intended to overcome the problem of national disunity and domestic conflicts, but ultimately resulted in the concentration of political power in the hands of Sukarno and a number of army officers. The new Sukarno government eliminated democratic ideas with institutionalized opposition, which was perceived as a main source of social unrest and disunity. The Western-style democratic ideas were replaced by "deliberation" to adopt a traditional way of discussion and consensus for governmental decisions and—if no consensus could be achieved—Sukarno himself, being the elderly political leader, made the final decision.[71]

Guided Democracy instantly restored domestic political and security order—at least momentarily—in the late 1950s, as Sukarno and the ABRI effectively put down regional rebellious activities and political opposition activities were strictly restrained. Sukarno cancelled elections and banned political activities by the main opponents of the president's leadership—namely, PNI and *Partai Sosialis Indonesia* (PSI, Indonesian Socialist Party).[72] Instead, he distributed half of the seats in the parliament to "functional groups" that represented various occupational interests, including the ABRI.[73]

With the installation of Guided Democracy, Sukarno became a stronger and increasingly authoritarian leader. The expansion of presidential power was evident in the growing power and role of the ABRI. The army chief of staff, Major General Nasution, elaborated upon an ideological rationalization for the ABRI's political role with the concept of the Middle Way doctrine.[74] The Middle Way principle dictated that the ABRI would neither pursue taking over the governmental power nor remain politically inactive.

Instead, the military would have the right to express its own political positions in the government, legislature, and state administrations. General Nasution maintained that the infusion of governmental bodies with the ABRI, which had excellent managerial and technical skills, would improve the administrative efficiency of the country.[75] The doctrine pointed to the fact that the civilian leadership and the top brass in the ABRI had equal rights and authority to participate in the governing process. The Middle Way doctrine in its original form had moderate and limited political goals for the ABRI when it was first declared. However, the doctrine developed into the idea of *dwifungsi* (dual function) doctrine. According to the *dwifungsi*, "The participation of ABRI in the political process may be seen from two angles, namely in its position as a defense and security force . . ., while as a social force it has rights and obligations as any other ordinary citizen . . . in taking part in the legislative bodies, occupying certain offices in the executive and judicial branches."[76] In September 1982, President Suharto made the doctrine law.

All the conditions of Guided Democracy, the declaration of martial law, and the Middle Way doctrine supported the ABRI's role in the government in the late 1950s. Under the provisions of the state of siege, local military commanders came to have almost unrestrained powers to maintain regional security and order. Yet the ABRI officers' presence in politics was more prominent in the organs of central government. For example, more than 30 percent of the ministers appointed in 1959 came from the ABRI, although it had had no military presence at the minister level before 1958.[77] The ABRI continued to increase its power in the civilian government by implementing emergency powers under martial law until 1963, when a modified form of martial law was reintroduced.

The ABRI's role expansion in government accompanied military officers' involvement in economic affairs. When the Sukarno government nationalized Dutch companies in Indonesia in the midst of violent uprisings by nationalist demonstrators in 1957, several military officers assumed the management task for these new state-owned business enterprises, including plantations, mining, banking, and trade. ABRI officers' involvement in business management continued to expand further in the 1960s, especially when British and American companies were put under military supervision. In particular, the state-owned oil corporation founded in 1957 was directly administered by the army leadership. Less noticeably, local military units built up their own business industries, mostly in connection with ethnic Chinese.[78] ABRI officers' participation in local economic affairs produced a corrupt officer corps that the central government found ever more difficult to control. Due to the military officers' economic activities in several lucrative industries, the military's defense spending as a percentage of the governmental budget did not correctly reflect the real amount of the defense spending as the greatest portion of the military budget came from the industries that ABRI officers controlled.[79] Army officers' engagement in economic transactions increased even further under Suharto's New Order regime in the late 1960s.

Guided Democracy during the late 1950s seemed to momentarily restore political order and domestic security, but subsequent crises and Sukarno's failure to manage them provided ABRI officers with opportunities to assume more politically influential positions in the final years of the Sukarno government. President Sukarno wanted to manage his political leadership by creating a balance of power among the three politically influential groups—namely, the ABRI, the *Partai Komunis Indonesia* (PKI, Communist Party of Indonesia), and the Muslims. But Sukarno's political scheme backfired as antagonism and power struggles between ABRI officers and the PKI intensified. The domestic political crisis resulted in a coup d'état on September 30, 1965, when a group of young officers kidnapped and killed six of the highest-ranking officers. General Suharto assumed leadership to put down the coup forces several days later. Suharto's military forces blamed the PKI for the coup attempt and killed more than half a million people suspected of being communists.[80] By this time, the helpless president had no choice but to transfer all political power to General Suharto.

The security challenges that Indonesia faced during the early years of the state-building had tremendous impacts on the domestic political processes and the ABRI's role in them. As previously discussed, the ABRI's political influence had been deeply entrenched even before the independent republic was declared in 1949. The ABRI's role in the independence war with the Dutch forces created strong beliefs among military officers that the ABRI was the army that would truly reflect and defend the people's interests. Due to such conditions, President Sukarno's attempt to control the military was frail at best. Growing domestic security threats and the parliamentary regime's inability to deal with the problems made the top brass in the army ever more vocal and assertive in the civilian political decision-making process. The ABRI forced Sukarno to replace the parliamentary democracy with a more authoritarian Guided Democracy, in which army officers' influence further increased. The next chapter will explain in detail the process of Sukarno's step-down and the installment of the military-dominant Suharto regime in the late 1960s.

Conclusions

This chapter has examined how security challenges brought about the rise of the armed forces' domestic political influence during the early years of the state-building process in four Asian countries—namely, South Korea, Taiwan, the Philippines, and Indonesia. After decades of colonial rule, these countries—except for the Philippines—faced the task of building a sovereign statehood after World War II ended and, in the process, confronted grave security challenges, whether domestic or international—or both. South Korea proclaimed its formal independence in 1948 after 35 years of Japanese colonial rule and three years of U.S. military occupation. The Republic of China on Taiwan lost the civil war with the communists on the mainland and established its government on Formosa Island in 1949. Meanwhile, the Philippines achieved independence from American occupation in 1935 and acquired full sovereignty in 1946. Finally, Indonesia proclaimed its full sovereignty in 1949 after fighting an independence war against the Dutch colonial power.

In the transition process from the colonial rule to the sovereign statehood, these Asian countries had to deal with extreme security threats. The Korean peninsula was divided into two hostile camps by the occupation forces, which ended in the bitter Korean War (1950–1953) and subsequent military confrontations. In Taiwan, the KMT faced imminent threats from the CCP armed forces externally and violent uprisings by native Taiwanese internally. Indonesia fought for five years against the Dutch and, even after gaining independence, continued to suffer from religious, ethnic, and regional conflicts and rebellions spearheaded by regional army commanders allied with Islamic groups. The Philippines was the only country that benefited from the absence of tangible security threats due to its geographic location and U.S. security commitment. However, the Philippines eventually followed the same path as other Asian countries as the AFP had to address various domestic uprisings, such as the Huk rebellion in the 1950s, the CPP and its NPA from the late 1960s, and the MNLF during the 1970s. In South Korea and Taiwan, security challenges came from both international and domestic arenas, while the main sources of threats in the Philippines and Indonesia resided within the domestic arena.

These security challenges during state-building years resulted in several noticeable domestic political outcomes, especially in regard to the character of civilian political power, the military's organizational temperament, and its political roles. The first direct outcome of internal and/or external threats was the vast expansion of military organizations in the Asian countries under study. The South Korean military witnessed an immense increase in the number of military personnel within five years of the birth of the republic; furthermore, the three years of the Korean War transformed the military organization into the best organized and trained institution in the country, promoting a strong anticommunist ideology. Similarly, the AFP in the Philippines was created as a small military unit but underwent a major expansion while fighting various rebellious forces from the 1960s through the 1980s. In contrast, Taiwan and Indonesia had large and relatively well-trained militaries at the time of independence due to their previous experience of civil war and independence war, respectively. The experiences of Asian countries during the early years of state-building reveal that, unlike what institutionalist theories of civil–military relations have simply assumed, not all militaries began as well-organized and politically influential organizations. Rather, as this chapter has clearly illustrated, the armed forces as a security institution reflected the particular security conditions a country faced. In this respect, it is worth examining the processes in which the military expands its institution under certain security conditions, rather than treating the presence of a strong army in society as a given.

Another important outcome of the presence of domestic and/or external threats was the centralization of political power within one or a small number of political leaders—usually the head of the executive branch. Since threats to the national security also mean threats to the regime survival in many cases, civilian leaders have strong inducement to mobilize the military for political purposes, eventually leading to the politicization of military officers. In all the cases discussed herein, the presence of significant threats nullified democratic institutions and processes and brought about more powerful and authoritarian civilian leadership. During the three years of the Korean War, President Rhee consolidated his repressive leadership by actively exploiting the North Korean threat and anticommunist ideology. Similarly, Chiang Kai-shek was able to monopolize power within the KMT government under extreme threat conditions on both mainland China and Taiwan due to his connection and control over the Whampoa Military Academy and its graduates. In the Philippines, violent domestic turmoil from the late 1960s enabled President Marcos to declare martial law and extend his presidential term beyond the constitutional limit. Under Marcos' authoritarian rule, the AFP organization and its political role significantly increased. Finally, threats of national disunity and regional rebellions in Indonesia forced President Sukarno to abolish the parliamentary democracy and install authoritarian Guided Democracy with a strong presidential power. Guided Democracy and the declaration of martial law further

Table 2.3 Security Threats and State-Building

	Threats	Changes in Political Regime	Changes in Military's Role
S. Korea	N. Korea/Korean War	Democracy to Rhee's Dictatorship	Subordination to Participation
Taiwan	Civil War/PRC Threat	Chiang Kai-shek and KMT Dictatorship	Subordination/ Participation
Philippines	CPP/NPA & MNLF	Democracy to Marcos Dictatorship	Subordination to Participation
Indonesia	Independence War/ Muslim Separatism	Democracy to Guided Democracy	Subordination to Participation

expanded the already assertive officers' political power. Table 2.3 summarizes these threats and resulting changes.

In the four Asian countries, civilian leaders invited the militaries to participate in civilian politics to promote both national security and regime security. However, once invited into civilian politics, the militaries' interventions in politics were quite different from case to case. In South Korea and Indonesia, army officers removed the civilian leadership via coups d'état and replaced it with a military dictatorial rule. Meanwhile, army officers in Taiwan and the Philippines during the same period exercised political power as the previous two cases did, but maintained civilian oversight. The next chapter discusses the domestic political dynamics that resulted in different modes of the military's political intervention—either coup d'état and military dictatorship or authoritarian civilian leaders' management of politicized officer corps.

Notes

1 The first National Assembly elections were held on May 10, 1948. The first National Assembly wrote the first written Korean Constitution.
2 For detailed information about the formation of the two Koreas, see Sungchul Yang, *The North and South Korean Political Systems: A Comparative Analysis* (Boulder: Westview Press, 1994).
3 John P. Lovell, "The Military and Politics in Postwar Korea," in *Korean Politics in Transition,* ed. Edward Reynolds Wright (Seattle: University of Washington Press, 1975), 153–99; Sejin Kim, *The Politics of Military Revolution in Korea* (Chapel Hill: University of North Carolina Press, 1971).

4 Even before the inauguration of the First Republic in South Korea, pro-communist guerrilla forces were expanding their influence. One of the most significant incidents was Cheju Uprising, in which communist guerrillas swept police stations and government buildings. The South Korean constabulary forces put down the rebels. However, by the end of the incident, about 60,000 people, or one-fifth of the total population in Cheju Island, were killed by the government forces. John Merrill, "The Cheju-do Rebellion," *Journal of Korean Studies* 2 (1980), 139–97.
5 Secretariat, House of Representatives, Republic of Korea, *The National Security Law* (December 1, 1948); also see Won-sun Pak, *Gukga Boanbup Yongu (The Study of the National Security Law) Vol. 2* (Seoul: Yoksa Bipyongsa, 1992), 15–16.
6 *The United Nations Document*, A/936, Add. I, Vol II, Annexes, 36.
7 Dean Acheson, *Speech on the Far East* (January 12, 1950).
8 Kenneth G. Clare, et al., *Area Handbook for the Republic of Korea* (Washington DC: GPO, 1969), 300–1.
9 For detailed information about the expansion of the military forces in South Korea, see Hochul Sohn, "Hanguk Jeonjaeng-gua Ideology Ji-hyung (The Korean War and the Ideological Terrain)," *Hanguk-gua Gukje Jeongchi (Korea and International Politics)* 6 (1980), 22; Myunglim Park, "Hanguk-eui Gukga Hyungsung, 1945–1948 (State-Building in South Korea, 1945–1948)," *Korean Political Science Review* 29: 1 (1995), 220.
10 Among the 100,000 military personnel, only about 65,000 men were equipped with guns, but without tanks and planes. In contrast, North Korean armed forces numbered 150,000 trained by Soviet military advisors and equipped with about 240 Soviet-made tanks, more than 200 planes, and other heavy equipment from the Soviet Union. Robert T. Oliver, *Why War Came in Korea* (New York: Fordham University Press, 1950), 1–22; Yong-ho Lee, "The Politics of Democratic Experiment: 1948–1974," in Wright ed., *Korean Politics in Transition*, 19–21.
11 During the 1950s, South Korea's government expenditure on defense amounted to 50.9 percent, while civilian sectors consumed 38.4 percent of the governmental spending. The Bank of Korea, *Economic Statistics Yearbook* (1962), 24–5.
12 Sung-joo Han, "South Korea and the United States: The Alliance Survives," *Asian Survey* 20 (1980), 1076.
13 Yong-won Han, "Gunbu-eui Jedojeok Sungjang-gua Jeongchi-jeok Haengdongju-eui (The rise of the military institution and its political activism)," in *Hanguk Hyondae Jeongchiron 1 (Modern Korean Politics I)*, ed. Bae-ho Han (Seoul: Orum, 2000), 289–92.

14 South Korea, *History of the Department of National Defense* (Seoul: Sungkwang-sa, 1956), 373.
15 Se-jin Kim, *The Politics of Military Revolution in Korea* (Chapel Hill: University of North Carolina Press, 1971), 40–63.
16 Joseph S. Chung, "North Korea's Seven Year Plan (1961–1970): Economic Performance and Reforms," *Asian Survey* 12 (1972).
17 Hung-mao Tien, *Government and Politics in Kuomintang China, 1927–1937* (Stanford: Stanford University Press, 1972), 9.
18 Taiwan had three major subethnic groups: (1) about 166,000 aborigines (non-Chinese); (2) Taiwanese Chinese who migrated during the Ming Dynasty in the seventeenth century; and (3) mainland Chinese who came to the island around 1947–1949 along with the KMT government. As of the 1940s, mainland Chinese consisted of about 12–15 percent of total population of the island. For Taiwan's ethnic groups and identity issues, see, John F. Cooper, *Taiwan: Nation-State or Province?* (Boulder: Westview Press, 1990).
19 Monte R. Bullard, *The Soldiers and the Citizen: The Role of the Military in Taiwan's Development* (New York: M.E. Sharpe, 1997), 76.
20 George H. Kerr, *Formosa Betrayed* (Boston: Riverside Press, 1965); Peter R. Moody, *Political Change on Taiwan: A Study of Ruling Party Adaptability* (New York: Praeger, 1992). Some records indicate that more than 10,000 Taiwanese were killed in the February 28th Uprising. See Alan M. Wachman, *Taiwan: National Identity and Democratization* (New York: M.E. Sharpe, 1994).
21 Hung-mao Tien, "The Transformation of an Authoritarian Party-State: Taiwan's Developmental Experiences," *Issues and Studies* 25 (1989), 116.
22 In addition to the National Assembly that has constitutional authority to elect the president, the Taiwanese political system consists of five governmental branches (Yuan): (1) Legislative Yuan that passes laws (The membership of the National Assembly and the Legislative Yuan were frozen until the KMT government retake the mainland China and hold new elections in all the provinces of China); (2) Executive Yuan that, headed by the President, holds the power to execute laws; (3) Judicial Yuan that is the highest court; and (5) Control Yuan that is responsible for evaluating the public officials; and (5) Examination Yuan that administers the recruitment and selection of civil servants. Gary M. Davidson, *A Short History of Taiwan: The Case for Independence* (Westport: Praeger, 2003), 83–5.
23 See Ming-min Peng, *A Taste of Freedom: Memoirs of a Formosan Independence Leader* (New York: Holt, Reinhart and Winston, 1972).

24 Jon W. Huebner, "The Abortive Liberation of Taiwan," *The China Quarterly* 110 (1987), 272.
25 Chiao C. Hsieh, *Strategy for Survival: The Foreign Policy and External Relations of the Republic of China on Taiwan, 1949–1979* (London: The Sherwood Press, 1985), 81.
26 John Lewis Gaddis, *The Cold War: A New History* (New York: Penguin Press, 2005), 37.
27 In addition, PRC signed a security pact with the Soviet Union in February 1950. With the signing of the pact, the Soviet Union returned Soviet-held properties in Manchuria and promised a $300 million loan to CCP. See Michael B. Yahooda, *China's Role in World Affairs* (London: Croom Helm, 1978), 43–64.
28 Huebner, 1987, 261.
29 Hollington K. Tong, *Chiang Kai-shek* (Taipei: China Publishing Company, 1953), 522.
30 Hsieh, *Strategy for Survival*, 91–2.
31 Republic of China on Taiwan, *The China Yearbook* (Taipei: China Publishing Company, 1979), 88.
32 For more detailed records on the Quemoy and Matsu crises, see, Tsou Tang, *The Embroilment over Quemoy: Mao, Chiang, and Dulles* (Salt Lake: University of Utah Press, 1959).
33 After Sun Yat-sen died, the KMT split along with three powerful political figures, Chiang Kai-shek, Hun Han-min, and Wang Ching-wei. Chiang became the most influential figure because of his control over the Whampoa Military Academy. Hu died in 1936, Wang in 1944. See, Hsieh, *Strategy for Survival*, 17.
34 Keith Maguire, *The Rise of Modern Taiwan* (London: Ashgate, 1998), 19–21.
35 Patrick Cavendish, "The 'New China' of the Kuomintang," in *Modern China's Search for a Political Form,* ed. Jack Gray (London: Oxford University Press, 1969), 175.
36 Maguire, *The Rise of Modern Taiwan*, 34.
37 M. Taylor Fravel, "Towards Civilian Supremacy: Civil–Military Relations in Taiwan's Democratization," *Armed Forces and Society* 29: 1 (2002), 62.
38 Viberto Selochan, "The Armed Forces of the Philippines and Political Instability," in *The Military, the State, and Development in Asia and the Pacific,* ed. Viberto Selochan (Boulder: Westview Press, 1991), 85.
39 For the United States' role in the establishment of democracy in the Philippines, see Jose Veloso Abueva, "Filipino Democracy and the American Legacy," *Annals of the American Academy of Political and Social Science* 428 (1976), 114–33.

40 Carl H. Lande, "The Political Crisis," in *Crisis in the Philippines: The Marcos Era and Beyond*, ed. John Bresnan (Princeton: Princeton University Press, 1986), 130.
41 Gretchen Casper, *Fragile Democracies: The Legacies of Authoritarian Rule* (Pittsburgh: University of Pittsburgh Press, 1995), 88.
42 Richard J. Kessler, *Rebellion and Repression in the Philippines* (New Haven: Yale University Press, 1989), 54.
43 Rizal G. Buendia, "The Secessionist Movement and the Peace Process in the Philippines and Indonesia: The Case of Mindanao and Aceh," *Asia-Pacific Social Science Review* 5 (2005), 51–67.
44 Lela G. Noble, "Muslim Separatism in the Philippines, 1972–1981: The Making of a Stalemate," *Asian Survey* 21 (1981), 1098.
45 Lela G. Noble, "The Moro National Liberation Front in the Philippines," *Pacific Affairs* 49 (1976), 408.
46 Ivan Molloy, "Revolution in the Philippines: The Question of an Alliance between Islam and Communism," *Asian Survey* 25 (1985), 825.
47 For a detailed report on the strengths of NPA and MNLF, see Larry A. Niksch, *Insurgency and Counterinsurgency in the Philippines* (Washington D.C.: Library of Congress, July 1, 1985).
48 For detailed information about the AFP's nonmilitary roles during Marcos administration, see Albert F. Celoza, *Ferdinand Marcos and the Philippines: The Political Economy of Authoritarianism* (Westport: Praeger, 1997), 77–82.
49 Mark R. Thomson. *The Anti-Marcos Struggle: Personalistic Rule and Democratic Transition in the Philippines* (New Haven: Yale University Press, 1995), 42.
50 Lela G. Noble, "Politics in the Marcos Era," in Bresnan, ed., 1986, 82.
51 Ibid, 84.
52 The Office of the President of the Philippines, September 22, 1972.
53 Ibid.
54 Felipe B. Miranda and Ruben F. Ciron, "Development and the Military in the Philippines: Military Perceptions in a Time of Continuing Crisis," in *Soldiers and Stability in Southeast Asia*, ed. J. Soedjati Djiwandono and Yong Mun Cheong (Singapore: Institute of Southeast Asian Studies, 1988), 172.
55 Carolina Galicia-Hernandez, "The Extent of Civilian Control of the Military in the Philippines: 1946–1976" (PhD diss., State University of New York at Buffalo, 1979), 217.
56 Kessler, *Rebellion and Repression in the Philippines*, 126.
57 Casper, *Fragile Democracies*, 95.

58 Harold W. Maynard, "The Role of the Indonesian Armed Forces," in *The Armed Forces in Contemporary Asian Societies,* ed. Edward Olson and Stephen Jurika, Jr. (Boulder: Westview Press, 1986), 188.
59 Clifford Geertz, The Integrative Revolution," in *Old Societies and New States: The Quest for Modernity in Asia and Africa,* ed. Clifford Geertz (New York: Free Press, 1963), 108.
60 Damien Kingsbury, *The Politics of Indonesia* (New York: Oxford University Press, 1998), 45.
61 Maynard, 1986, 188.
62 David Bourchier and Vedi R. Hadiz, *Indonesian Politics and Society: A Reader* (New York: RoutledgeCurzon, 2003), 4.
63 Herbert Feith, "Constitutional Democracy: How Well Did It Function?" in *Democracy in Indonesia: 1950s and 1990s,* ed. David Bourchier and John Legge (Monash University, Centre for Southeast Asian Studies, Monash Papers on Southeast Asia No. 31, 1994).
64 Harold Crouch, *The Army and Politics in Indonesia,* 2nd edn. (Ithaca: Cornell University Press, 1988), 30.
65 Ulf Sundhaussen, *The Road to Power: Indonesian Military Politics, 1945–1967* (New York: Oxford University Press, 1982), 70.
66 Herbert Feith, *The Decline of Constitutional Democracy in Indonesia* (Ithaca: Cornell University Press, 1962), 262.
67 Anders Uhlin, *Indonesia and the "Third Wave of Democratization": The Indonesian Pro-Democracy Movement in a Changing World* (Richmond: Curzon Press, 1997), 54–5.
68 Steven Drakeley, *The History of Indonesia* (Westport: Greenwood Press, 2005), 88–94.
69 Ibid., 97–8.
70 For more detailed analysis of the origins and development of Guided Democracy in the 1950s, see Baladas Ghoshal, *Indonesian Politics 1955–1959: The Emergence of Guided Democracy* (New Delhi: K. P. Bagchi & Co. 1982).
71 Feith, *The Decline of Constitutional Democracy in Indonesia,* 515.
72 Ibid., 18.
73 Uhlin, *Indonesia and the "Third Wave of Democratization,"* 39.
74 Damien Kingsbury, *Power Politics and the Indonesian Military* (New York: Routledge, 2003), 51–4.
75 Sundhaussen, *The Road to Power: Indonesian Military Politics,* 127.
76 J. Soedjati Djiwandono, "The Military and National Development in Indonesia," in Djiwandono and Cheong, eds, 77.
77 Crouch, *The Army and Politics in Indonesia,* 47.

78 Ibid., 39.
79 J. Kristiadi, "The Armed Forces," in *Indonesia: The Challenge of Change*, ed. Richard W. Baker et al. (New York: St. Martin's Press, 1999), 101.
80 Benedict Anderson and Ruth McVey, *A Preliminary Analysis of the October 1, 1965 Coup in Indonesia* (Ithaca: Cornell University Press); Robert Cribb, ed., *The Indonesian Killings 1965–1966: Studies from Java and Bali* (Monash University, Centre of Southeast Asian Studies, Monash Papers on Southeast Asia No. 21, 1990).

CHAPTER THREE

The Dynamics of Military Intervention

The previous chapter surveyed the rising political role of the armed forces in the four Asian countries under study—namely, South Korea, Taiwan, the Philippines, and Indonesia—during the early years of the state-building period. The discussion explored how growing security threats to the states shaped domestic political structures, culminating in the collapse of democratic regimes and the installation of civilian authoritarian ones. These Asian countries began with democratic political systems, including popular elections and free political oppositions. Yet before long, mounting security threats brought about a concentration of political power within one political strongman who mobilized the armed forces to strengthen both state and regime security. As a result, growing security challenges and the installation of authoritarian regimes in these countries gave rise to the expansion of the military's political influence.

However, once brought into domestic political turf, the ways in which politicized officers became engaged in politics differed from case to case. Army officers in South Korea and Indonesia toppled civilian leadership via coups d'état and installed military-dominant dictatorial rules, whereas the top military brass in Taiwan and the Philippines remained under the supervision of civilian authoritarian leadership. According to the classification scheme presented in Chapter One, the military's role in the first two cases was one of *control*, while the other two cases were one of *participation*. Thus, this chapter will focus primarily on identifying the factors that resulted in this difference across the cases.

This chapter attempts to single out major structural factors that led to the different modes of military engagement in domestic politics, whether through a coup d'état and the installment of military dictatorship (*control*) or the military's involvement in politics as a junior partner of authoritarian civilian leadership (*participation*). The structural theory discussed in Chapter One suggests that, in order to explain different modes of military intervention in politics, it is important to look at the dynamics of the interactions among major political actors at the domestic level—namely, the military, civilian leadership, and civil society—under a specific condition of security threats. More specifically, the theory argued that army officers are likely to topple civilian leadership and dominate the civilian politics through military dictatorship when three domestic political conditions come together: (1) the armed forces suffer from the lack of organizational unity and engage in factional struggles; (2) civilian leadership loses political legitimacy due to its failure to maintain security and political order; and (3) civil society groups endorse a radical political ideology and adopt a strategy of physical violence. Meanwhile, the top brass in the army is likely to come under civilian control when (1) the military institution retains organizational cohesiveness through an effective command structure; (2) civilian leaders are able to sustain their political leadership and manage security and social order; and (3) civil society groups do not provoke domestic disorder and violent political movements.

The structure of this chapter is slightly different from the previous chapter, as it discusses the cases of coup d'état and military dictatorship (South Korea and Indonesia), followed by those of civilian authoritarian rules in which the army participates politically as a junior partner (Taiwan and the Philippines). The following two sections discuss the dynamics of the military coup and installment of military regimes in South Korea (1961) and Indonesia (1965). Section I focuses on South Korea from the fall of the Rhee regime in the late 1950s to the declaration of *Yushin* in early 1972. Section II examines the political development of Indonesia from the 1950s to the late 1960s, in which Sukarno's Guided Democracy failed to provide domestic order, the ensuing political crisis included an aborted coup attempt, and General Suharto took control of the country through a military dictatorship. Sections III and IV analyze the Taiwanese and Philippine cases, where civilian leadership invented control mechanisms over politicized army officers during the 1960s and 1970s. The conclusion summarizes major findings and compares and contrasts the cases.

Coup d'État and Military Dictatorship: South Korea and Indonesia

I. South Korea: From Student Revolution to Yushin

Throughout his presidential tenure, President Rhee Syngman had been successful enough to consolidate his political power by strengthening authoritarian rule through personal charisma and tactful political maneuvering. And army officers were always instrumental in achieving the president's political ambition. However, the increasingly oppressive, corrupt, and incompetent government eventually eroded Rhee's popularity among both the general public and the armed forces. Army officers ultimately played a decisive role in overthrowing the Rhee regime in the midst of the April Student Revolution that erupted after the Rhee regime's irregularities in the 1960 presidential election. The student revolution successfully removed the Rhee regime and restored democracy with a parliamentary system. However, the new democratic regime only contributed to intensifying political disorder and national security crisis. The short democratic trial ended in military coup d'état by a small number of young officers led by Park Jung-hee. This section explores the historical routes from the demise of the Rhee regime in April 1960 to the political turmoil under the short-lived parliamentary democracy of Prime Minister Chang Myon (1960–1961), Park Jung-hee's subsequent coup d'état in 1961, and finally the consolidation of military dictatorship with the declaration of the *Yushin* (revitalization) constitution in 1972.

Downfall of Rhee Syngman

By the late 1950s, President Rhee and his ruling Liberal Party (LP) faced growing resistance from both opposition political elites such as the opposition Democratic Party (DP) and, more intensely, radicalized college students' demonstrations. The general public's support for the Rhee regime quickly evaporated for several reasons. First, Rhee nullified the constitution and democratic processes by amending the constitution twice, in 1952 and 1954. The 1952 constitutional amendment, as discussed in the previous chapter, changed the presidential election method from a National Assembly vote to popular referendum. Two years later, Rhee amended the constitution to abolish the two-term restriction on presidential tenure for the first president of the Republic of Korea. In these constitutional amendment processes, Rhee used the armed forces to intimidate opposition leaders.[1]

The authoritarian rule by terror and physical violence continued against opposition elites who posed as potential challenges to his power. For example, Vice President and DP leader Chang Myon was shot in the hand during the DP convention in September 1956. The police arrested the gunman, who later confessed that he had been hired by the National Police Chief. In 1958, Cho Bong-am, the Progressive Party leader, was arrested and charged with espionage and subversion; he was subsequently sentenced to death and hanged. One year later, *Kyungsang Shinmun* (a daily newspaper) was charged with the violation of the National Security Law; two reporters were arrested, and the newspaper's publishing license was revoked.[2] When faced with growing criticism and opposition from domestic audiences, Rhee and other hard-liners in the ruling LP adopted more authoritarian strategies to ensure the regime's survival.

At the age of 85, the unpopular president ran for his fourth term in the 1960 presidential election. By this time, Rhee himself and his political aides were certain to lose the election because the regime had already lost support from the people; moreover, the opposition DP was gaining momentum in building its political influence. The DP nominated Cho Byong-ok as its presidential candidate and Chang Myon as its vice-presidential candidate. Both candidates were prominent political figures who had gained wide-ranging popular support. Given this situation, the hard-liners in the ruling LP engaged in systemic election fraud, including the invalidation of opposition ballots, group voting, ballot stuffing, intimidation, and physical terror inflicted on the opposition election campaigns.[3] Such serious electoral fraud led the opposition candidates to proclaim that the election was fraudulent and, therefore, not valid. The election resulted in Rhee's victory by substantial margin, garnering 89 percent of the vote while vice-presidential candidate Yi Ki-bung won 79 percent of the vote.[4]

The irregularities in the election prompted nationwide demonstrations, especially among high school and college students. Anti-Rhee demonstrations started in southeastern cities, rapidly proliferating to Seoul and other major cities. Violent clashes between the demonstrators and the police resulted in the deaths of more than 100 demonstrators and more than 1,000 serious injuries. The students were soon joined by middle class citizens as well as more than 300 university professors.[5]

The Rhee regime declared martial law and brought heavily armed military forces to the capital, claiming that "devilish hands of communists" had infiltrated South Korea to instigate commotion throughout the country.[6] However, Rhee's oppressive apparatus did not work this time as the police and the armed forces were not willing to follow orders of the martial law commander, the Army Chief of Staff General Song Yo-chan. Outnumbered and disheartened, many policemen abandoned their duties while the dispatched military forces simply disregarded the martial law commander's order, trying to maintain neutrality between the Rhee regime and the demonstrators. Furthermore, several high-ranking officers, including General Song and Defense Minister Kim Jung-youn, personally met with the president to demand his resignation.[7] President Rhee stepped down on April 26, 1960, concluding 12 years of his presidential job; he left the country and lived in Hawaii until his death.

Chang Myon's Second Republic

After Rhee stepped down, South Korea restored democracy by inaugurating the Second Republic with a parliamentary system after amending the 1948 constitution on June 15, 1960. On July 29 of the same year, the new system held a national election to vote for a new National Assembly that would, in turn, form a new executive. In the election, the Democratic Party—now the ruling party—gained 175 of the 233 seats in the House of Representatives as well as 31 of the 58 seats in the House of Councilors.[8] In August 1960, after five months of an interim government led by Heo Jung, the Second Republic was proclaimed and Chang Myon named prime minister. Yun Po-sun was named president with ceremonial—but little actual—power. According to the 1960 constitution, the prime minister served as chief of executive and head of the State Affairs Council (the cabinet). The new constitution drastically increased the democratic components of South Korean politics by weakening presidential powers and decentralizing the powers into the executive and the legislative branches.

While the new constitution and political systems were certainly more democratic than the previous Rhee government, the Chang regime was not effective enough to withstand serious challenges from both within and outside the government. The Chang government was too weak and incompetent to deal with social and political problems that had become rooted within the Rhee regime, such as a deteriorating economy, factional struggles within the ruling DP, and empowered but impatient, radical, and frequently violent student protestors. The weak political institution was unable to resolve the growing demands for political participation; furthermore, it immediately exacerbated the security conditions in both domestic and international arenas as North Korea took no time to expand its influence in South Korea during the domestic crisis.

One of the major challenges facing the new regime was the economy, which showed no sign of improvement, but rather was further impaired by continuing social and political disorder and rampant corruption of the civilian government. Inflation skyrocketed; the price of rice jumped 60 percent and that of oil 23 percent. Meanwhile, industrial production declined by 12 percent under the Chang regime.[9] Consequently, the Chang government's first priority was to overcome its economic difficulties and, as such, tried to reduce the size of the armed forces, whose personnel numbered more than 600,000 and consumed almost 50 percent of government expenditures. During the 1960 election campaign, one of Chang's pledges was to cut 200,000 military personnel, including up to 100,000 in his first year alone.[10]

However, Chang's plan to reduce the military encountered strong opposition not only from the top brass in the South Korean army, but also from the Kennedy administration, which was concerned about communist expansion in East Asia. As a result, the plan to downsize the army was quickly revoked; nevertheless, the incident created deep distrust of the civilian government among high-ranking officers.[11]

A more serious and immediate challenge to Chang came from the politically empowered but impatient college students. The April Student Revolution originally sought to dethrone Rhee and the ruling LP and then restore democracy in South Korea. However, six months after Rhee's ouster, students were still influential enough to decide the direction of South Korean politics. College students demanded drastic and wide-ranging political reforms, including the punishment of those LP members who manipulated the 1960 presidential election. When the Chang government failed to respond to their demands, the students went to the streets to demonstrate. In one event in October 1960, for example, student demonstrators occupied the parliamentary building and urged thorough punishment for election fraud.[12] Within a year of the Second Republic's inauguration, more than 2,000 demonstrations occurred involving more than one million participants.[13] Thus, a more pressing task for the new regime was not the guarantee of political freedom and participation, but rather what Huntington called "the creation of a legitimate public order."[14]

However, the ruling DP was incompetent at best in handling the national crisis, primarily due to the intra-party factional struggles that continued throughout the Second Republic. The DP was formed as a loose political coalition among diverse social forces, including intellectuals, student organizations, and anti-Rhee opposition leaders who represented both liberal and conservative elements of society. Consequently, the party did not form a clear ideological or political identity—not to mention party discipline or integrity. The party's only raison d'être was to overthrow the old regime. In Gregory Henderson's words, the ruling circle in the Second Republic was "a marriage of convenience between two interest groups, not of belief and loyalty."[15] Naturally, the ruling DP broke into two factions. Members of the new faction—representing the spirit of the April Student Revolution—challenged the old conservative leadership and urged more extensive political reforms. Meanwhile, the old faction—the less influential components of the ruling DP—broke away to form the New Democratic Party (NDP), a new opposition party.

Such political fragmentation created two difficult challenges for the Chang leadership. The first task was to create a new concrete political organization that could consolidate the ruling class, especially the DP. The next step was to find a balancing point between two extremes of political groups: (1) left-leaning college students and intellectuals who pushed for more radical reforms and punishment for the old crooks who had served the Rhee regime and (2) conservative elites and army officers whose primary concern was political stability and national security. Chang was not successful in any of these tasks. Weak and divided, the nascent democracy was further damaged by political and economic turmoil. The crime rate doubled after Rhee stepped down, and the corrupt police did not obey civilian leadership. In this situation, the general public became deeply disillusioned with the democratic regime, which was incompetent, factionalized, and highly corrupt, thereby aggravating social disorder.

The political mess heightened the sense of a national security crisis, especially as pro-communist groups rapidly proliferated under the Chang regime. The Socialist Party was formed, and the left-wing newspaper, *Minjok Ilbo* (People's Daily) began publishing in February 1961. The newspaper reportedly received financial support from an unknown communist organization based in Japan.[16] In addition, college students' proposal for national unification with North Korea further intensified the national security crisis. College students demanded that South Korea pursue a foreign policy of nonalignment and neutrality between the two superpowers by distancing itself from the United States and cultivating a closer relationship with the Soviets. Furthermore, these students urged an immediate dialogue with North Korean representatives for peaceful reunification. North Korea lost no time in welcoming the students' proposal, urging for free elections throughout the Korean peninsula and reducing both sides' military forces to 100,000. Although Chang flatly rejected the proposals, the left-leaning political groups instigated outrageous reactions from the conservative anticommunist groups that charged the Chang leadership with inconsistency and pro-communist policies. In effect, North Korea's political propaganda and armed infiltrations substantially increased during the Second Republic, expanding its influence in South Korean society.

Radical college students and the growing influence of socialist groups offended the general public's and high-ranking military officers' staunch anticommunist sentiment stemming from the experience of the Korean War. Army officers perceived the burgeoning leftist groups in society as a grave security challenge to the state. The sense of widespread national security crisis and Chang's loss of popular support eventually provided justification for the May 1961 coup d'état. Consequently, the first and foremost pledge by the military junta stated that "Positive, uncompromising opposition to communism is the basis of our policy."[17] Furthermore, coup forces justified their takeover of political power by charging that the civilian leadership was incapable of carrying out economic development and maintaining political order.[18] When a group of army officers staged a coup on May 16, 1961, the general public provided little resistance; instead, people seemed to accept the coup as an inevitable remedy for the country's political, economic, and security predicaments.

Installation of Military Dictatorship

The South Korean army's political activism in general and Park Jung-hee's desire for a coup in specific dated back to 1952, when President Rhee mobilized military forces to terrorize political leaders opposed to the constitutional revision. After the ruling LP's election fraud in 1960, Park and a small number of young Turks in the army planned a coup on May 8, but it did not materialize due to the outbreak of the April Student Revolution. Two days later, eight officers were arrested and charged with plotting to topple the civilian government; all of them were released a few days later.[19] Park and his followers continued attracting supporters within the army by initiating a so-called "purification campaign" in the military. During the military campaign, Park demanded that Army Chief of Staff Song resign in order to take responsibility for the military's engagement in the 1960 election fraud. Although Park's coup attempt did not materialize at the time, young army officers' support for Park rapidly spread during the political turmoil of the Second Republic.

In the early hours of May 16, 1961, a group of approximately 250 officers—supported by 5,000 soldiers—undertook a speedy and bloodless coup d'état. The military action effectively overthrew the nine-month-old parliamentary democracy in South Korea. Park justified the coup by criticizing the Chang regime's pervasive corruption, its inability to defend the country from communist threats, and the absence of a viable plan for social and economic development. The coup forces arrested several old politicians, student activists, opposition politicians suspected of endorsing pro-communist ideology, and a number of corrupt businessmen. The military junta set up a Revolutionary Court and Prosecution on July 12 to try 697 civilians for their pro-communist activities and political-economic corruption; 15 of them were sentenced to death, 16 to life imprisonment, and 276 to long-term prison sentences.[20] In less than two months after the coup, Park founded the Korean Central Intelligence Agency (KCIA) and seated Kim Jong-pil, his brother-in-law, as the head to facilitate the military's dictatorial rule.

The KCIA possessed virtually all-encompassing power, carrying out surveillance over not only army officers, but also civilian politicians, students, intellectuals, and the press. Meanwhile, the Military Revolutionary Committee proposed six pledges to the people that included, among others, anticommunism as the prime national policy objective, industrial revolution, closer military alignment with the United States, and "a spiritual regeneration of the people."[21] Promises also included the transfer of the government to civilians and the coup officers' return to the barracks as soon as they completed their revolutionary missions.

Although the execution of the coup encountered virtually no organized resistance, the junta was not strong enough to accomplish complete control over the military or gain support from the people. One of the distinctive characteristics of the May 1961 coup was that it was staged not by the military as an institution, but by a small number of young officers with similar regional, educational, and career backgrounds.[22] UN Commander-in-Chief General Carter Magruder declared that "all military personnel in his command support the duly recognized Government of the Republic of Korea headed by Prime Minister Chang Myon" and asked President Yun Po-sun to mobilize 40,000 soldiers to suppress the coup plotters.[23] However, President Yun did not respond to General Magruder's request and opposed carrying out a countercoup, arguing that it could lead to civil war. In addition to the lack of recognition, the junta suffered from factional struggles within the coup leadership.[24]

Due to the lack of support from within and outside the military, the junta promised to go back to its original duties as early as possible. However, in reality Park planned to consolidate his dictatorial rule through what S. E. Finer termed "quasi-civilianization" by calling for a popular presidential election on October 15, 1963.[25] Right before the election, General Park retired from active military duty and ran in the election as a "civilian" candidate. He hastily organized the Democratic Republican Party (DRP), which was filled with retired army officers. Park won the presidential election by a close margin, garnering 42.6 percent of total votes while his competitor, Yun Po-sun, gained 41.2 percent. Four years later, Park won again in the 1967 presidential election.

Despite the Park regime's quasi-civilianization measures, army officers became deeply involved in every aspect of political and economic processes. For example, a number of retired officers occupied about 20 percent of the seats in the National Assembly throughout the Park regime.[26] Similarly, the Park government's 314 ministers between 1964 and 1979 featured 118 with an active military background. In addition to consolidating his control over the government, Park tightened his dominance over the military by appointing senior officers to key governmental positions or sending them to foreign countries as ambassadors.[27] The military regime also further militarized the entire society by mobilizing all adult male civilians into militia forces and training them for domestic defense—in addition to more than 600,000 regular military personnel.

In October 1972, Park finally consolidated his dictatorial rule by declaring the *Yushin* (revitalization) constitution, which gave the president all-encompassing power with no political opposition. With the *Yushin*, Park declared martial law, eliminated the National Assembly, and outlawed any type of political activity. Thus, the *Yushin* in effect changed the constitution to enable the president to be elected not by the popular vote, but by a small number of congregations chosen by Park himself, institutionalizing his lifetime presidency.

An interesting point of discussion is how Park's military junta—a small factional segment of the Korean army—managed to control all of society and the military. At least two major factors—namely, national economy and security threats—contributed to the consolidation of the military dictatorial regime in South Korea. First, the military regime was exceptionally successful in economic development and social order. Although democratic values were sacrificed with the brutal dictatorship, the country restored high levels of sociopolitical order and stability that had beleaguered the previous governments. Furthermore, the Park administration brought unprecedented economic development; during Park's dictatorial rule (1961–1979), the country's GNP per capita rose from $82 in 1961 to $1640 in 1979 while economic growth averaged 8.8 percent per year.[28] Park's victory in three consecutive presidential elections (1963, 1967, and 1971) was possible mainly due to such remarkable economic success and social stability.

Another, and presumably more significant, factor that enabled Park to declare the 1972 *Yushin* was the degenerating security environments surrounding the Korean peninsula starting in the late 1960s. The Vietnam War and the United States' "abandonment" of South Vietnam forced Park to rethink the credibility of Washington's security commitment to South Korea. To make matters worse, the Nixon administration announced a rapprochement toward communist China, simultaneously revealing the news that one-third of American troops stationed in South Korea would be withdrawn by 1971. Thus, the country's security conditions became increasingly ominous as North Korea drastically increased its armed infiltration into South Korea. During the five years immediately preceding the *Yushin* regime,

North Korea made more than two thousand attempts at armed infiltration into the southern territory.[29] Meanwhile, anti-Park demonstrations also heightened domestic instability to both the state and the regime in the early 1970s. In particular, college students posed the greatest threat to the dictatorial regime. Student demonstrations began as resistance to the lengthening of compulsory military education in universities; the students also demanded the immediate termination of the military dictatorship and the restoration of democracy. Anti-Park demonstrations reached their peak in 1971, when approximately 300 such demonstrations occurred. The Park government declared the Garrison Decree over Seoul and temporarily closed all universities in the city. As a result of these issues, during the late 1960s and early 1970s, South Korean society was burdened by a sense of insecurity.

The *Yushin* constitution consolidated Park's military dictatorship until October 1979, when he was assassinated by Kim Jae-kyu, head of the KCIA and one of his closest confidants. As noted, the failure of civilian leadership—by both Rhee and Chang—provided the military with important momentum for the 1961 coup and the installation of a military dictatorship in South Korea. In particular, the Chang government's failure to provide social, political, and economic stability served as a direct cause of the coup d'état. Furthermore, the extension and consolidation of the military's dictatorial rule was possible in the presence of worsening security conditions both domestically and internationally. In the aftermath of Park's death, another coup d'état occurred as well as a military dictatorship led by Chun Doo-hwan and his followers in the Korean army, which lasted until 1987.[30]

II. Indonesia: The 1965 Coup

Chapter Two discussed how internal security threats during Indonesia's state-building process resulted in the failure of parliamentary democracy and the installation of an authoritarian regime with Guided Democracy and martial law and, in this political transition, how the *Angkatan Bersenjata Republik Indonesia* (ABRI, Republic of Indonesia Armed Forces) became deeply involved in domestic political and economic affairs. The Guided Democracy attempted to overcome domestic political disorder arising from the ill-functioning parliamentary democracy and secure the territorial integrity of the state. At the same time, the declaration of martial law presented the central command of the ABRI with extensive powers to suppress regional rebellions against the central government. The martial law regime enabled the army to be deeply engaged in civilian administration and the management of several lucrative economic sectors. Consequently, Guided Democracy and martial law resulted in the army officers' deeper penetration into domestic politics and the growth of ABRI's corporate economic interests.

Guided Democracy along with strong presidential power provided Indonesia with a certain level of political and security stability for a short period of time in the late 1950s. During this time, President Sukarno secured his political leadership by maintaining a delicate but unstable power balance between the two most influential and competing political actors: the *Partai Kommunis Indonesia* (PKI, the Indonesian Communist Party) and the ABRI. The PKI emerged as an influential political force in Indonesia in the 1950s by supporting liberal democracy and political freedom as a strategy to broaden its support base among the Indonesian people. Political freedom and free elections during the parliamentary democracy era enabled the PKI to emerge as one of the most influential political groups from the elections, winning 17 percent of the vote in 1955 and 27.4 percent in the 1957 provincial elections in Java.[31] However, once Guided Democracy was proclaimed, the PKI changed its political strategy from supporting liberal democracy to endorsing the *Partai Nasional Indonesia* (PNI, Indonesian Nationalist Party) and Sukarno's authoritarian leadership.

Sukarno, the PKI, and the ABRI: An Unstable Power Balance

President Sukarno fabricated a power balance between the PKI and the ABRI, strengthening his political ties with the PKI while simultaneously developing a cooperative relationship with the ABRI as a way of counterbalancing the PKI. Initially, political stability under Guided Democracy was possible due to army officers' active support of the authoritarian rule. The martial law regime significantly strengthened the ABRI's political influence in central and provincial administrations by launching a territorial command structure that stretched from central army headquarters in Jakarta down to the local levels.[32] As a result, provincial army officers exercised an executive authority equal to that of civilian administrators.

President Sukarno and the central army leadership formed a strategic partnership to put down regional insurrections and strengthen the president's power. In return, the ABRI entrenched its influence in political and economic arenas, which were legitimatized by General Abdul Haris Nasution's "middle way" doctrine (as discussed in the previous chapter). The middle way doctrine declared that the ABRI would not limit its mission within the role of national defense. Rather, army officers would assume a more active role at all levels of government to safeguard the territorial integrity of the state.[33] Maintaining a closer relationship with the authoritarian president would provide ABRI officers with the justification for their engagement in civilian political affairs. For Sukarno's part, the ABRI was instrumental in preserving both state and regime security as well as balancing the growing influence of the PKI in the governing process.

Soon after all regional insurrections were effectively under control under the martial law regime, Sukarno and the ABRI marched together to recover West Irian, which was still occupied by the Dutch and, therefore, remained a symbol of national humiliation for both civilian politicians and ordinary citizens. The recovery campaign had the potential to become a means for garnering support from domestic audiences and unifying diverse political interests. This campaign eventually resulted in strengthening the ABRI's political position as it escalated from a diplomatic dispute to an armed battle. In December 1961, Sukarno set up the Supreme Command for the Liberation of West Irian under his leadership, appointing General Nasution as his deputy and Major General Suharto as commander of the military operation.[34] The West Irian campaign, with United States' diplomatic support, culminated in success in 1963.

The West Irian campaign awarded the ABRI with more prestige and political muscle in the Sukarno government, which made Sukarno feel threatened by the military's growing influence and his excessive dependence upon army officers. The increasing role of the ABRI in the Sukarno government forced the president to strengthen his ties with other political groups—namely, the PKI, the *Nahdlatul Ulama* (NU, Muslim Teachers' Party, a conservative Sunni Islamic group), and the PNI—as a means of curbing the ABRI's political dominance. Sukarno's political scheme of power balancing is clearly symbolized by the doctrine of "Nasacom," which included nationalism, religion, and communism as the organizing principles of national unity. Sukarno believed that the Nasacom doctrine would become a channel for national unity by incorporating diverse political and religious forces into a cooperative political association.

Power Struggles between the PKI and the ABRI

The unstable balance between the ABRI and the PKI until the early 1960s quickly began to destabilize the Sukarno regime as the president embraced several policy initiatives that the PKI endorsed. The PKI became influential enough to challenge the ABRI's prerogatives in the government. The antagonism between the two groups further deepened with the creation of an independent Malaysia. The movement of Malaysian state-building was seen by the president and the PKI as a British project to create a puppet regime to perpetuate neocolonial rule in the neighboring territory. Sukarno and the PKI set off a "Crush Malaysia" campaign, called *Konfrontasi*, which escalated into a military campaign in August 1964.[35]

While the PKI enthusiastically supported Sukarno's "Crush Malaysia" from the beginning, the ABRI followed it only hesitantly. Army officers, with a strong self-image about the military as the only institution that truly represented and defended the nation, could not oppose the campaign openly due to the fact that—like the West Irian campaign—it was closely connected with the Indonesian people's sense of national prestige. If the ABRI opposed the "Crush Malaysia" campaign, it was almost certain to damage the persona of the military.

The *Konfrontasi* was not highly popular among the moderate political groups in Indonesia, but the PKI vehemently carried out a campaign to shift the Indonesian people's hostility toward the PKI to western colonial powers such as Britain and the United States.[36] The PKI charged that the federation of Malaysia was nothing more than a "form of neocolonialism" and a British strategy to extend influence in the Southeast Asia Treaty Organization (SEATO).[37] In January 1964, PKI members occupied several British plantations in Indonesia, simultaneously launching a campaign against the United States' support for the independence of Malaysia. The anti-Western demonstration peaked when the U.S. military forces started massive air raids on North Vietnam. The *Konfrontasi* ended only after General Suharto gained control of the government with the 1965 coup d'état, with Indonesia and Malaysia ultimately signing a peace treaty in 1966.

The PKI's influence in the Sukarno government extended further into other domestic issues, including land reform and the reduction of the size the ABRI and its economic role. The PKI's land reform campaign (*aski sepihak*, unilateral action) emerged from Central and East Java, soon stretching to other regions in West Java and Sumatra. Major targets of the land reform campaign included not only regional landlords who had close ties with the PNI and the NU, but also government-owned properties managed by ABRI officers.[38] The PKI's land reform initiative caused violent conflicts between PKI-led peasants and regional landlords who aligned with regional military units during the early 1960s. Such political movements on the part of PKI—including the *Konfrontasi* and the land reform—provoked the ABRI, as the former threatened the corporate interests of the latter.

The PKI's dominant position in the Sukarno regime also negatively affected Indonesia's position in foreign policy, isolating itself from major

Western powers by withdrawing its membership from the United Nations and forming closer ties with Moscow and Beijing.[39] In 1965, Sukarno himself announced his leadership role in the formation of an international alliance or "anti-imperialist" and nonalignment movement, including countries such as Indonesia, North Vietnam, China, North Korea, and other left-leaning countries. Meanwhile, the PKI established close ties with and gained financial support from the Chinese Communist Party. As such, the Sukarno government's foreign policy initiatives during the 1960s badly damaged its relationship with the United States and other major Western powers.

The direct impact of the PKI-initiated foreign policy, along with inconsistent domestic economic policies, led to the economic crisis of the 1960s. In response to Indonesia's withdrawal from the United Nations and the International Monetary Fund (IMF), the United States and the IMF decided to withdraw their economic aid from the country.[40] In the aftermath of the "Crush Malaysia" campaign, the IMF put off financial credits from Indonesia while the United States canceled its plan to provide new economic aid to the country. During the final year of the Sukarno presidency, inflation stood at 600 percent, the price of rice rose 900 percent, the budget deficit reached 300 percent of total governmental revenue, and poverty and hunger became widespread.[41]

During the early 1960s, at least two major events occurred to provoke the ABRI's organizational interest. In June 1962, Sukarno announced extensive structural and personnel changes in the ABRI. Sukarno himself became Supreme Commander of the Armed Forces, exerting more influence over the military. In regard to personnel changes, Army Chief of Staff Abdul Haris Nasution was forced to hand over his position to Major General Ahmad Yani, and officers of the Yani faction were promoted to commander positions in the ABRI, which was in turn directly controlled by Sukarno. This relegated General Nasution to a mere administrative head of the Ministry of Defense and the Armed Forces staff, without actual power in the ABRI.[42] Thus, it became evident that Sukarno had tried to restrain the ABRI's political power by removing the power of General Nasution, who had been a symbolic leader among army officers since the inception of the republic.

Another critical event that enraged the ABRI was Sukarno's lifting of martial law in 1963. Guided Democracy and martial law had been quite successful in suppressing various regional rebellious components, including Darul Islam in West Java, rebellions in Sulawesi, and the West Irian campaign. As domestic security threats had dwindled significantly by the early 1960s, President Sukarno lifted martial law and cut defense spending by 47 percent in 1963.[43] This reduction of the military budget put ABRI commanders in a difficult position because they had to downsize the organization but were not willing to do so given the growing domestic and international threats. By this time, senior officers were determined to fight back against the PKI-dominant Sukarno regime. Rumors were spreading that a group of top brass in the ABRI was receiving support from the United States and plotting a coup d'état to topple Sukarno and the PKI.

However, before the military coup took place, a group of pro-PKI officers, led by Lieutenant Colonel Untung bin Syamsuri and allied with two army battalions and the air force, launched a preemptive coup during the night of September 30, 1965.[44] The coup forces kidnapped and killed six of the highest-ranking officers of the ABRI, including General Yani. The Untung coup forces occupied part of Jakarta, declaring that they had seized power to protect President Sukarno and prevent a coup by army generals allegedly backed by the U.S. Central Intelligence Agency.[45] However, it took less than 24 hours for Major General Suharto to put down the Untung group and regain control over the ABRI. It was reported that the PKI was behind the coup attempt and, during the six months following the aborted coup, more than half a million PKI members and communist sympathizers were killed by the ABRI and other civilian groups, especially Muslim youth groups.[46]

Suharto and the "New Order"

The aborted coup attempt marked a sweeping power transition from the Sukarno-PKI coalition to a military-dominant authoritarian regime led by General Suharto, the highest-ranking general in the military hierarchy in the postcoup era. The years from 1965 to 1967 were a critical moment in Indonesian politics in which, under the Suharto leadership, the ABRI entrenched its hegemony in domestic politics and redirected the country's foreign policy from a leftist orientation to one integrated with the global capitalist system by rebuilding closer ties with major Western powers. In March 1966, President Sukarno was forced to step down and transfer power to General Suharto after being put under virtual house arrest. The National Consultative Assembly (or Provisional People's Consultative Assembly) endorsed Suharto's authority and, one year later, elected Suharto as acting President. Finally, Suharto became president in 1968 and was confirmed in his leadership by Indonesian voters in the 1971 elections.

The elimination of Sukarno and the PKI left the ABRI as the only dominant political force in the postcoup period. The first course of action that

Suharto and the army leadership took was to ban the Communist Party and dismiss 14 ministers from the government. Suharto also reorganized the ABRI to strengthen his commandership by purging officers with pro-communist ideology and pro-Sukarnoism while taking away powers from the regional military commanders. Suharto tightened his control over the ABRI by eliminating the chief of staff's power to command troops and by downsizing the elite troops. Instead, Suharto filled key positions in the army with officers whom he personally trusted, so that two kinds of officers rose to power under Suharto's rule: officers personally loyal to Suharto and those who were politically inconsequential.[47]

Suharto's New Order regime further militarized the country as the ABRI became more deeply engaged in domestic political, administrative, and economic affairs. Suharto dispatched army officers throughout the archipelago to maintain internal security by repressing any possibility of opposition to the central government. The ABRI played a vital role in strengthening the central government's control over local governments and regional military units. President Suharto also issued limited tours of duty for regional commanders and appointed officers from outside the region to the commandership positions.[48] Moreover, the ABRI was automatically entrusted with 20 percent of seats in the legislative body at all levels of government. In the area of economy, military officers' role were expanded under the New Order regime, as Suharto extended preferential treatment to the military-owned businesses.[49] Some officers were appointed as directors of public corporations (including the state-owned oil companies) while others founded joint ventures with civilian businessmen (predominantly those of Chinese ethnicity). Consequently, the ABRI's political role further increased throughout Suharto's leadership from the late 1960s up until 1998, when he stepped down from his presidency.

While safeguarding his political power through the use of the ABRI, Suharto also organized the political party Golkar (*Golongan Karya*, Functional Group) to serve as his own electoral machine and institutionalize his authoritarian rule over society.[50] Unlike other political parties organized in a more general sense, the Golkar was organized as a federation of various functional groups (e.g., youth, farmers', and women's organizations) arranged by elites in Indonesian society. These loose organizations had existed before Suharto rose to power, but he mobilized the diverse functional groups into a political party-type entity. Suharto managed tight control over the Golkar Party by appointing party leaders from the top to the lower levels and exerting heavy influence over the party's decision-making process. ABRI officers were instrumental in building the Golkar, as it was originally organized in 1964 by army officers to compete with the PKI. Although active ABRI officers were not allowed to take leadership roles in the Golkar, an advisory council of retired generals directed the party from behind the scenes. The Golkar Party functioned as the most instrumental element for Suharto's rule by controlling the bureaucracy, the military, and civil society in general as all members of the bureaucracy and the army had to be members of the Golkar.

Suharto's military-dominant authoritarianism successfully controlled various components of domestic instability. Major sources of domestic security threats at the local levels were effectively suppressed using the more centralized military commandership under Suharto, who was welcomed by countries of the noncommunist world.[51] The restoration of Indonesia's relations with major Western powers had the effect of stabilizing the domestic economy. Furthermore, as OPEC hiked oil prices in the 1970s, Indonesia's economic conditions improved considerably, thereby reducing its dependence on foreign aid. Suharto's success in economic and security areas enabled him to maintain his authoritarian rule until 1998, when he stepped down in the middle of the economic crisis.

Authoritarian Rules and the Military's Political Role: The Philippines and Taiwan

The previous two sections examined the military coups in South Korea and Indonesia during the 1960s, in which the armed forces overthrew fragile civilian leadership and established military dictatorships. In these cases, the militaries' political domination was not transient, but an institutionalization of military dictatorial rules that lasted for decades (South Korea, 1961 to the 1980s; Indonesia, 1965 to the 1990s). Meanwhile, the armed forces in the Philippines and Taiwan from the 1970s through the 1980s reveal somewhat different modes of political intervention—namely, army officers' political participation under the guidance of civilian authoritarian leadership. The question that the remaining two sections of this chapter will discuss is which factors contributed to preventing the military's coup and political domination? In other words, what kinds of control mechanisms did the authoritarian leaders employ to circumvent army officers' attempt to dominate civilian politics? The following sections will examine similarities and differences between the two cases in terms of civilians' control of the military.

I. The Philippines

From the inception of the republic to the overthrow of Marcos in 1986, the political roles of the Armed Forces of the Philippines (AFP) evolved in three distinct stages. In the first historical stage, the AFP was created as a politically neutral and professional organization under American tutelage. President Marcos subsequently declared martial law and turned politically neutral officers into politically influential actors. Finally, a group of politically active generals withdrew their support for Marcos and played a decisive role in Marcos' downfall.

This section explains the ways in which President Marcos managed his authority over politicized AFP officers throughout his authoritarian rule, focusing on the factors that thwarted any military coups during his rule and why Marcos ultimately lost support from a group of officers. In particular, this section explores how Marcos' personalistic control over the senior officer corps severely undermined the AFP's military professionalism, promoted factional struggles, and ultimately led to the withdrawal of officers' support for him. Although no coup occurred during Marcos' rule, his manipulation of the AFP leadership made them even more politically conscientious, which led to a highly unstable and incomplete democratization under President Corazon Aquino in the late 1980s.

Martial Law and the AFP

During the early years of martial law, Marcos and AFP officers maintained a cordial and cooperative relationship. The declaration of martial law and Marcos' authoritarian rule was possible only through the support of a dozen high-ranking officers, called the "twelve disciples." These officers included, among others, Secretary of Defense Juan Ponce Enrile, Armed Forces Chief of Staff Romeo C. Espino, Philippine Army commanding officer Fidel V. Ramos, and the Philippine Navy Commander Favian Ver.[52] Marcos consulted with these officers before the declaration of martial law and, in turn, these officers helped fortify Marcos' authoritarian rule.

After the martial law regime eliminated all politically influential actors—namely, opposition political parties, Congress, student organizations, and labor unions—from the political scene, the AFP was the only politically dominant institution that became a primary power machine enabling the president to govern the country. Consequently, Marcos presented AFP officers with various preferential benefits, including promotions, higher pay, upsurges in military budgets, the extension of officers' tenures beyond term limits, and other numerous economic benefits. As such, Marcos served as the AFP's patron, guaranteeing its organizational interests and justifying its participation in domestic political and economic affairs. As a result, Marcos and the army's top brass managed an accommodating relationship during the early years of martial law.

However, Marcos was simultaneously well aware of the danger of his becoming too dependent upon the armed forces to maintain his presidency. Although the AFP was the only institution that Marcos could use for his political purposes, it nevertheless posed the greatest threat to his power.[53] Thus, the first thing Marcos did after declaring martial law was to make army officers dependent upon his authority to prevent them from developing into a politically autonomous institution that could challenge his power.

Marcos designed a delicate personalistic control mechanism over the AFP officers throughout his presidential tenure. Although Marcos awarded all military officers one-grade promotions immediately after declaring martial law, their subsequent tenure and promotions were to be renewed once every six months, depending upon a review of their allegiance to the president. President Marcos appointed the officer corps from his hometown in the Ilocos region to the highest and most important posts of the AFP—a process begun during his constitutional presidency (1965–1971), when he served concurrently as Secretary of Defense for the first 13 months of his term, and that remained in effect throughout the martial law period.[54] Among officers from the Ilocos region, General Ramos and Major General Ver were the most influential figures under Marcos' rule as Ramos was appointed the new commanding general of the Philippine Constabulary and Ver commanded the Presidential Security Command.[55] Thus, officers either from Ilocos or with personal connections with Marcos and his wife were promoted to the highest positions in the AFP hierarchy, whereas officers outside the Marcos circle were discriminated against.

Factional Struggles within the AFP

The Marcos regime's personalistic control over the AFP had a destructive impact on military professionalism and intensified factional struggles among army officers. Whereas officers from the Ilocos region received enormous benefits and monopolized key commandership positions, officers not from Ilocos or unclear in their loyalty to the president were assigned to areas outside metro Manila to conduct dangerous counterinsurgency missions with the New People's Army (NPA) and the Moro National Liberation Front

(MNLF).[56] Consequently, officers outside Marcos' inner circle became increasingly frustrated as they found themselves fighting the flourishing insurgent forces without proper equipment or training. In particular, junior officers' frustration deepened as Marcos was not seriously concerned about the nation's security in general, but rather the security of his regime and his cronies.

Marcos was able to control the AFP leadership by tactfully using factional competition based on education, region, and religious-linguistic identities. The top brass was divided almost evenly between graduates of the Philippine Military Academy (PMA) and four-year university graduates with ROTC commissions. Two senior officers symbolized the two factions and led the factional struggles: General Ver, who was a graduate of the University of Philippines and was supported by the highly politicized ROTC officers, and General Ramos, who—although not a PMA alumnus, graduated from West Point in the United States and gained great respect from junior-level and more professionalized army officers. By the beginning of the 1980s, the factional struggles had clear-cut lines between the PMA and non-PMA officers.[57]

As time passed, the power balance between the two factions began to slowly change in favor of General Ver's side, while the Ramos faction became marginalized in Marcos' ruling circle. Marcos took steps to distance himself from senior officers such as Defense Minister Enrile, AFP Chief of Staff Espino, and Philippine Constabulary Commander Ramos by removing them from AFP's chain of command.[58] Meanwhile, Marcos trusted General Ver and gave him prevailing powers, positioning him to head the Presidential Security Command (PSC) and the National Intelligence Coordinating Agency (NICA). In turn, General Ver tightened his control over the PSC by placing his three sons—Colonel Irwin Ver, Lieutenant Col. Rexor Ver, and Major Wyrlo Ver—in key positions within the PSC. The PSC and NICA functioned as Marcos' secret police and were responsible for eliminating any anti-Marcos movements within both the armed forces and civil society.

The chasm between Marcos and a group of junior officers loyal to General Ramos became increasingly pronounced in the late 1970s, when the president faced multiple challenges on the domestic front. Marcos had to struggle with deteriorating economic conditions, intensifying opposition from Catholic Church leaders, growing domestic insurgency movements as the NPA and MNLF gained momentum and expanded their sphere of influence, and emerging political opposition from civil society groups. Nevertheless, the most serious blow to the legitimacy of the Marcos regime stemmed from the assassination of Benigno Aquino, the former Senator and presidential competitor to Marcos in the early 1970s.[59]

Meager Performance of the Marcos Regime

Marcos' justification for the extension of his presidential tenure and martial law relied predominantly upon his regime's commitment to economic development and national security. During the 1970s, the Marcos regime successfully improved economic conditions, as evidenced by the 6.4 percent growth in real GNP along with reduced trade and fiscal deficit from 1975 to 1979, mainly due to sound economic policies designed by technocrats.[60] The rejuvenated economy in the early years of martial law gave rise to broad-based support for Marcos' rule. However, the Philippine economy suffered a continuous decline with the beginning of the 1980s. The second oil shock in 1979, the worldwide economic recession, and domestic economic scandals contributed to the economic decline. The economic growth rate plunged drastically, while foreign debt and the governmental budget deficit multiplied until Marcos stepped down in 1986.[61] Furthermore, the 1983 political crisis caused by the assassination of former Senator Aquino resulted in a massive exodus of foreign capital. During the final two years of Marcos' rule, the GDP growth recorded a significant drop (−7 percent), inflation recorded 50 percent increase, the unemployment rate rose to 36 percent, and external debt hit a record high at US$28.2 billion.[62]

The economic crisis of the early 1980s seriously damaged Marcos' political standing in several ways. First of all, the continuous economic decline quickly dissolved support for Marcos from business communities that had previously maintained affable relationships with the president. Marcos established a patron–client relationship with wealthy business families by providing them with enormous preferential benefits during the martial law years. In turn, these business elites offered important financial support to the Marcos regime.[63] However, the economic crisis and the massive exodus of foreign capital in the 1980s hit these families hard, especially Makati-based and Filipino-Chinese businesses. To make matters worse, Marcos' relationship with the business elites of Chinese ethnicity deteriorated as the president tried to track their currency transactions in order to generate governmental revenues. Originally, these Manila-based business owners did not oppose Marcos' authoritarian rule as long as the president did not negatively impact their businesses. However, the economic crisis forced Marcos to interfere in conglomerates' corruption and tax evasion practices. In response, the business elite resisted Marcos' policy by organizing street demonstrations, in which more than 100,000 workers marched through the streets on September 14, 1983. Furthermore, Filipino-Chinese businesses began to secretly provide financial support to anti-Marcos opposition political groups.[64]

The economic crisis also negatively impacted national security conditions, as both the NPA and MNLF insurgency movements gained popularity and strength throughout the archipelago. During the early years of martial law, Marcos' counterinsurgency efforts in the southern provinces had been effective enough to drastically weaken the insurgency operations. However, starting in the late 1970s, the NPA and MNLF gained the momentum necessary to regroup in the middle of the economic crisis. The CPP and NPA quickly expanded their member recruitment efforts and influence not only in provincial areas, but also in the metro Manila area, while the strength of the Muslim MNLF was rather stagnant due to the lack of foreign support and a leadership crisis within the organization.

While the growing CPP/NPA and MNLF insurgencies posed serious challenges to the country's national security, the general public's withdrawal of support for the Marcos dictatorship intensified the sense of the regime's security crisis. In particular, the Catholic Church's leadership exerted tremendous influence over the shaping of public opinion, given that more than 85 percent of the population was Catholic.[65] In the early years of the Marcos rule, church leaders were ambivalent about martial law and tried to avoid political involvement, although they formed a Church-Military Committee during the early years of martial law and focused on investigating the mistreatment of political prisoners and other human rights violations by armed forces personnel.[66] The Church–Marcos relationship grew antagonistic as the AFP arrested several church leaders who joined or secretly supported the NPA rebellion. During the final years of the Marcos rule, the Catholic Church—especially Manila's Jamime Cardinal Sin—provided critical leadership in the anti-Marcos struggle that ultimately led to the fall of Marcos and the subsequent democratization in the Philippines.

Rise of the RAM and Fall of Marcos

As the political, economic, and security environments were turning against the authoritarian regime, Marcos became ever more dependent upon army officers, especially General Ver and his followers. The most significant challenge to the regime came with the news that former Senator Aquino was returning to the Philippines after a decade-long exile in the United States. However, he was assassinated by a gunman upon his return to the Manila airport on August 21, 1983. Initially, it was suspected that first lady Imelda Marcos and General Ver had planned the assassination, which caused massive anti-Marcos demonstrations involving millions of Filipinos. The Catholic Church leaders and Manila-based business elites took leading roles in organizing the so-called "Parliament of the Streets."[67]

However, the ultimate source of the Marcos regime's collapse came from the president's personalistic control over and ensuing factionalization of the AFP, which resulted in the loss of control over certain segments of the army. Deeply disappointed with political corruption, factional struggle, and the loss of professionalism in the AFP, a group of junior officers headed by Colonel Gregorio Honasan organized a secret fraternity, named Reform the Armed Forces of the Philippines Movement (RAM). As early as 1978, a group of the PMA graduates formed the clandestine fraternity; two years later, approximately 200 soldiers were arrested for their participation in an attempted coup.[68] Most RAM members were PMA graduates who had combat experience against communist and Muslim insurgents throughout the 1970s yet remained outside Marcos' inner circle. These RAM officers' grievances about the promotion system in the AFP continued to grow as they were systematically excluded from the higher ranks while Manila-based officers who were responsible for the security of Marcos monopolized most of the senior generalship. The RAM officers demanded improved training, better equipment, a merit-based promotion system, and military professionalism by stressing that professionalization of the army was the only way to restore its ability to succeed in counterinsurgency missions.[69]

After Aquino's assassination, the RAM officers went so far as to demand that Marcos step down from his presidency. Meanwhile, RAM members devised a coup plan to overthrow the Marcos government and, if necessary, assassinate him in order to establish a military junta, planning a target date of mid-1987. However, the coup plan did not materialize because Marcos unexpectedly announced a presidential election to be held in early 1986. In February 1986, General Ramos and General Enrile hastened the coup plan, leading to the disintegration of army officers' rally for Marcos. When the 1986 presidential election result was inconclusive, with both Marcos and his competitor Corazon Aquino declaring victory, the RAM officers played a decisive role in the ouster of Marcos and establishment of a new democratic government led by Aquino, the widow of former Senator Aquino.

Unlike the cases of South Korea and Indonesia, where the armed forces executed coups and installed military dictatorial regimes, the AFP did not attempt to establish a military-dominant regime but rather stayed under Marcos' authoritarian rule until the final moment when the Marcos rule ended in 1986. The absence of a coup in the Philippines during this period was largely due to Marcos' ability to maneuver the political power of high-ranking officers by exploiting factional struggles in the AFP. However, the president's personalistic control over army officers severely damaged military professionalism and organizational cohesiveness while intensifying factional struggles within the AFP. Consequently, while there was no successful coup during the Marcos tenure, the top brass in the military became politicized further so that a group of officers in the RAM faction sided with the pro-democracy group to topple Marcos. Yet the RAM was never a pro-democracy group; indeed, it became a stumbling block for the democratization process in the Philippines, as RAM officers and other segments of the AFP staged no less than seven major coup attempts within the first four years of the Aquino presidency. The next chapter discusses how different factions within the AFP made the democratization process highly unstable and incomplete by trying to subvert the new democratic regime.

II. Taiwan

Of the four cases under study, Taiwan demonstrated the most stable civilian control of the military from the 1960s through 1980s, as the Taiwanese army remained under strong civilian supervision—first by Chiang Kai-shek and later by his son Chiang Ching-kuo. In this respect, the Taiwanese case during the given period provides quite a different path of political development than the Philippine case, in which Marcos further politicized the AFP officers. Although the Taiwanese armed forces were deeply engaged in the country's political, social, and economic aspects, they retained a high level of organizational unity and professionalism, which made a significant difference during the country's democratization from the 1980s to 1990s. This section discusses the factors that promoted the strong civilian guidance over the Taiwanese army when the officers had a strong presence in domestic politics. More specifically, it discusses how a confluence of several conditions—namely, changes in security environments, the strength of civilian leadership, and the control mechanism of the political commissar system—produced strong civilian control over the military.

After losing mainland China to Mao Tse-tung's Chinese Communist Party (CCP) and retreating to Formosa Island at the end of the civil war in 1949, the Kuomintang (KMT) government's immediate task was to build a strong military capable of contending with severe domestic and international threats and ultimately retaking the mainland territory. To achieve the task of building a strong state, Generalissimo Chiang Kai-shek's first mission was to reform the highly corrupt and factionalized KMT party into a political institution based on ideological indoctrination and strong leadership. The party reform focused on centralizing the leader's power and placing the party under the direct control of Chiang Kai-shek (1927–1975) and subsequently Chiang Ching-kuo (1975–1988). Meanwhile, the Chiang government established a single-party authoritarian state in which the military served as the party's army and was directly subordinate to the KMT party and ultimately to Chiang Kai-shek.[70]

Reforming the Party

Chiang Kai-shek had the strong conviction that the dismal defeat in the civil war with the CCP and its army was due not to the nationalists' military weakness, but to rampant political corruption, lack of discipline, factional struggles within the KMT party and the army, and ultimately the loss of the people's support. Therefore, Chiang's first policy priority after retreating to Taiwan was a thorough organizational restructuring of the party and the government. The factional struggle within the party had become a chronic problem since the death of Sun Yat-sen, founding father and devout leader of the KMT, in 1925. The most influential factions in the party included the C. C. Clique, Whampoa Military Clique, Western Hills Group, Political Study Group, and local military leaders.[71] On the mainland, the center of the party lost control over its local branches, and party elites' corruption became an easy pathway for communist infiltration into the KMT party's hierarchy. Chiang strongly believed that the nationalist forces' defeat on the mainland was due to the KMT's organizational weakness compared to its communist counterpart.

Consequently, Chiang's party reorganization plan focused on removing factions and establishing a highly centralized and ideologically indoctrinated political body. In 1949, Chiang retired from the presidency when his troops lost the mainland, yet retained his leadership in the party behind the scenes. In 1950, the Legislative Yuan asked him to carry on his presidential leadership; thus, he regained his position. Chiang subsequently created a Central Reorganization Commission (CRC) consisting of 16 members handpicked by Chiang himself who would supervise the direction of the KMT party's reform. The first reform move was to purge the Chen brothers, who were the leaders of the C. C. Clique and responsible for endemic corruption in the party. The reform initiative also removed many of Chiang's long-time political allies, such as T. V. Soong and H. H. Kung, from their positions in the party.[72]

The party reorganization focused on six principles asserting that the party should (1) be a revolutionary democratic party; (2) spread out into various social groups such as farmers, workers, youth groups, and intellectuals; (3) be democratic centralist; (4) adopt the Leninist party's organizational structure; (5) provide political leadership in all areas of governmental policies; and (6) pledge allegiance to Sun Yat-sen's Three Principles of the People (nationalism, democracy, and the People's welfare).[73] The KMT organization followed the Soviet Union's Leninist party model because Chiang himself as well as his son Ching-kuo had been trained in Soviet military academies and learned the ideological and organizational advantages of a Leninist party. Thus, Chiang reorganized the KMT party into one based on the principles of "democratic centralism," meaning that all the important powers were concentrated in the hands of the party chairman (i.e., Chiang) and the Central Standing Committee (CSC).[74]

Reforming the Army

As a crucial component of the party reorganization drive, Chiang also restructured party–army relations by introducing a "political commissar system" (i.e., "political warfare system") to the Taiwanese military. To implement the system, Chiang created the General Political Warfare Department (GPWD) and appointed his son Chiang Ching-kuo as the GPWD's first director. The primary role of the branch was to check and reinforce the political reliability of military officers, youth (high school and university students), and ordinary citizens. One of Chiang's primary concerns was preventing communists from infiltrating the armed forces. During the early 1950s, several high-ranking generals were found to be agents of the CCP—including, among others, the Chief of Military Conscription, the vice-minister of National Defense, and the Chief of Army Supply Services. However, the GPWD simultaneously became so powerful that it could charge anyone in the party or military who was critical of Chiang's rule as being "pro-Communist." In 1964, Chiang Ching-kuo boasted that about "50,000 regular policing agents [worked] in the many organizations under his control, and that the number of paid informants active on Formosa might be ten times that figure."[75] Throughout the 1950s, the GPWD purged numerous senior officers in the army whose loyalty to Chiang was not clear. As a result, Chiang Ching-kuo, the GPWD head, entrenched the party cells in the military hierarchy in order to indoctrinate officers with anticommunist and antiseparatist ideologies.

In addition to the KMT party's penetration into the armed forces with the political commissar system, the Chiang government also attempted to solve the chronic problem of the military's factional struggles by adopting universal conscription and mandatory retirement rules for politically influential senior high-ranking officers. The universal conscription system was applied to all Taiwanese males on their 18th birthday. As Table 2.1 in

Chapter Two illustrates, ethnic Taiwanese became predominant at the junior officership and the private soldier levels. The integration of ethnic Taiwanese into the army effectively reduced the problem of personal loyalty and factionalism. Since the enlisted soldiers were mostly ethnic Taiwanese, higher-ranking officers from the mainland would find it difficult to execute a coup d'état as the deep ethnic cleavage curtailed the officers' trust of their troops and limited the Taiwanese soldiers' obedience.[76] Chiang Ching-kuo's military reform also targeted senior commanders who had been politically influential figures since the very early years of the KMT on the mainland. The GPWD decreed that high-ranking generals at the commandership level could not keep their position for more than seven years. The mandatory retirement rule thereby eliminated the possibility of senior officers' political intervention.[77] These party reorganization and reform drives enabled the KMT to gain strong control over the state, the military, and society until the late 1980s, when democratization began.

With the rebuilding of the KMT under Chiang's strong and centralized leadership, the KMT government launched a long-term economic development program on the island beginning in the early 1950s. In 1951, the KMT set up the Economic Stabilization Board (ESB) to formulate and implement economic policies. The ESB carried out a series of long-term economic plans, starting with the first plan for Economic Rehabilitation (1953–1956) and culminating in the tenth medium-term plan (1990–1993). These economic plans were extremely successful throughout the five decades of KMT's rule in Taiwan, averaging annual GNP growth rates of 9.2 percent. In addition to the fastest economic growth among the Newly Industrialized Economies (NIEs) in East Asia, the KMT government also maintained some of the lowest levels of unemployment and economic inequality rates in the world.[78]

Taiwan's Security Conditions, 1950s–1970s

One of the immediate and significant impacts of this phenomenal economic growth under the KMT leadership was the reduction of internal security threats, especially from the ethnic Taiwanese who had held emotional grievances and antagonism toward the mainlanders since the February 28th Uprising, in which KMT forces massacred thousands of Taiwanese. The continued economic prosperity during the 1950s and 1960s changed Taiwanese islanders' evaluation of the KMT leadership, resulting in them accepting the government as a legitimate authority rather than choosing the communist rule of mainland China. Within a decade of the KMT's move to Taiwan, domestic security conditions had significantly improved primarily due to the success of the drastic reforms in the party and the military as well as the growing economic prosperity.

While the KMT was building political stability and economic wealth in the domestic area, changes in international security arrangements in the 1970s and 1980s surrounding Taiwan also transformed the KMT regime's external security conditions, especially from the CCP and its People's Liberation Army (PLA). At first glance, developments in international security order seemed to harm Taiwan's security position. Richard Nixon announced the Guam Doctrine, which proposed a gradual de-escalation of the U.S. military's commitments abroad, particularly in East and Southeast Asia.[79] Within the first two years in office, Nixon secretly dispatched Secretary of State Henry Kissinger to arrange the Sino-American summit meeting,[80] ultimately producing the Shanghai Joint Communiqué of February 27, 1972 that declared "The United States acknowledges that all Chinese on either side of the Taiwan Strait maintain there is but one China and that Taiwan is part of China. The United States government does not challenge the position . . . the United States reaffirms the ultimate objective of the withdrawal of all U.S. forces and military installations from Taiwan."[81]

The United States subsequently took actions to support the Joint Communiqué by reducing American military personnel with the withdrawal of two squadrons of F-4 Phantom jet fighters and the remaining military installations from Taiwan by May 1975. Furthermore, the United States pulled its embassy out of Taipei and opened a new one in Beijing in January 1979, which resulted in an automatic termination of the Mutual Defense Treaty of 1954 and the official diplomatic relationship with Taiwan—although unofficial ties continued under such agreements as the Treaty of Friendship, Commerce and Navigation. The United States also continued to sell its weapons to Taiwan.[82] Washington's rapprochement with Communist China and the de-recognition of the KMT regime were downright shocks to Chiang Kai-shek, considering that the United States had been the guarantor of Taiwan's security against communist attacks.

Another diplomatic setback for the KMT government came in October 1971, when the United Nations General Assembly voted by a large majority to expel the Taiwanese delegates, replacing the seat with the delegates of the PRC as the legitimate representatives of the Chinese people. Thus, the KMT regime not only lost its security benefactor but also its diplomatic ties with other major powers. Until the end of the 1960s, the KMT regime had been increasingly gaining diplomatic recognition from other countries—more so than the mainland Communist regime did. However, over time, more countries switched to recognize the growing influence of mainland China.

Taiwan's strategy of providing foreign aid for developing countries—especially Latin American and African nations—in exchange for diplomatic support in the UN was ultimately unsuccessful.[83] Consequently, Taiwan became isolated while the CCP gained more influence in international relations.

Yet an unexpected and ironic effect of Taiwan's diplomatic isolation was reduced security threats from the mainland. When the KMT retreated to Taiwan, its biggest priority was retaking the mainland territory through a military counterattack. Thus, during the 1950s, all available domestic resources were mobilized for military buildup, as discussed in the previous chapter. However, starting in the 1960s, Chiang's strategy of retaking the mainland became less feasible as the CCP on the mainland strengthened its control over the territory and expanded its influence in foreign relations.

Changes in international security and—more importantly—on the mainland forced Chiang to adopt alternative foreign policy strategies in the 1960s. The new strategy was expressed as early as 1959, when Chiang stated in his New Year's Message: "Now the task of mainland recovery is to be accomplished by efforts which are 70 percent political and only 30 percent military."[84] This address marked an important change in Taiwan's foreign policy direction from a military to a political counterattack that focused on winning diplomatic battles. The Nixon Administration's subsequent rapprochement with the CCP and Taiwan's ejection from the UN made the KMT regime's strategy of political counterattack an unachievable policy option; thus, the KMT turned its strategic priority to the economic development of Taiwan. By this time, recovering mainland China by military means became a distant possibility, and residence on Formosa Island appeared permanent.

Meanwhile, the CCP's approach to the KMT regime on Taiwan showed noteworthy changes from its strategy of armed liberation to peaceful unification. Throughout the 1970s, Beijing authorities approached Taipei for a dialogue on national unification, despite the fact that the Chiang regime repeatedly rejected Beijing's proposals for peace talks. As a gesture of appeasement, the CCP released nationalist war criminals in March 1975; the KMT refused to allow them to enter Taiwan.[85] The CCP's conciliatory approach to Taiwan continued throughout the 1980s under the leadership of Deng Xiao-ping, who made a series of recommendations such as the "Nine-Point Unification Proposal," "Three Exchanges" (postal service, trade, and tourism), and "Four Contacts" (academic, cultural, scientific, and sports activities). The communist regime publicly guaranteed that Taiwan would preserve a high degree of autonomy as a special administrative region and the current socioeconomic system would not be interrupted. Likewise, structural changes in international relations during the 1960s and 1970s resulted in diplomatic isolation of the KMT regime in Taiwan, while the PRC become an increasingly influential actor. However, these changes ironically contributed to a more favorable security environment for the Taiwan government while its defensive position led it to abandon the military-first strategy and adopt a more peaceful *money-first* approach throughout the 1970s and 1980s.

Chiang Ching-Kuo and Taiwanization, 1975–1988

While domestic and international security conditions significantly improved, the KMT regime also provided strong and stable leadership for the country. The smooth transition of power from Chiang Kai-shek to his son Ching-kuo did not raise any succession problems or a power vacuum that would have given the armed forces an opportunity to intervene in politics. The political stability that Chiang Ching-kuo provided during the power succession was primarily a result of his control over the Taiwanese armed forces as a long-time superintendent and the director of the GPWD under the political commissar system entrenched in party–army relations from the 1950s.

The political stability and legitimacy of the Chiang Ching-kuo regime stemmed from his Taiwanization of the KMT, governmental branches, and the military. As discussed in Chapter Two, Chinese mainlanders as minorities in Taiwan monopolized the seats in all the important positions in the KMT party and the government as well as in the military hierarchy. However, once Chiang Ching-kuo assumed the presidency, ethnic Taiwanese slowly began to fill the membership seats in several governmental bodies, including the CSC. Before Chiang Ching-kuo took the leadership, ethnic Taiwanese occupied only 3 seats in the 21-member CSC in 1973; that number rose to 9 at the end of the 1970s and 16 (out of 31) in the final year of the Chiang presidency in 1988.[86] The Taiwanization process was similar in the armed forces, where officers of Taiwanese origin began to fill the higher-ranking positions. During the early years of KMT rule in Taiwan, Chinese mainlanders monopolized the generalship positions, whereas Taiwanese islanders were recruited as private soldiers or lieutenants. By the end of Chiang's Taiwanization initiatives, ethnic Taiwanese officers accounted for 15.8 percent of generals and 32.6 percent of colonels (see Table 2.1 in Chapter Two).

Civilian control of the military in Taiwan from the 1960s to 1980s remained the most stable among all four cases examine herein. In Taiwan, a number of factors contributed to strong civilian control of the military, although army officers became as deeply involved in domestic politics as officers in other countries did. First, decreasing internal and external security threats brought about changes in the Taiwanese military's mission and doctrine, leading leadership to abandon the strategy of a military counterattack to retake the mainland by military means. Furthermore, far-reaching political reform and rapid economic growth strengthened the KMT government's legitimacy and political support from ethnic Taiwanese. One of the notable components of the political reform was the elimination of factional struggles within both the party and the army, which made civilian oversight of the military more effective. Finally, Chiang Ching-kuo's *Taiwanization* paved the way for subsequent liberalization and democratization in the 1980s and 1990s, in which Lee Teng-hui—a Taiwanese native—assumed the presidency and initiated democratic reforms without a serious setback. The next chapter explains civil–military dynamics in Taiwan during this democratization period.

Conclusions

This chapter provided an overview of the second historical stage of the military's domestic political role in four Asian countries—namely, the dynamics and different modes of the politicized officers' engagement in domestic political process. In doing so, the discussion divided the cases into two distinct types: the military's political control via a coup d'état and military dictatorship in South Korea and Indonesia on the one hand and army officers' participation in politics under civilian supervision in the Philippines and Taiwan on the other. The latter two cases further revealed differences in the ways in which civilian leaders mobilize and control the politically attentive officer corps: a "professionalized pattern" in which civilian leadership removed military factionalism and supported the military's organizational integrity (in Taiwan) and a "politicized type" in which civilian leadership managed control over the armed forces utilizing personal control over top brass in the military and manipulating factional struggles (in the Philippines).[87]

Moreover, this chapter identified at least four key causal factors that resulted in different patterns of the military's political intervention across the cases. In South Korea and Indonesia, a confluence of four contextual conditions resulted in military coups and military dictatorship in the 1960s: (1) civilian leaders' inability to provide political-security order, (2) factional struggles in the military leadership, (3) the ideological radicalization of civil society, and (4) growing domestic and/or security threats.

In South Korea, the Chang Myon government's inability to maintain domestic political order and the ensuing political crisis led to the 1961 military coup. After Rhee Syngman stepped down from his presidency during the April Student Revolution of 1960s, South Korea restored a democratic political system with a parliamentary government. However, Chang Myon failed to provide political order, instead fomenting further crisis, as radicalized student protestors hijacked the country's political route. Meanwhile, the South Korean army was further factionalized as a result of Rhee's manipulation of factional struggles in the military as a way of controlling politically influential officers. The 1961 coup was a revolt by a small number of junior officers in the army, not by the whole military as an institution. Park Jung-hee's military junta effectively consolidated the military dictatorship by declaring martial law and the *Yushin* constitution in 1972, when threats from North Korea continued to increase while the United States simultaneously tried to reduce its security commitment to the region.

Indonesia shared several domestic conditions with South Korea that led to the 1965 coup d'état. Sukarno's Guided Democracy ultimately failed to balance the two polarizing political forces (i.e., the PKI and the ABRI) in the early 1960s. Sukarno and the empowered PKI further jeopardized the national security by implementing several pro-communist policies in domestic and foreign policy areas, especially the PKI-initiated land reform (unilateral action) and the "Crush Malaysia" campaign (*Konfrontasi*). When ABRI leadership planned to purge the Sukarno-PKI coalition, a group of junior officers (the *Untung* group) staged a preventive coup against the ABRI officers who opposed Sukarno and the PKI, killing most of the highest-ranking generals. The ABRI, led by General Suharto, put down the coup attempt, placed Sukarno under house arrest, and banned the PKI. Likewise, the coups in both South Korea and Indonesia arouse under similar structural circumstances (e.g., high security threats, civilian leadership failure, radical civil society, and factionalized armed forces). Table 3.1 shows the modes of political intervention by the military in the four Asian countries under discussion.

Army officers in the Philippines and Taiwan were as politically prominent as those in South Korea and Indonesia, yet they did not overturn the civilian leadership but rather participated in politics under civilian supervision. For all the differences, the two countries shared at least one crucial similarity: the presence of a strong civilian authoritarian leadership and its control over the military. In the Philippines, the absence of a coup during Marcos' authoritarian rule (1972–1986) was largely due to his ability

Table 3.1 Modes of Military's Political Intervention

	Threats	Changes in Political Regime	Changes in Military's Role
S. Korea	Domestic chaos North Korean threats	Democratic failure and coup d'état	Yushin and military's political domination
Taiwan	Decrease in internal and external threats	Chiang Kai-shek/ Ching-kuo authoritarianism	Military's participation under civilian guidance
Philippines	Growing CPP/NPA insurgencies	Marcos' personal dictatorship	Military's participation under civilian guidance
Indonesia	Internal threats due to PKI	Sukarno regime's failure, coup and countercoup	Military's political domination

to exercise supervision over high-ranking officers. Marcos positioned officers from his hometown in the Ilocos region and those who were personally loyal to key posts in the AFP, promoting them to the highest-ranking positions with preferential benefits. Furthermore, he tried to keep the AFP weak and divided by manipulating and elevating factional struggles between the Philippine Military Academy (PMA) graduates led by General Ramos and the ROTC officers headed by General Ver. The balance between the two factions ultimately turned to General Ver's favor, as President Marcos tried to reduce the influence of General Ramos. However, the personalistic control and factionalization of the AFP seriously harmed military professionalism, resulting in the formation of a secret faction, Reform the Armed Forces of the Philippines Movement (RAM) among a group of junior officers outside the Marcos circle. RAM played a decisive role in the regime transition after the fall of Marcos dictatorship, leading to the installation of a democratic government by Aquino in 1986. Furthermore, the RAM officers and other military factions staged numerous coup attempts during the early years of democratization in the Philippines. Thus, despite the lack of coup attempts by AFP officers during Marcos' authoritarian rule, Marcos's approach to controlling the military eventually resulted in the factionalization of the military and officers' political activism.

Finally, Taiwanese civil–military relations demonstrated the most stable civilian control over politicized officers among the four cases during the same period. Throughout the authoritarian rules by Chiang Kai-shek and later his son Ching-kuo, the presence of a strong and efficient civilian leadership served as a crucial factor that prevented the military's political domination in Taiwan. The institutionalization of civilian control of the military in Taiwan dates back to the early 1950s, when Generalissimo Chiang reformed party–army relations as a vital part of reorganizing the KMT party. He adopted the political commissar system and positioned his son Ching-kuo as the first director of the General Political Warfare Department (GPWD), which closely monitored army officers' ideological orientation and political allegiance to Chiang Kai-shek. The commissar system reformed Taiwanese armed forces as an ideologically indoctrinated and cohesive organization. Moreover, Chiang Ching-kuo's dominance over the army contributed to a smooth power transition from Chiang Kai-shek, with no major political crisis or instability. Changes in international security environments also simultaneously contributed to stable civilian control in Taiwan during the 1970s and 1980s.

Notes

1 Jungwon Kim, *Divided Korea: The Politics of Development, 1945–1972* (Cambridge: Harvard University Press, 1976).
2 For detailed description of Rhee's authoritarian rule, see Sungju Han, *The Failure of Democracy in South Korea* (Berkeley: University of California Press, 1974); Yong-pyo Hong, *State Security and Regime Security: President Syngman Rhee and the Insecurity Dilemma in South Korea, 1953–1960* (New York: St. Martin's Press, 2000).
3 David W. Reeves, *The Republic of Korea* (London: Oxford University Press, 1963), 49.
4 Republic of Korea, *Daehanminguk Seongo-sa (History of Elections in Korea)* (Seoul: Central Election Management Committee, 1964), 481–3.
5 Gregory Henderson, *Korea: The Politics of Vortex* (Cambridge: Harvard University Press, 1968), 175.
6 John Kie-chiang Oh, *Korean Politics: The Quest for Democratization and Development* (Ithaca: Cornell University Press, 1999), 41.
7 Kyung-cho Chung, *New Korea: New Land of the Morning Calm* (New York: McMillan, 1962), 71.
8 Oh, *Korean Politics*, 44.
9 Bank of Korea, *Monthly Report*, March 1961.
10 Dae-kyu Lee, Kyu-hui Hwang, and In-hyuk Kim, eds, *Bigyo Gunbu Jeongchi Gaeip-ron (Comparative Analysis of Military Intervention in Politics)* (Busan: Dong-A University Press, 2001), 357.
11 Some scholars explain the 1961 coup in South Korea as a result of the military's effort to secure its corporate interest. For example, see Jinseok

Jun, "South Korea: Consolidating Democratic Civilian Control," in *Coercion and Governance: The Declining Political Role of the Military in Asia*, ed. Muthiah Alagappa (Stanford: Stanford University Press, 2001), 122–5.
12 William A. Douglas, "Korean Students and Politics," *Asian Survey* 3 (December 1963); Byung-hun Oh, "Students and Politics," in *Korean Politics in Transition*, ed. Edward Reynolds Wright (Seattle: University of Washington Press, 1975), 107–52.
13 Stephen Bradner, "Korea: Experiment and Instability," *Japan Quarterly* 8 (1961), 414.
14 Samuel P. Huntington, *Political Order in Changing Societies* (New Haven: Yale University Press, 1968), 7.
15 Henderson, *Korea*, 304.
16 Se-jin Kim, *The Politics of Military Revolution in Korea* (Chapel Hill: University of North Carolina Press, 1971), 30.
17 Secretariat, The Supreme Council for National Reconstruction, *Military Revolution in Korea* (1961), 11.
18 Jung-hee Park, *Uri Minjok-eui Nagal Gil (Future of our Nation)* (Seoul: Koryo Inc., 1965), 174–5.
19 Se-jin Kim, *The Politics of Military Revolution in Korea*, 78.
20 Robert Scalapino, "Which Route for Korea?" *Asian Survey* 2 (1962), 3.
21 Republic of Korea, Military Revolutionary Committee, *A Statement by the Military Revolutionary Committee* (May 16, 1961).
22 For detailed information, see Yong-won Han, *Hanguk-eui Gunbu Jeongchi (Military Politics in Korea)* (Seoul: Daewang-sa, 1993), 210–11.
23 Walter Briggs, "The Military Revolution in Korea: On Its Leader and Achievements," *Korea Quarterly* 5 (1963), 30.
24 For detailed information about factional struggles in the Korean army, see Se-jin Kim, *The Politics of Military Revolution in Korea*, 36–76.
25 Samuel E. Finer, *The Man on Horseback* (New York: Praeger, 1962), 176–90.
26 Kwang-oong Kim, "Hanguk Min-gun Gwanryo Elite eui Ideology-wa Jeongchi (Ideology and Politics of the Civilian and Military Elites in South Korea)," *Kyegan Kyunghyang* (Spring, 1988), 33.
27 Heung-soo Han, ed., *Hanguk Jeongchi Dongtae Ron (Political Behavior in Korea)* (Seoul: Orum, 1996), 271–3.
28 Bank of Korea, *Gyongje Tonggye Nyonbo (Economic Statistics Yearbook)* (various volumes).
29 Chang-hon Oh, *Yushin Cheje-wa Hyundae Hanguk Jeongchi (Yushin and Contemporary Korean Politics)* (Seoul: Orum, 2001), 78.

30 This book does not cover the 1980 coup d'état in South Korea. For detailed information about the 1980 coup, see Chong-sik Lee, "South Korea in 1980: The Emergence of a New Authoritarian Order," *Asian Survey* 21 (1981), 125–43; Kyungkyo Seo, "Military Involvement in Politics and the Prospects for Democracy: Thailand, the Philippines, and South Korea in Comparative Perspective," (PhD diss., University of Southern Illinois, 1993).
31 Ulf Sundhaussen, "Indonesia: Past and Present Encounters with Democracy," in *Democracy in Developing Countries, Volume Three: Asia*, ed. Larry Diamond, Juan Linz, and Seymour Martin Lipset (London: Adamantine Press Limited, 1989), 434.
32 For detailed analysis of the ABRI's territorial command structure, see Damien Kingsbury, *Power Politics and the Indonesian Army* (New York: RoutledgeCurzon, 2003), 67–139; Thomas E. Sidwell, *The Indonesian Military: Dwi Fungsi and Territorial Operations* (Fort Leavenworth: Foreign Military Studies Office, 1995).
33 William R. Liddle, "Indonesia's Democratic Past and Future," *Comparative Politics* 24 (1992), 446.
34 Rudolf O. G. Roeder, *The Smiling General: President Soeharto of Indonesia* (Jakarta: Gunung Agung, 1969), 195.
35 Harold Crouch, *The Army and Politics in Indonesia*, 2nd edn (Ithaca: Cornell University Press, 1988), 57.
36 John O. Sutter, "Two Faces of Konfrontasi: 'Crush Malaysia' and the 'Gestapu,'" *Asian Survey* 6 (1966), 527.
37 Justus M. van der Kroef, *The Communist Party of Indonesia* (Vancouver: University of British Columbia Press, 1965), 273.
38 Crouch, *The Army and Politics in Indonesia*, 64.
39 Rex Mortimer, *Indonesian Communism Under Sukarno: Ideology and Politics, 1959–1965* (Ithaca: Cornell University Press, 1974).
40 Jamie, A. C. Mackie, *Konfrontasi: The Indonesia-Malaysia Dispute, 1963–1966* (London: Oxford University Press, 1974).
41 David Bourchier and Vedi R. Hadiz, *Indonesian Politics and Society: A Reader* (New York: Routledge, 2003), 6.
42 Ulf Sundhaussen, *The Road to Power: Indonesian Military Politics, 1945–1967* (Oxford: Oxford University Press, 1982), 163–4.
43 Donald Hindley, "Indonesia's Confrontation with Malaysia: A Search for Motives," *Asian Survey* 4 (1964), 904.
44 Daniel S. Lev, "Indonesia in 1965: The Year of the Coup," *Asian Survey* 6 (1966).

45 Anders Uhlin, *Indonesia and "The Third Wave of Democratization": The Indonesian Pro-Democracy Movements in a Changing World* (New York: Palgrave Macmillan, 1997), 40.
46 Sutter, 1966, 534.
47 Salim Said, "Suharto's Armed Forces: Building a Power Base in New Order Indonesia, 1966–1998," *Asian Survey* 38 (1998), 536–8.
48 John M. Allison, "Indonesia: The Year of the Pragmatists," *Asian Survey* 9 (1969), 132.
49 For the ABRI's economic role under the Suharto regime, see J. Kristiadi, "The Armed Forces," in *Indonesia: The Challenge of Change*, ed. Richard W. Baker, et al. (New York: St. Martin's Press, 1999); Robert Lowry, *Indonesian Defense Policy and the Indonesian Armed Forces* (Canberra: Strategic and Defence Studies Center, Australian National University, 1993).
50 For the formation and development of Golkar, see David Reeve, *Golkar of Indonesia: An Alternative to the Party System* (London: Oxford University Press, 1985).
51 Peter D. Scott, "The United States and the Overthrow of Sukarno," *Pacific Affairs* 58 (1985), 239–64; Geoffrey Robinson, "Indonesia: On a New Course?" in *Coercion and Governance: The Declining Political Role of the Military in Asia*, ed. Muthiah Alagappa (Stanford: Stanford University Press, 2001), 227.
52 Carolina G. Hernandez, "The Extent of Civilian Control of the Military in the Philippines, 1946–1976," (PhD diss., State University of New York at Buffalo, 1979), 217.
53 Richard J. Kessler, "Development and the Military: Role of the Philippine Military in Development," in *Soldiers and Stability in Southeast Asia*, ed. Soedjati Djiwandono and Yong Mun Chong (Singapore: Institute of Southeast Asian Studies, 1988), 222.
54 For detailed information about the *Ilocanization* of the Philippine Armed Forces, see Carl H. Lande, "Political Crisis," in *Crisis in the Philippines: The Marcos Era and Beyond*, ed. John Bresnan (Princeton: Princeton University Press, 1986), 134–6; also see Chapter Two of this volume.
55 David Wurfel, *Filipino Politics: Development and Decay* (Ithaca: Cornell University Press, 1988), 147.
56 Benjamin Muego, *Spectator Society: The Philippine Under Martial Rule* (Athens: Ohio University Center for International Studies, 1988), 148.
57 Eva-Lotta Hedman, "The Philippines: Not So Military, Not So Civil," in Alagappa, ed., *Coercion and Governance*, 177–8.

58 Cecilio T. Arillo, *Breakaway: The Inside Story of the Four-Day Revolution in the Philippines, February 22–25, 1986* (Manila: CTA, 1986), 132.
59 Albert F. Celoza, *Ferdinand Marcos and the Philippines: The Political Economy of Authoritarianism* (Westport: Praeger, 1997), 24.
60 Patricio N. Abinales and Donna J. Amoroso, *State and Society in the Philippines* (Lanham: Rowman & Littlefield, 2005), 205–7.
61 See Stephan Haggard, "The Political Economy of the Philippine Debt Crisis," in *Economic Crisis and Policy Choice: The Politics of Adjustment in the Third World*, ed. Joan M. Nelson (Princeton: Princeton University Press, 1990), 235.
62 Bernardo Villegas, "The Economic Crisis," in Bresnan, ed., 145.
63 John F. Doherty, *Who Controls the Philippines Economy: Some Need Not Try as Hard as Others* (Honolulu: University of Hawaii Press, 1982).
64 Lewis M. Simons, *Worth Dying For* (New York: William Morrow, 1987), 55–6; also see Sandra Burton, *Impossible Dream: The Marcoses, the Aquinos, and the Unfinished Revolution* (New York: Warner Books, 1989), 277.
65 For information on state–church relationship under the Marcos rule, see Richard P. Hardy, *The Philippine Bishops Speak (1968–1983)* (Quezon City: Maryknoll School of Theology, 1984); Pasquale T. Giordano, *Awakening to Mission: The Philippine Catholic Church, 1965–1981* (Quezon City: New Day, 1988).
66 Kessler, *Soldiers and Stability in Southeast Asia*, 137.
67 Mark R. Thomson, *The Anti-Marcos Struggle: Personalistic Rule and Democratic Transition in the Philippines* (New Haven: Yale University Press, 1995). 8.
68 Kessler, *Soldiers and Stability in Southeast Asia*, 128.
69 Rodney Tasker, "The Hidden Hand," *Far Eastern Economic Review* (August 1, 1985), 10–11.
70 Monte R. Bullard, *The Soldier and the Citizen: The Role of the Military in Taiwan's Development* (New York: M. E. Sharpe, 1997), 3.
71 For more detailed information about the KMT party reorganization in the 1950s, see Bruce J. Dickson, "The Lessons of Defeat: The Reorganization of the Kuomintang on Taiwan, 1950–1952," *The China Quarterly* 133 (1993), 56–84.
72 Keith Maguire, *The Rise of Modern Taiwan* (Sydney: Ashgate, 1998), 32.
73 Simon Long, *Taiwan: China's Lost Frontier* (London: Macmillan, 1991); also see Maguire, *The Rise of Modern Taiwan*, 32–3.
74 Ching-cheng Lo, "Taiwan: The Remaining Challenges," in Alagappa, ed., *Coercion and Governance*, 145–6; Hsiao-shih Cheng, *Party-Military*

Relations in the PRC and Taiwan: Paradoxes of Control (Boulder: Westview, 1990); Hsiao-shih Cheng, "The Polity and the Military: A Framework for Analyzing Civil–Military Relations in Taiwan," *Journal of Social Sciences and Philosophy* 5 (1990).
75 George H. Kerr, *Formosa Betrayed* (Boston: Houghton Mifflin, 1965), 395.
76 Hung-mao Tien and Tun-jen Cheng, "Crafting Democratic Institutions in Taiwan," *The China Journal* 37 (1997), 9.
77 Steve Tsang, "Chiang Kai-shek and Kuomintang's Policy to Reconquer the Chinese Mainland, 1949–1958," in *In the Shadow of China*, ed. Steve Tsang (Honolulu: University of Hawaii Press, 1993); Edward W. Ross, "Taiwan's Armed Forces," in *The Armed Forces in Contemporary Asian Societies*, ed. Edward Olson and Stephen Jurika, Jr. (Boulder: Westview Press, 1986).
78 Peter Ferdinand, "The Taiwanese Economy," in *Take-off for Taiwan*, ed. Peter Ferdinand (London: Royal Institute of International Affairs, 1996); Hung-mao Tien, "Social Change and Political Development in Taiwan," in *Taiwan in a Time of Transition*, ed. Harvey Feldman, Michael Y. M. Kau, and Ilpyong Kim (New York: Paragon House, 1988).
79 *International Herald Tribune* (January 21, 1969), 4.
80 For Nixon's détente policy in East Asia, see Raymond L. Garthoff, *Détente and Confrontation: American-Soviet Relations from Nixon to Reagan* (Washington D.C.: Brookings Institution, 1985); Robert D. Schulzinger, *Henry Kissinger: Doctor of Diplomacy* (New York: Columbia University Press, 1989).
81 Congressional Quarterly, ed., *China: U.S. Policy since 1945* (Washington DC: Congressional Quarterly Inc., 1980), 323–5.
82 Harvey J. Feldman, "Development of US-Taiwan Relations, 1948–1987," in Feldman et al., 129–73.
83 Chiao Chiao Hsieh, *Strategy for Survival: The Foreign Policy and External Relations of the Republic of China on Taiwan, 1949–1979* (London: The Sherwood Press, 1985), 175–229.
84 Loh I-Cheng, *The China Yearbook, 1959–1960* (Taipei: China Publishing Company, 1959), 974.
85 Peter P. Cheng, "Taiwan 1975: A Year of Transition," *Asian Survey* 16 (1976), 63.
86 Hung-mao Tien, "Social Change and Political Development in Taiwan," in Feldman et al., 13.
87 Zoltan Barany, "Democratic Consolidation and the Military: The East European Experience," *Comparative Politics* 30 (1997), 21.

CHAPTER FOUR

Democratization and Building Democratic Armies

As examined in the previous two chapters, the four countries under study have experienced several decades of military involvement in politics, although the ways in which the armed forces became engaged were quite different. In South Korea (1961) and Indonesia (1965), the top brass in the army toppled flagging civilian leadership and dominated the civilian politics until democratization replaced the military-dominant regime with one of democratically elected civilians. In these two cases, the militaries involved themselves in politics by overthrowing their civilian masters. In contrast, generals in Taiwan and the Philippines participated in political processes just as much as the first two cases, but did not attempt to overthrow their authoritarian regimes. In the latter cases, the armed forces' political involvement was one of participation, in which politicized officers were firmly controlled by authoritarian civilian leaders.

The structural change in international politics at the end of the Cold War in the 1980s brought about changes in domestic political conditions in these countries and, more specifically, a reevaluation of the armed forces' roles in domestic politics. In societies where national security is a primary concern, domestic audiences are likely to enter into a kind of implicit "social contract" in which the general public is willing to sacrifice political freedom under an authoritarian or military-dominant regime inasmuch as the regime provides important public goods, such as national security and economic development.[1] However, the social contract itself has enervating effects irrespective of the authoritarian regimes' performance success or failure. For example, in South Korea and Taiwan, authoritarian leaders successfully managed to provide security order and achieved phenomenal economic success for decades. These authoritarian rulers' performance success in turn strengthened civil society and pro-democracy movements, thereby destabilizing the existing regime. In contrast, the Philippines' Marcos and Indonesia's Suharto suffered from performance failure in economic issues and domestic security, which also strengthened civil society groups' pro-democracy movements. All in all, these oppressive regimes, with the support of the military forces, faced challenges from pro-democracy movements in the 1980s (and 1990s in Indonesia). One of the biggest challenges for these democratizing nations was to depoliticize the military, reorganize it as a professionalized and politically neutral body, and place it under democratically elected civilian authority.

This chapter moves on to the third historical juncture of civil–military dynamics in the four countries: the military's withdrawal from politics during democratization and the subsequent establishment of civilian supremacy over the military hierarchy. All four countries (except Indonesia in the late 1990s) experienced democratic regime transitions in a similar time span during the late 1980s. However, these cases reveal quite different patterns in the way in which politicized officers withdrew from politics and relinquished their roles to newly elected civilian leadership. South Korea and Taiwan experienced more stable and thorough democratization, with little backlash from the politically influential officer corps, whereas the other two countries encountered a strong resistance from praetorian solders, thereby making democratization highly unstable, violent, and less complete. This chapter clarifies the factors behind the major differences that emerged when establishing stable democratic regimes in which the armed forces were willing to submit themselves to their new civilian masters.

This chapter is composed of four sections. The first section examines the military's political disengagement in South Korea between the 1980s and 1990s, which covers the limited liberalization measures carried out by dictator Chun Doo-hwan, the democratic opening in 1987, the transition to a quasi-civilian government (1988–1992), and Kim Young-sam's military reform (1993–1997). The second section explores democratization in Taiwan, including liberalization under Chiang Ching-kuo (1975–1988), democratic reforms under the Lee Teng-hui (1988–2000) presidency, and the inauguration of the Chen Shui-bian presidency (2000–2008). The third section explores the Philippines from Marcos' fall in 1986 to the transition to the Aquino presidency (1987–1991), the AFP's coup attempts, and the inauguration of the Ramos leadership (1992–1998). The fourth section discusses the Indonesian regime transition that covers Suharto's loss of support from the army leadership and the public in 1998 and subsequent democratization. The conclusion compares and contrasts the four cases and provides some theoretical and empirical reflections.

I. South Korea: From Military Dictatorship to Democracy

Since the inception of the republic in 1948, South Korea experienced two military coups—one in 1961 by Park Jung-hee and the other in 1979 by Chun

Doo-hwan—and three decades of military dictatorship (from 1961 to 1987). As the second military dictator, Chun suffered from a serious legitimacy crisis from the beginning as he and his followers in the army brazenly crushed democratic movements in the process of taking over power in 1980. One prominent example of Chun's cruelty was his use of the military forces to put down pro-democracy demonstrations in Gwangju in southwest South Korea in May 1980, in which more than 100,000 people participated and hundreds of people were killed.[2] Throughout the eight years of Chun's dictatorial rule, pro-democracy groups leveraged incessant and growing resistance, forcing the Chun regime to introduce limited political and economic liberalization measures in the mid-1980s to soften the brutal image of the dictatorial rule. Although Chun did not implement liberalization on his own will, he remained quite confident about his regime's performance, especially in economic and security policy areas. For example, from 1983 to 1987, South Korea's economy recovered from the world oil shock and economic recession, achieving an average annual economic growth rate of 9.5 percent whereas the average inflation rate was a low 2.8 percent.[3] Meanwhile, in foreign and security policy areas, the Chun regime enjoyed the most favorable security environment since the inception of the republic, surpassing North Korea in terms of military capability and reinvigorating its alliance with the Reagan administration. Yet contrary to the dictator's expectations, the limited liberalization measures provided opposition political leaders and pro-democracy groups with a window of opportunity to push the dictatorial regime for more thorough political reforms.

The democratization process in South Korea evolved in four phases: (1) opposition leaders' and pro-democracy demonstrators' push for the military elites to declare the "June 29 Declaration" for democratic reform (1987); (2) the first democratic presidential election and the Roh Tae-woo presidency as a quasi-military and quasi-civilian government (1988–1993); (3) the Kim Young-sam presidency as the first true civilian leadership (1993–1998); and (4) democratic consolidation in which the opposition leader, Kim Dae-jung, succeeded the presidency (1998–2003). The following section discusses the four phases of democratization and the military's depoliticization in South Korea.

Liberalization under Chun Doo-hwan

As briefly mentioned, Chun's limited liberalization in the mid-1980s aimed to alter people's image of him as a brutal dictator as well as mollify civil society's growing resistance to authoritarian rule. The liberalization measures included, among others, the reinstatement of expelled professors and university student activists who participated in anti-Chun demonstrations, the rehabilitation of over 200 opposition politicians, and the release of "security-related" political prisoners.[4] Throughout these efforts, Chun was confident that his regime could manage opposition political forces effectively by making them compete against one another for political hegemony among scattered opposition groups with different political ideals. However, the liberalization measures brought about an unexpected outcome of unifying and strengthening those opposition political forces. In the 1985 National Assembly election, Chun's ruling Democratic Justice Party (DJP) failed to gain the two-thirds majority in the legislature necessary for passing important laws, especially constitutional amendments and the electoral system for the presidency. In the election, out of 276 total parliamentary seats, the ruling DJP won 148 seats (35.2 percent), whereas the opposition New Korean Democratic Party (NKDP) garnered 67 seats (29.3 percent) and the Democratic Korea Party (DKP) 35 seats (19.7 percent).[5]

The immediate impact of the 1985 election was the empowerment of opposition politicians, including two of the most prominent pro-democracy leaders, Kim Young-sam and Kim Dae-jung, as well as civil society groups such as college students, labor unions, and dissident groups. At this critical juncture, Kim Young-sam and Kim Dae-jung provided important leadership to unify various opposition forces for a nationwide campaign for democracy, including a constitutional amendment for direct presidential elections.[6] The opposition forces' march for democratization began from radical and frequently violent student activists and labor unions, although it was subsequently joined by middle-class citizenry. Civil demonstrations reached their peak when Chun suspended any discussion over constitutional reform with the intention of nullifying the presidential election by popular vote. Instead, Chun nominated Roh Tae-woo, one of his cohorts in the 11th Korean Military Academy (KMA) and one of the key members of the 1979 military coup, as his handpicked successor through an indirect presidential election by an electoral college (the so-called "April 13 measure").

The April 13 measure instantaneously ignited waves of nationwide demonstrations. Various opposition forces united to form the National Coalition for a Democratic Constitution (NCDC), an umbrella organization that included most social sectors, including opposition politicians, intellectuals, religious groups, and the labor and farmers' unions. In June 1987, the NCDC organized the "People's Rally to Denounce the Cover-up of the Torture-Murder and the Scheme to Maintain the Current Constitution," in which more than 240,000 people participated. During the first half of 1987, several reports emerged concerning the torture and death of protesters, which reinforced the public's belief that the Chun regime was nothing more than a brutal military dictatorship. For instance, on May 26, a Catholic priest revealed that Park Jong-cheol, a Seoul National University student, had been tortured to death by the police.[7] The anti-Chun and pro-democracy demonstrations effortlessly turned into a political outpouring that the dictator could not control or reverse. In this political crisis situation, the ruling elites—including leading army officers—had two options: make concessions to the opposition forces and further democratic openings or bring the armed forces to quell the demonstration movements and tighten the military's dictatorial rule. This critical political moment divided senior army officers into two groups: hardliners who were willing to use physical terror against the opposition movements to secure the military regime and soft-liners who were afraid of a nationwide political turmoil and thus willing to initiate democratic reforms. The Chun regime and the military chose the soft-liners' option and proclaimed the June 29 Declaration by Roh Tae-woo, which is discussed in the following section.

Why did the Chun regime and military leaders adopt the soft-liners' approach and decide to yield to the pro-democracy forces' demands? Several factors strengthened the soft-liners' voices in the military and prevented the army from intervening in domestic politics. First of all, international environments surrounding South Korea were not favorable to the hardliners' options. During the 1980s, external security threats significantly diminished as the military balance increasingly favored South Korea over North Korea. Continued economic development in South Korea facilitated its buildup of military capabilities that surpassed North Korea by the early 1980s. Furthermore, South Korea strengthened its security by reinvigorating its alliance with the United States, whereas North Korea lost its major allies as most of the socialist countries in Eastern Europe began to adopt a liberal democracy and market economy. Most importantly, continued social disorder and harsh repression against civil society groups provoked international criticism for the human rights violations and ultimately led to the withdrawal of some Western democracies from the 1988 Seoul Olympic Games. In the end, the Reagan administration—which had initially supported the Chun dictatorship—urged Chun to exercise restraint when dealing with pro-democracy demonstrators and continue negotiations with them.

Roh Tae-woo Presidency: Quasi-military, Quasi-civilian

On June 29, 1987, Roh Tae-woo, Chun's handpicked successor and the ruling DJP's presidential candidate, proposed an eight-point democratic reform measure called the Declaration of Democratization and Reforms.

The declaration included, among other components, a constitutional revision for direct presidential elections, fair election management, political amnesty and restoration of civil rights of political dissidents, and the lifting of press restrictions.[8] Two days after the declaration, Chun announced that he would accept Roh's reform proposals, which brought sudden political tranquility to Korean society. Shortly thereafter, Roh and opposition leader Kim Young-sam reached an agreement on a constitutional revision. The draft for a new constitution was written by an eight-member working group, submitted to the National Assembly, and approved on October 12, 1987. In this respect, although democratization movements in South Korea began from grassroots' protests, the democratization took off as a result of negotiations between the ruling elites in the authoritarian regime and the pro-democracy opposition elites—a process that Samuel P. Huntington termed a "transplacement" mode of transition.[9]

Pro-democracy movements finally gained critical momentum with a democratic presidential election based on the new constitution. However, at this critical juncture, opposition forces were split into two camps that followed two prominent opposition leaders—Kim Young-sam (Reunification Democratic party, RDP) and Kim Dae-jung (Party for Peace and Democracy, PPD)—as they failed to nominate a single opposition presidential candidate. Thanks to the opposition leaders' split, the ruling DJP candidate Roh won the first democratic presidential election with only 36 percent of the popular vote, while Kim Young-sam garnered 28 percent and Kim Dae-jung 27 percent.[10] Pundits speculated that, had there been a unified front and single candidacy in the pro-democratization camp, the opposition would have won the election with wide margins. As a former general and leading member of the 1979 military coup, Roh became the president elected in the first free and competitive election since 1961; democracy in South Korea seemed to have no choice but to wait another five years, when the next presidential election would occur in 1992.

In hindsight, however, the Roh presidency turned out to bring at least one significant positive effect to Korea's democratization, especially in terms of the Korean army's disengagement from politics. During the 1987 presidential election campaign period, several senior generals openly announced that they would not neglect the situation if the left-leaning candidate, Kim Dae-jung, became president.[11] Since Roh—a retired general—had close connections to and strong influence in the army hierarchy, senior army officers perceived Roh's presidency as the lesser evil and nonthreatening to their preestablished prerogatives. They expected President Roh to secure their organizational, financial, and political interests and protect them from possible prosecutions for the 1979 coup d'état and extensive human rights violations throughout the military dictatorship. As expected, upon Roh's becoming president in 1988, opposition leaders and civil society groups fiercely pressed for extensive investigation and punishment of former generals, including Chun. Yet Roh minimized such prosecution and guaranteed the military's institutional autonomy, resulting in two effects in regard to civil–military relations in South Korea.[12] On the one hand, senior officers' presence and influence in Roh's government were pervasive because the military's support for the regime served as a crucial component of the regime maintenance; consequently, retired military officers constituted 20 percent of the Roh cabinet and 7 percent of the National Assembly.[13] On the other hand, Roh's position in the military had the effect of precluding a possibility of resistance from senior officers in this early stage of democratization.

Meanwhile, changes in the external security environment in the late 1980s and the Roh government's so-called *Nordpolitik* discouraged army officers' political involvement. Since the end of the Korean War, South Korea had been under constant threat from North Korea, which had benefited from the political, economic, and military support of the Soviet Union and the People's Republic of China throughout the Cold War years. However, during the 1980s, Moscow's and Beijing's support for North Korea significantly decreased as Deng Xiao-ping and Mikhail Gorbachev engaged in their own domestic political and economic reforms. Furthermore, North Korea became diplomatically isolated from its East European allies who were also adopting democracy and free market economy. In this situation, the Roh administration, with a solid security commitment from the United States, actively sought to open diplomatic relations with these former communist states. Consequently, South Korea significantly improved its security conditions, while North Korea lost its own diplomatic backyard and economic partners. This détente mood surrounding the Korean peninsula consequently eliminated the military's decades-long rationale for political engagement as a way of defending the country from possible communist attack.[14]

Meanwhile, on the domestic political front, the changing nature of civil society and its political tactics deterred the armed forces' political intervention during the critical moment of the democratic regime transition. In the early stage of the democracy movement, all civil society activities were dominated by radical groups, such as college students, militant blue-collar labor unions, peasants, and the urban poor. Overall, these groups endorsed radical sociopolitical reforms—demanding not just liberal democracy, but also a far-reaching revolution in South Korea—and adopted violent tactics against the military dictatorship. Prior to the June 29 Declaration, the various civil society groups—despite their ideological and tactical differences—united under a common aim: ending the military dictatorship. However, after the June 29 Declaration and the ensuing presidential election, these radical civil society groups lost popularity among citizens and, as a result, were significantly weakened in their influence on the subsequent democratization process.[15]

While the radical and militant *Minjung* (people) movements lost ground in the political scene after June 1987, other types of civil society began to thrive and took over civil society movements in the post-democratization period. Representing white collar workers, professionals, intellectuals, and religious leaders, these groups—rather than pursuing radical social changes by violent means—focused on gradual institutional reforms by utilizing legal and nonviolent strategies to deal with a range of social issues, such as political corruption, consumer rights, environmental degradation, and free and fair elections.[16] Ultimately, these civil society groups contributed to the political and social stability in the newly democratized South Korea, which in turn prevented the military from intervening in politics.

Meanwhile, a "grand alliance" among conservative forces established on January 22, 1990, provided the Roh government with political stability and strong leadership. Although Roh was elected president through direct election in 1987, he failed to attain broad support from the public, winning only 36 percent of the popular vote. To make matters worse, the ruling DJP failed to secure a simple majority in the National Assembly election in 1988. In the 299-member Assembly, Roh's DJP won only 125 seats, while Kim Dae-jung's PPD captured 70 seats, Kim Young-sam's RDP took 59 seats, and Kim Jong-pil's New Democratic Republican Party (NDRP, the most conservative party) took 35 seats.[17] The 1988 National Assembly election results created the so-called *yosoyadae* (ruling minority and opposition majority), which led to political gridlock in the National Assembly. However, this stalemate was broken with the conservative grand alliance, as President Roh's ruling DJP, RDP leader Kim Young-sam, and NDRP leader Kim Jong-pil announced a three-party (DJP-RDP-NDRP) merger and the formation of a new Democratic Liberal Party (DLP), leaving Kim Dae-jung's PPD as the only opposition. The three-party merger minimized the role of the progressive political voices and enabled the conservative segments of South Korean politics to hijack the post-democratization political route, which included the key members of the previous dictatorial regime. However, the creation of the conservative grand alliance broke the political stalemate in the *yosoyadae* Parliament and restored political stability and effectiveness.[18] The ruling

LDP nominated Kim Young-sam as its presidential candidate for the 1992 presidential election.

Kim Young-sam's Presidency and the Military Reform

Democratization in South Korea reached another significant turning point in the 1992 presidential election, when Kim Young-sam, the ruling DLP presidential candidate, won the election. Prior to the election, President Roh had made two important decisions that ultimately became critical for a stable power transition.[19] First, during the campaign, Roh announced that he was resigning from his position as the DLP's leader to demonstrate his political neutrality and commitment to a fair election and peaceful regime change. His resignation removed the possibility for senior army officers to interfere in the election process. Second, he introduced strict election campaign laws, including a reduced campaign period and limitations on campaign spending. The campaign laws helped end secret political funds from big businesses (the so-called *Chaebol*). Thus, the Roh presidency helped solve what Huntington has called the "praetorian problem" of the military's intervention during a regime transition period. Kim Young-sam, although he had been an opposition leader and pro-democracy activist against military dictatorship for more than three decades, was accepted by army officers as the lesser evil since he represented the conservative ruling circle. He won the 1992 presidential election with 42 percent of the popular vote, while the opposition candidate, Kim Dae-jung, received 34 percent and Chung Ju-young, the owner of Hyundai Corporation, garnered 16 percent.[20]

President Kim Young-sam was in a better position to conduct extensive reforms, including those involving the army, than his predecessor Roh. Kim began his presidency with a ruling majority in the National Assembly and strong support from both the general public and various pro-democracy civil society groups.[21] As soon as he was inaugurated, President Kim wasted no time in embarking on wide-ranging political and economic reforms that included the armed forces, anticorruption, financial openness, and electoral reforms. The South Korean army was the first target of the reform drive.

Although Roh had been able to secure allegiance from the top brass, the officers' loyalty was in return for Roh's protection of the military's corporate interest. Therefore, army officers still possessed enormous influence in politics and institutional prerogatives throughout the Roh government. President Kim's first priority was to reduce the military's political power and establish institutionalized civilian control of the South Korean army. He began the military reform by reshuffling top personnel so that he could establish firm control over senior army officers. Shortly after his inauguration, Kim contacted several top-ranking senior officers to discuss these military reforms and received a positive response from army leadership. He removed two officers, Chief of Staff Kim Jin-young and Seo Wan-su, the head of the Defense Security Command (DSC)—the infamous agency headed by Chun Doo-hwan during the 1979–1980 coup d'état and the backbone of the military dictatorship. Furthermore, President Kim reformed the chain of command in the military intelligence agencies actively involved in policing domestic politics, including monitoring opposition activists and pro-democracy civil society movements.[22]

More importantly, to reinforce his control over the armed forces, Kim focused on disbanding the *Hanahoe* (one mind), a secret association created by Chun and Roh.[23] Originally organized in 1964, the *Hanahoe* increased its membership and influence under the patronage of Park Jung-hee in the 1970s. During the power vacuum after Park's assassination in 1979, the *Hanahoe* executed a military coup and established Chun's dictatorial rule. Under the Chun regime, *Hanahoe* members rose to the apex of power both within the military hierarchy and in civilian politics.[24] President Kim weakened the *Hanahoe* by adopting several strategies, including early retirements and the exclusion of its members from promotions. Within one year of being elected, President Kim reshuffled more than 50 of the highest-ranking officers. Eight non-*Hanahoe* officers quickly rose to division commanders whereas none of the *Hanahoe* members was included in the promotions.[25]

The Kim government effectively used a strategy of raising corruption issues in the military to purge corrupt officers and eliminate the *Hanahoe* faction in the army. A bribery scandal emerged when the wife of a navy officer publicly complained that her bribes to an admiral's wife were ineffective in her husband's promotion. When the scandal was publicized by the mass media, the Kim government took advantage of the opportunity to cleanse the system of politically minded high-ranking officers who were collecting bribes. The bribery scandal resulted in the arrest of more than a dozen senior officers. Another significant corruption scandal erupted in relation to the purchase of air fighters from the United States as a defense modernization plan. An investigation by the Board of Audit and Inspection revealed huge sums of secret funds in two bank accounts of two former defense ministers, which resulted in the further purge of politicized officers.

Kim's reform also included anticorruption drives in the economic and financial sectors, ultimately targeting corrupt high-ranking officers. The Kim government enacted the Real-Name Financial Transaction System in

1993 to monitor financial activities and real estate deals.[26] During the three decades of the military dictatorship, borrowed or false names were widely used for banking transactions and real estate registrations, thereby enabling big business owners (*Chaebol*) to donate large amounts of untraceable monies to politicians. The Kim government enacted the 1993 law to stop this flow of illegal money. Interestingly enough, one unexpected outcome of the law was that it enabled prosecutors to discover a huge amount of secret funds amassed by the former president. On October 19, 1995, opposition legislator Park Kye-dong disclosed that former president Roh held secret funds amounting to approximately $650 million under 40 false-name accounts.

This incident triggered massive demonstrations throughout major cities, demanding punishment for both Chun and Roh. With the strong support of the public led by civil society groups, the National Assembly passed a special law that dealt with the bribery scandals, the 1979 coup d'état, and the 1980 Gwangju massacre. Former presidents Chun and Roh as well as 14 other generals were found guilty of rebellion, conspiracy, and corruption. At the trial, Chun was sentenced to death, Roh to 22 years in prison, and the remaining officers to several years of incarceration. The punishment of the two military-turned-presidents and other high-ranking generals put an end to army officers' influence in politics. With this trial and a series of other institutional reforms, firm civilian control over the armed forces was achieved under Kim's presidency. Consequently, when long-time pro-democracy activist and opposition leader Kim Dae-jung rose to the presidency in 1997, the Korean army—unlike during the 1987 presidential election—expressed its allegiance to the new president.

Several factors enabled Kim Young-sam's success in military reform and allowed him to establish firm civilian control. First, from the beginning of his term, the Kim presidency received strong support from the general public, who hailed it as the first legitimate civilian government since the Second Republic by Chang Myon had fallen in the 1961 coup d'état. Although Roh became president through a free and competitive presidential election, his legitimacy was significantly undermined by his previous career in the military—especially given his leading role in the *Hanahoe*, his participation as one of the December 12 coup plotters, and his position as the second most powerful man in Chun's dictatorial rule. In contrast, Kim Young-sam boasted a decades-long career as a pro-democracy activist and prominent leader of the country's democratization. At the time of his inauguration, Kim enjoyed more than 80 percent approval rates and garnered support from a diverse spectrum of political forces by co-opting several former opposition leaders without losing support from conservatives. In the trial against the two generals-turned-presidents, more than 75 percent of people supported the prosecution.[27]

Second, ideologically moderate civil society groups that focused their efforts on institutional reforms also contributed to strengthening Kim's reform drive and deterring army officers' resistance to reform. During the democratization period, civil society movements drastically moved away from radical and violent street demonstrations, turning instead to moderate and middle-class dominant civil initiatives during the late 1980s and early 1990s. These new civil groups focused on issues such as economic justice, social welfare, environmental crisis, and women's rights.[28] They strongly supported Kim's reforms, and Kim consequently adopted the issues they raised. The decline of the radical *Minjung* movements and the rise of middle-class civil groups contributed to a significant decline in physical violence by both the government and civil society groups, precluding any possibility of the armed forces' political involvement.

Finally, the existence of a cohesive and professionalized army encouraged stronger civilian control over the armed forces. During their presidential terms, Chun and Roh maintained the military as a cohesive institution, with the *Hanahoe* dominating the army hierarchy. Although South Korea experienced three decades of military dictatorship, the military as an institution never intervened in politics. Rather, two coups were staged by a small number of army officers. During his presidential term, Kim Young-sam focused on reforming the South Korean army to be a unified organization by removing politically influential *Hanahoe* officers from the military leadership. When Kim reorganized the army, the military as an institution did not exert veto power except for a small number of *Hanahoe* officers. The *Hanahoe*, in turn, was effectively eradicated and banned under the Kim government.

II. Taiwan: Officers' Loyalty from the Party to the State

During its decades-long rule in Taiwan, the Kuomintang (KMT) government evolved from a quasi-military government in the 1950s to a one-party authoritarian state up until the 1980s, finally becoming a democratic regime with a multiparty system in the 1990s. In all the stages of its political development, the Republic of China (ROC) on Taiwan maintained very firm civilian control of the armed forces. Prior to democratization, civilian control of the ROC army was attributable to the presence of a strong civilian leadership by the Chiang family—namely, Chiang Kai-shek and his son Ching-kuo—and to the KMT party's penetration into the military hierarchy using the political commissar system.²⁹ During this period, army officers were more committed to the KMT party than to the state or the people in general, just as in many communist states, as previous chapters have shown.

On the other hand, establishing democratic control of the military is a crucial component of democratization. In Taiwan, this entailed changing army officers' loyalty from the KMT party to the constitution and the state. Although curbing the army's political power has been an essential element of successful democratization in Taiwan, insufficient scholarly attention has been devoted to addressing this aspect.³⁰ This section explains how Taiwan successfully achieved a stable democratic transition and, in the process, created firm civilian control over the armed forces. To have a better understanding of civil–military relations in Taiwan, we need to go back to Chiang Ching-kuo's limited liberal reforms in the 1970s and 1980s and the power transition to Lee Teng-hui.

Chiang Ching-kuo's Reforms

Developments in international politics during the 1970s, especially the Nixon Doctrine and Sino-US rapprochement, brought two contrasting consequences to Taiwanese politics. The country found itself in a difficult international position during the 1970s due to diplomatic isolation—namely, diplomatic de-recognition by most countries, expulsion from the United Nations, and, most importantly, the loss of the U.S. security commitment. This situation marked the KMT's most humiliating defeat against communist China since it lost the civil war in 1949. These international developments created a deep legitimacy crisis in the Chiang government. With international de-recognition, the KMT government could no longer claim itself to be the only legitimate regime in China. However, a new détente was simultaneously taking shape around the Taiwan Straits in the 1970s.³¹ The rapprochement between the United States and China significantly reduced the communist threats to the KMT regime. Furthermore, generational changes in both Taiwan and on the mainland (including the death of Chiang Kai-shek and Mao Tse-tung) diminished the severity of hostility between the two governments. Generational changes and interethnic marriages gradually blurred the ethnic gap between Taiwanese islanders and mainland Chinese. By the mid-1970s, about 55 percent of Chinese ethnics had been born after the KMT had retreated to Taiwan.³² Meanwhile, on the mainland side, Deng Xiao-ping's pragmatism and economic reform drives led to China's conciliatory approach to Taiwan, constructing a favorable security environment for the Chiang Ching-kuo regime. By the 1970s, the prime objective of the KMT regime was not to retake the mainland territory by military force, but to build a stable and legitimate political entity with a strong economy and robust defense.[33]

Decreasing security threats enabled Chiang Ching-kuo to embark on a slow but steady political liberalization that aimed to strengthen the KMT's legitimacy among ethnic Taiwanese. The focal point of Chiang's reform was the *Taiwanization* of the KMT party, legislative branches, and the army hierarchy (see Chapter Three). As a result of Chiang's reform drives in the 1970s until his death in 1988, KMT rule transformed the island from hard-authoritarianism to soft-authoritarianism, during which time political oppression was significantly diminished and Taiwanese ethnics expanded their participation and influence in the government and the military.

Although the KMT regime initiated the early stage of liberal reforms, it was the opposition political forces that pushed for a more thorough and profound democratization. Chiang's liberalization brought about a rapid increase in the political opposition movement, known as *tangwai* (literally meaning "outside the party"). *Tangwai* began as a grassroots coalition formed by ethnic Taiwanese who demanded political freedom and independence for the island.[34] *Tangwai* became an important and influential force for democratization, running for seats in local and provincial assemblies and raising numerous issues such as farmers' interests, religious rights, environmental preservation, and consumers' rights.[35] In pushing the KMT government for more reforms, *tangwai* members adopted a moderate strategy and dealt with less politically sensitive issues such as economic justice, environmental preservation, and labor rights. In 1983 and 1987, according to Fan's survey, just 11 percent of *tangwai*'s initiatives were considered political, while other nonpolitical issues accounted for the rest.[36] *Tangwai*'s democratic initiatives slowly transformed the authoritarian society without intimidating the old conservatives in the KMT and the army.

In September 1986, 135 members of the *tangwai* announced the formation of a new political party, the Democratic Progressive Party (DPP), with legislator Fei Hsi-ping as the party leader. Surprisingly enough, rather than prosecuting DPP organizers, the KMT regime took no action. Indeed, Chiang made an interesting announcement in early 1986 during an interview with the *Washington Post*, when he said he would lift martial law as soon as a new national security law could be put into place.[37] With the formation of the DPP, Taiwan had the first multiparty election in the 1986 National Assembly and Legislative Yuan elections. In addition, earlier that year, President Chiang appointed an ad hoc committee for further democratic reforms. The committee recommended several important reform objectives, such as ending the ban on opposition parties, reorganizing the National Assembly and the Legislative Yuan, and furthering the *Taiwanization* and structural reform of the KMT party.[38] The committee's recommendation set the foundation for democratization in the late-1980s and early-1990s.

Chiang followed the committee's suggestion to lift the four-decade-long martial law in July 1987, which positively impacted Taiwan's democratization in several ways. With the lifting of martial law, opposition parties became legal; a number of opposition parties were formed, including the Social Democratic Party, the Green Party, the Workers Party, the Labor Party, and in 1993 the Chinese New Party—none of which became influential enough to offer a serious challenge to the KMT until the 1996 presidential election.[39] In addition, the KMT government lifted the ban on travel to mainland China, enabling Taiwanese businesses to invest in and trade with the mainland. Finally—and most significantly in terms of the military's political roles—the end of martial law prohibited army intelligence agencies from interfering in civilian affairs, thereby reducing the armed forces' political influence.

The Lee Teng-hui Presidency

Before lifting martial law, Chiang Ching-kuo carefully prepared for a smooth power transition by declaring that the Chiang family would never assume leadership in Taiwanese politics and subsequently appointing Lee Teng-hui as his successor upon his death.[40] A technocrat with a doctoral degree from Cornell University, Lee served as the mayor of Taipei City and governor of Taiwan Province from 1978 to 1981; in 1982, he was handpicked by Chiang to serve as vice president. Lee's appointment as the next president was a genuine surprise both within and outside the KMT as he was an ethnic Taiwanese who did not have a significant support base in the party. Until Chiang's death, anxiety about the power succession and possible political crisis continued, with some apprehensions about a possibility of military coup. However, against these backdrops, several factors contributed to a smooth power transition from Chiang to Lee. First, Chiang himself made it clear that there would be no military government or another "Chiang Dynasty" after his death and that Lee would be his successor. Second, Chiang's *Taiwanization* drives within and outside the KMT party long before his death provided Lee with favorable conditions for securing his power base in the party and the army. Third, one year before Lee rose to the presidency, martial law was lifted so that army officers could not overtly intervene in the succession process. Finally, right after rising to power, Lee appointed General

Hau Pei-tsun, the most influential figure in the ROC army, as premier.[41] As a result of these factors, 24 senior army officers, including Chief of Staff General Hau, swore loyalty to Lee upon his inauguration.

Democratic reforms were further accelerated under Lee's leadership. From 1988 until 1996, when the direct presidential election took place, were the most critical years for Taiwan's democratization and the army's depoliticization. In the summer of 1990, Lee convened a National Affairs Conference (NAC)—an advisory council for the president—to create a national consensus on democratic reforms. The NAC reached an agreement on key reform issues, including: (1) lifting the Temporary Provisions (or "Period of Mobilization for Suppression of Communist Rebellion," an emergency legislation passed by the National Assembly in May 1948); (2) retiring the "old guards" in the Legislative Yuan (legislative branch) and National Assembly (a governmental branch with the power to amend the constitution and elect the president and vice-president), who had been elected in mainland China before retreating to Taiwan; (3) constructing proportional representation seats in the Legislative Yuan; and, most importantly, (4) electing the president through direct popular election.[42]

Based on the NAC's recommendation, President Lee abolished the Temporary Provisions, officially ending the half-century-long civil war with the mainland regime. The official termination of the civil war drastically softened Taiwan's approach to its mainland counterpart. In January 1991, the KMT government founded the Mainland Affairs Council (MAC) to plan and implement policies toward the mainland. In addition, the ending of the Temporary Provisions notably reduced the ROC army's domestic security roles. In 1992, the KMT disbanded the Taiwan Garrison Command (TGC), which had performed the army's internal security and policing responsibilities throughout the Cold War years.[43] Meanwhile, all military training programs for university students were also eliminated, fostering further de-militarization of civilian society in Taiwan. In addition to curbing the military's political and domestic security roles, President Lee reformed the legislative bodies. He forced older members of the Legislative Yuan and National Assembly into retirement and reformed the electoral systems so that representatives were chosen through popular election. Finally, he announced that Taiwan would have a popular presidential election in 1996. Lee's democratic reforms were so orderly and well-executed that no significant political crisis occurred during the democratic reform period.

Several important elements enabled President Lee's successful democratic reforms and the depoliticization of army officers. The first and most significant factor was the diminishing external security threats surrounding the island during the democratic reforms. As previously mentioned, authorities from mainland China had been offering conciliatory gestures to their counterparts on the island ever since Deng Xiao-ping rose to power and initiated economic reforms. In response, the KMT leadership—although slow to react—permitted economic transactions and family visits to the mainland. The amount of Taiwan–PRC trade reached $1 billion in 1987, although it was an indirect trade with the mainland via Hong Kong.[44] The business community led the subsequent expansion of economic cooperation with the mainland, quite free of political and security constraints.

As Table 4.1 summarily illustrates, economic transactions across the Taiwan Straits increased rapidly, leading Taiwan and the PRC toward a deep economic interdependence. By the time the first democratic presidential election was held, mainland China had become the second largest trading partner for Taiwan. In addition, Taiwanese businessmen's foreign direct investment to the mainland increased in the 1990s, amounting to more than $1.2 billion in the final year of the Lee presidency. Such a rapidly forming economic interdependence was not interrupted by strained political–security relations between the two governments in the mid- to late-1990s. Rather, growing economic cooperation became the most significant factor stabilizing Taiwan–PRC relations.

The second element conducive to Taiwan's smooth democratic regime transition was the way in which the country launched the democratization, especially the role of elections, which resulted in an absence of physical violence between civil society groups and the government. Although free and competitive elections were originally not allowed for most positions in the

Table 4.1 Taiwan–PRC Economic Exchanges, 1990–1996 (in US$ millions)

Year	Taiwan's Exports to PRC	% of Taiwan's Total Exports	Taiwan's Trade Surplus with PRC
1990	4,395	6.54	3,629
1991	7,494	9.84	6,368
1992	10,548	12.95	9,429
1993	13,993	16.47	12,889
1994	16,023	17.22	14,164
1995	19,434	17.40	16,342
1996	20,727	17.87	17,668

Source: Tse-kang Leng, "Dynamics of Taiwan-Mainland China Economic Relations: The Role of Private Firms," *Asian Survey* 38: 5 (1998), 494–509.

central government, including the president and other representative bodies, elections at the local and provincial levels were held from the time the KMT party moved to the island in 1949. During the democratization era, major democratic reforms revolved around the expansion of elections—both for the presidency and the legislative bodies. The effect of elections in Taiwan's democratization was twofold. Elections at the local levels provided ethnic Taiwanese elites with an opportunity to expand their political bases at the local and provincial levels; these elites subsequently became influential political actors at the national level after they joined *tangwai*, a predecessor of the DPP, the first opposition party in Taiwan. The local elections also fostered the grassroots' rise as an influential force for democratization. As political development in Taiwan progressed through the KMT's elite-initiated reforms and opposition elites relied on elections for their political purposes, the democratization evolved without street demonstrations involving physical violence.

Meanwhile, electoral politics in Taiwan also served to legitimize KMT's one-party dominant rule even after democratization. Chiang Ching-kuo's political reforms and the *Taiwanization* of the KMT government aimed to overcome the legitimacy crisis stemming from Taiwan's diplomatic setbacks in the 1970s. Throughout the 1980s and 1990s, the KMT's electoral success at all levels created political stability and legitimacy for its rule. Although the *tangwai* nominated legislative candidates at all levels, its winning percentage was minimal. Even after the party became the DPP in 1989, the

Table 4.2 Distribution of Popular Votes/Seats in Legislative Elections, 1986–1995

Year/Elections		KMT	Tangwai/DPP*
1986	Popular Vote	66.9	33.1
	Percentage of Seats	77.2	22.8
1989	Popular Vote	58.5	27.2
	Percentage of Seats	71.3	20.8
1992	Popular Vote	53.0	31.0
	Percentage of Seats	62.7	31.7
1995	Popular Vote	46.1	33.2
	Percentage of Seats	51.8	32.9

Note: *In the 1986 election, the DPP candidates were identified as *Tangwai* because the DPP was not formally legalized until 1989.

popular support for the opposition party was far from being influential enough to challenge the KMT's dominance. As evident in Table 4.2, the KMT never lost its majority in the legislative elections; its main opposition, the DPP, won only a small number of seats in the Legislative Yuan during the democratic regime transition.[45] The KMT's electoral victories in the legislative bodies from the top all the way to the local governments presented the party with broad-based public support and legitimacy, with little serious challenge from opposition forces. The KMT's electoral victories enabled the government to execute slow but smooth and carefully planned democratic reforms.

Lee Teng-hui's Military Reform

Another effect of the KMT's electoral victories was that they strengthened Lee Teng-hui's position within the party and against the military leadership. President Lee overcame the obstacles of his ethnic Taiwanese background and narrow support base in the party through electoral victories as well as the careful manipulation and purging of old guards in both the party and the army. During this process, strong support from civil society groups was vital for Lee's success in implementing democratic reforms.

When Lee took the political leadership in 1988, the major challenges to his leadership and democratic reform came from within the ruling party and the army leadership. During the early years of his leadership, the KMT realigned itself into two factions with different policy directions: a mainstream group led by Lee himself and a nonmainstream faction represented by General Hau Pei-tsun. The two factions clearly differentiated their political identities based on their ethnic backgrounds and foreign policy positions. The mainstream faction included ethnic Taiwanese and young reform-minded technocrats in the KMT who were ideologically moderate, while the nonmainstream faction was composed of ethnic Chinese mainlanders and represented conservative elements of the party. In foreign policy, the mainstream had adopted an ambivalent position, although it later moved closer to the opposition DPP's pursuit of Taiwanese independence by denying the "one China" formula. Meanwhile, the nonmainstream politicians strongly attached themselves to the "one China" principle and placed greater emphasis on unification with the mainland.[46] The ROC army leadership constituted an influential element of the nonmainstream forces in the KMT, opposing the idea of Taiwan's independence. Thus, Lee's political missions included curbing the influence of not only the nonmainstream party members, but also senior army officers who had strong influence in the party.

In order to overcome resistance from the nonmainstream faction and senior officers within it, President Lee retired the former Chief of Staff, General Hau pei-tsun, who represented the nonmainstream and the military, and appointed him as premier in 1990. General Hau had been the most influential figure in the ROC army, having appointed 75 percent of the generals when he was on active duty. He opposed further democratic reforms and Taiwanese independence, suggesting that the army would not tolerate the independence movement even though it occurred through a popular referendum.[47] Premier Hau and the nonmainstream elites demanded that President Lee take legal action against the DPP and some of the mainstream members by charging them as secessionists. The nonmainstream faction further insisted that members of foreign-based Taiwanese independence movements be barred from entering the island. In regard to political reform, the nonmainstream faction wanted democratic reforms to remain at a minimum, including the constitutional amendment that would adopt direct presidential election. Likewise, opposition to further democratic reforms revolved around major domestic and foreign policy areas, including national identity, independence issues, and democratic reforms within the ruling KMT party.

Yet, against this backdrop, President Lee successfully strengthened his position in the KMT by mobilizing support from mainstream KMT members, the DPP moderates, and the general public, marginalizing the nonmainstream faction in the political processes. The influence of the nonmainstream faction in the party was marginalized after General Hau was dismissed from the premiership and Lee embarked on military reform and party–army split. In the 1992 Legislative Yuan election, members of the mainstream KMT party and the DPP formed a grand coalition to oust Hau from the premiership. During this process, the KMT mainstream faction and the DPP marshaled support from the native Taiwanese elites and the general public.

Lee's democratic reforms culminated in military reforms. For the first three years of his presidency, he had to appease senior army officers to secure his political position. The president diminished General Hau's influence over senior army officers by retiring him from active military service, appointing him as defense minister in 1989, and assigning him to the premiership one year later to silence the conservative elements in the ROC army. After the expulsion of Hau from the premiership, the army officers' political influence also declined. Lee trimmed the military budget, which led to a reduction of military personnel. Furthermore, he reduced the military's representation in the Central Standing Committee of the KMT. The Lee government institutionalized civilian oversight of the military by establishing an Intelligence Committee in the Legislative Yuan to administer the National Security Bureau and control the armed forces.[48] While reducing military officers' presence in civilian affairs, the KMT also withdrew its influence from the army, augmenting the military's institutional autonomy and professionalism. In October 1993, the Legislative Yuan passed a law prohibiting political parties from establishing their organizations in the army, effectively terminating the political commissar system.[49]

President Lee's political position was finally secured and democratic reforms reinforced with the 1996 presidential election. In this election, the ruling KMT candidate Lee won 54 percent of the popular vote, while the DPP candidate Peng Ming-min garnered 21 percent.[50] Meanwhile, Hau Pei-tsun, together with Lin Yang-kang, formed the New Party and garnered 14.9 percent of popular vote. Four years later, in 2000, Taiwan's democratization was finally consolidated when opposition DPP leader Chen Shui-bian was elected to the presidency. Clear evidence of the establishment of democratic control over the military was the army officers' allegiance to the new president, who endorsed radically different foreign and security policies than what the ROC army had traditionally espoused.[51]

III. The Philippines: AFP's Role under the Aquino Presidency

The preceding two sections have elucidated how a combination of structural factors—favorable security environments, a strong civilian leadership backed by vibrant civil society, and a cohesive military organization—brought about stable regime transition and the depoliticization of the armed forces in South Korea and Taiwan in the 1980s and 1990s. The remaining two cases—the Philippines and Indonesia—reveal a different pattern of democratic regime change—namely, incomplete/unstable democratization with politically influential armed forces. In contrast to the previous two cases, the remaining cases depict a democratic regime transition in which civilian leaders failed to provide stable leadership and politicized army officers became a stumbling block for democratic consolidation.

In South Korea and Taiwan, democratic regime transitions began with a limited liberalization under strong authoritarian regimes and subsequent elite compromise, thereby signifying slow but stable transitions. However, in the mid-1980s, the Philippines experienced a regime transition without prior liberal reforms or elite compromise under Marcos' authoritarian regime. Instead, democratization was prompted after the Reform the Armed Forces of the Philippines Movement (RAM)—whose relationship with Marcos had reached its lowest point—sided with Corazon Aquino to topple

Marcos at the critical juncture of political crisis in 1985 and 1986. The RAM's decision was vital for the end of the authoritarian rule and the installation of a democratic regime. However, the Armed Forces of the Philippines (AFP) was never a pro-democracy group, as RAM members or Marcos loyalists staged no less than seven major coup attempts within the first four years of the Aquino presidency. This section focuses on Marcos' ouster and the subsequent regime transition under the Aquino leadership to explain why the Aquino leadership failed to achieve stable democratization and institutionalization of firm civilian control over the AFP.

End of Marcos' Authoritarianism

The assassination of former senator Benigno S. Aquino in 1983 marked an important turning point in the downfall of the Marcos authoritarian regime, as discussed in Chapter Three. The assassination provoked sweeping demonstrations by the general public for the first time since the declaration of martial law in 1972. Aquino's assassination led Filipinos to call "for justice for Aquino, national reforms, an end to the role of the U.S. in the Philippines, and Marcos' resignation."[52] The Philippine Catholic Church, under the leadership of Jaime Cardinal Sin, played a critical role in organizing anti-Marcos demonstrations referred to as the People's Power movement.[53] The Catholic Church leadership played an especially important role in channeling communication among the disorganized and often competing opposition forces for the common political cause: the abolition of Marcos authoritarianism and the installation of a new democratic government. Continuing domestic political crises after the assassination caused a massive flight of foreign capital, leading to a serious economic downturn in the final years of Marcos' rule. Immediately after Aquinos' assassination, more than $700 million capital left the country; foreign currency reserves plunged from $2.4 billion to $600 million, foreign debt rose to $26 billion, and the GNP declined by 5 percent in the following year.[54] More damaging still, economic difficulties elevated the armed insurgency operations by the Moro National Liberation Front (MNLF), a Muslim separatist movement, and the New People's Army (NPA), an armed apparatus for the Communist Party of the Philippines (CPP). The strength and operation of the two insurgency groups reached its highest point in 1986, seriously threatening the security of both the nation and Marcos' regime.

The most serious blow to the authoritarian regime came from Marcos' loss of support in the army leadership. His personalistic control over AFP leadership gave rise to factional struggles among army officers, especially between the Philippine Military Academy (PMA) and non-PMA graduates. The PMA faction that initiated the RAM withdrew its support for Marcos and sided with the pro-democracy group represented by Corazon Aquino. As noted in the previous chapter, RAM members planned a coup against Marcos as early as October 1985. The shaky support from the AFP forced the president to declare, on November 3, 1985, that a snap election be held on February 7, 1986.

The announcement of the presidential election was a huge surprise to the unprepared and disorganized opposition forces. Among various opposition leaders, Corazon Aquino and Salvador Laurel were the most prominent figures. Both were willing to run in the presidential election, creating the concern that the opposition's vote might be split, leading Marcos to win the popular vote. In this situation, prominent opposition leaders such as Vincente Puyat, Francisco Rodrigo, and Cardinal Sin mediated between Laurel and Aquino to form a united front in the election. Laurel yielded to Aquino for the presidential candidacy on the condition that they run under the United Democratic Opposition (UNIDO), an opposition umbrella group.[55] It was almost certain that Aquino and Laurel would win the 1986 presidential election considering Aquino's tremendous popularity among the general public and united opposition forces.

Since Marcos knew he was heading for a loss, he engaged in various kinds of electoral fraud, including buying votes through bribery, mobilizing bureaucrats' votes, and using AFP officers to terrorize pro-opposition voters.[56] Marcos was estimated to have spent more than $500 million to buy popular votes. In addition, General Ver and the ruling Kilusang Bagong Lipunan (KBL) party devised a plan to put AFP forces into heavy pro-opposition districts for psychological terror. Consequently, the first presidential election since 1972 came to be one of the most violent elections in the Philippines as 264 people were reportedly killed and 227 injured during the election campaign.[57]

Even with these extensive election irregularities, the results of the 1986 presidential election remained inconclusive, leading both Marcos and Aquino to declare victory. The Commission on Elections (COMELEC), which was controlled by the ruling KBL party, declared Marcos' victory with 54 percent of the popular vote, while the National Movement for Free Elections (NAMFREL), a citizen watchdog group, announced Aquino's victory. In light of this situation, Aquino held a People's Victory rally, in which approximately one million people participated to support Aquino's win.[58]

The biggest momentum for democratic regime transition came when RAM members revolted against Marcos on February 22, 1986, and publicly supported Aquino. Defense Minister Juan Ponce Enrile and Vice Chief of Staff General Fidel V. Ramos played leading roles in this development. Prior to the mutiny, Marcos ordered the AFP to arrest RAM members, including these two leaders. However, before the arrest could be carried out, Enrile and Ramos learned of the order and decided to rise up against Marcos. They resigned their positions in the Marcos government and declared that the 1986 election was fraudulent and that Aquino was the legitimate winner.[59] Not long after Enrile and Ramos announced their withdrawal of support from Marcos at Camp Aguinaldo, more than 80,000 people surrounded the camp to protect the "rebels" from Marcos loyalists' attempt to take them into custody.[60] A massive defection of AFP officers to the RAM's side ensued. Consequently, Marcos' plan to attack Camp Aguinaldo failed because of the large human blockade around the camp and the AFP's refusal to follow Marcos' order. On February 25, Marcos fled Malacanang, the presidential palace, and Aquino and Laurel organized a provisional government, formally ending the Marcos authoritarian rule.

Inauguration of the Aquino Presidency

As the first democratically elected president of the Philippines since 1965, Aquino faced an enormous number of reform imperatives to remove vestiges of authoritarian rule and reestablish democratic political institutions. One of the most pressing tasks was to purge Marcos loyalists from both the government and the army and subsequently rebuild democratic institutions with a new constitution—efforts that had been halted with the 1972 martial law. In addition, the president had to deal with the economic difficulties that the Philippines had endured throughout the latter half of Marcos' rule. Closely related to the economic conditions and political unrest were the rising insurgency operations by the NPA and the MNLF throughout the country. However, the Aquino government could not exert strong political leadership because Aquino failed to unite various political forces that had contributed to overthrowing Marcos. Eventually, inexperience and Aquino's lack of strong leadership thwarted democratic reform programs in the Philippines, giving AFP officers the opportunity to challenge the democratic regime with numerous coup attempts.

The Aquino government comprised loosely aligned political forces espousing different ideologies and political interests, including RAM officers, conservative politicians, business elites, religious groups, moderate liberal democrats, and the general public that formed the People's Power, among others. These diverse political interests constituted three major political factions in the Aquino regime: (1) conservative politicians and business elites who were deprived of their political positions and economic interests under the Marcos dictatorship; consequently, their stake in the new democratic politics was to regain their political and economic privileges; (2) RAM officers led by Enrile and Ramos, who provided decisive momentum for the fall of Marcos; and (3) progressive liberal democrats who supported Aquino's political reforms but were the most marginalized political force in the government.[61] The first two groups were predominant in the Aquino government, whereas the liberal democrats were the weakest. Although these diverse and competing forces contributed to political pluralism and democratic elements in the government, the acute competition among them deepened elite fragmentation and became a source of weak and inefficient leadership in the newly born regime.

One of the most pressing tasks for the Aquino government was to introduce economic reform in general and land reform in particular, which in turn was closely related to the growing insurgency problem in the southern provinces of the Philippines. Yet economic reform went nowhere as it was hampered by the influence of conservative politicians and business elites in both Congress and the Aquino administration. Rather than undertaking wide-ranging economic reforms, these individuals were only interested in recovering their properties that had been confiscated under the martial law regime. The land reform program clearly illustrates the Aquino government's problem. Land-owning groups led by Congressman Jose Cojuangco Jr., President Aquino's brother, initiated and implemented a new land reform law in the legislative branch.[62] The so-called Comprehensive Agrarian Reform Program (CARP) was introduced in 1988 to solve the chronic problems of land ownership in rural areas; in reality, it focused on recovering Aquino's and other conservative land owners' agricultural estates that had been confiscated under the Marcos regime. The conservative elites' influence in the Aquino government became even stronger after the 1987 congressional elections, in which 130 of the 200 congressmen belonged to conservative factions called "traditional political families," while another 39 had close ties with these families. Only 37 congressmen had no electoral record prior to 1971.[63] The election resulted in a return to politics by "dynastic" families who controlled the pre-martial law politics; given this situation, political and economic reforms were hardly far-reaching.

Civil–Military Friction and Coup Attempts

Meanwhile, the AFP grew to be a more serious stumbling block for the Aquino government. Although RAM's decision to turn against Marcos was perhaps the most crucial contributor to Marcos' overthrow and the installation of a democratic regime, the RAM was never a pro-democracy group. The RAM had simply chosen to support pro-democracy forces to unseat the Marcos regime, which had marginalized RAM officers from key positions in the AFP. Regardless of its motivation, the RAM's decision to support Aquino had been vital for the installation of a new government and, as such, RAM officers believed that they had the right to participate in the Aquino government as an equal partner of the civilian leadership. Miranda and Ciron's survey of 452 AFP officers clearly shows army officers' political attitudes.[64] In the survey, approximately 96 percent of the respondents agreed that the AFP should play an active role in national development that included a secure political environment (72 percent) and sustained economic growth (71 percent). Furthermore, 61 percent of officers believed that army officers had more germane capabilities in managing administrative jobs in civilian government than their civilian counterparts.

At the outset of the Aquino presidency, AFP officers pronounced their allegiance to the new democratic leadership. However, before long, these officers' support for Aquino quickly dissolved due to civil–military frictions in key policy areas. First, as previously discussed, the Aquino government failed to conduct major economic reforms, including land reforms; consequently, economic difficulties continued. In addition, Aquino failed to strengthen her political position by mobilizing the People's Power into her presidential leadership. Strong and united civil society groups that had real enthusiasm for democratic reform quickly dispersed after Marcos stepped down, leaving old conservative factions to hijack the post-democratization political scene. In this set-up, the president was not strong enough to eliminate the Marcos loyalists and the politically influential officers from her government. Finally, the civil–military friction centered on defense and security policies, especially when dealing with the growing insurgency operations.

Aquino and the AFP disagreed on the counterinsurgency strategy toward the communist CPP/NPA and the Muslim MNLF. The AFP insisted on strengthening the counterinsurgency program by adopting tough measures to crack down on insurgencies, whereas the civilian leadership preferred more peaceful negotiations. Aquino enraged the AFP by releasing political prisoners, including CPP leader Jose Maria Sison. Furthermore, the new government called for a ceasefire and initiated peace talks with the CPP and the MNLF secessionists. In the ceasefire talks, the Aquino government selected government negotiators from civilian representatives, but did not include any AFP officers. The Aquino government reached a ceasefire agreement with the National Democratic Front (NDF), an umbrella organization of underground leftist groups, agreeing upon a 60-day truce effective on December 10, 1986. However, the truce did not last long due to a dispute over key issues. The NDF presented unacceptable demands to Aquino, such as a share of seats in the Aquino government and the integration of the NPA militias into the regular AFP organization. The Aquino government's peace talks with Muslim Moro secessionists similarly failed, as the MNLF demanded autonomy of Mindanao and its armed forces independent of AFP command.[65]

·After the Aquino government's peace efforts with the insurgents ended in failure in the late 1980s, the NPA and the MNLF resumed their armed uprisings. According to Sison and the CPP Central Committee, the CPP/NPA possessed about 230,000 fighters and 10 million people who joined communist-organized groups.[66] In such a perilous security situation, the Aquino government further antagonized the AFP by cutting 14 percent of the military budget during Aquino's first year in office. To make matters worse, Aquino provoked the AFP by founding a Presidential Human Rights Commission to investigate human rights violations by the AFP during the martial law regime. AFP officers came to believe that the Aquino government systematically marginalized the AFP's role in the governing process while favoring the leftists' political agenda.

Before long, segments of the AFP withdrew their support from the Aquino government and began staging numerous coup attempts. As Table 4.3 illustrates, numerous major coup attempts were organized either by RAM members or by Marcos loyalists within the first four years of the Aquino presidency. As previously discussed, several of Aquino's policies aggravated the government's relationship with the AFP during a short period of time: Aquino's decision to investigate the military's human rights abuses under martial law,

Table 4.3 Major Coup Attempts during the Aquino Presidency, 1986–1989

Date	Military Groups
July 1986	Loyalists, supported by RAM
November 1986	RAM
January 1987	Loyalists, supported by RAM
April 1987	Loyalists
July 1987	Loyalists
August 1987	RAM
December 1989	RAM and Loyalists

Source: Mark R. Thomson, *The Anti-Marcos Struggle: Personalistic Rule and Democratic Transition in the Philippines* (New Haven: Yale University Press, 1995), 169.

the cease-fire and peace negotiations with the CPP/NPA, several left-leaning members in the administration, and—most importantly—the Aquino government's mishandling of security issues.[67]

In the first coup attempt in July 1986, Arturo Tolentino—Marcos' running mate in the 1986 presidential election—and several other pro-Marcos officers occupied the Manila Hotel and declared Marcos to be the legitimate president. The coup failed and was effectively contained, but none of the officers participating in the coup were punished. Four months later, General Ramos uncovered a second coup plan, this time organized by RAM officers. Enrile was suspected to be behind the two coup plans. Therefore, after the second coup attempt, Aquino fired Enrile. In the following year, Marcos loyalists, the RAM faction, or a combination of different factions made at least four coup attempts,[68] during which time the Aquino government failed to formulate any workable policies to carry out the institutional reform of the AFP. Moreover, these numerous coup attempts significantly weakened Aquino's control over the AFP, forcing her government to give way to the AFP in political initiatives and accept the officers' demands, which included (1) increasing AFP's counterinsurgency power; (2) dismissing left-leaning cabinet members; (3) reinstituting the National Security Council; and (4) firing corrupt officials in the government.[69] The recurring coup attempts forced the Aquino government to accept most of the AFP officers' demands. Aquino increased the military budget and payment by 60 percent and adopted the AFP's counterinsurgency plan, which had previously been dismissed. In addition, she was forced to fire several cabinet members who were charged by the military as being leftist sympathizers. As such, the coup attempts seriously damaged Aquino's leadership, destabilized the post-democratization politics, and ultimately aggravated the economic conditions in the Philippines throughout the late 1980s.[70]

Civilian control over the AFP was established only after Fidel Ramos was elected president in the 1992 election. As the former chief of staff who gained solid support from PMA graduates, Ramos successfully curbed the RAM's veto power in domestic politics. However, his control over the AFP was secured by bringing several senior AFP officers into his government. Even after Ramos claimed his political authority over the military, he did not attempt to dismantle different factions in the AFP and reorganize it into a cohesive organ. Due to civilian leaders' lack of ability or willingness to reform the AFP, factional groups lingered in Philippine politics, and rumors of coups continued to haunt the society even after two decades of democratic rule.

Although the Philippines did not return to military-dominant dictatorial rule, its democratization process was tainted by numerous coup attempts.

Severe security threats from the growing CPP/NPA and the MNLF insurgency movements created a structural condition for the AFP to be politically influential. The country's security threats became further exacerbated by the Aquino government's inappropriate handling of the insurgency movements. Meanwhile, Aquino's weak leadership provided AFP officers with the opportunity to challenge civilian authority repeatedly. The once-strong People's Power movement did not turn into pro-democracy forces in the Aquino government; rather, conservative political and economic elites dominated the new regime and thwarted political and economic reforms. Finally, the new democratic leadership failed to reorganize the AFP into a cohesive and professionalized military institution, resulting in the armed forces continuing to suffer from factional struggles that had been fostered by Marcos as a way to secure his control over the AFP. The factionalized AFP staged numerous coup attempts when the Aquino government failed to provide strong political leadership.

IV. Indonesia: Democratization and the ABRI's Role

Once Major General Haji Mohammad Suharto and the army officers toppled President Sukarno in 1965, the *Angkatan Bersenjata Republik Indonesia* (ABRI, Armed Forces of the Republic of Indonesia) became a dominant player in Indonesian politics, remaining so until Suharto stepped down from his presidency in 1998. Throughout Suharto's presidency, ABRI officers became deeply engaged in domestic political, administrative, and economic affairs under the *dwifungsi* (dual function) doctrine. Army officers were guaranteed seats in the National Parliament and in the People's Representative Council, an electoral college that selected the president and vice president once every five years. In addition, President Suharto assigned military officers to various governmental positions at both national and provincial levels to facilitate his authoritarian rule. Furthermore, retired officers also held various governmental positions; approximately 50 percent of the provincial governors and more than 30 percent of district heads had prior military backgrounds. By the mid-1990s, Suharto employed about 14,000 officers outside the area of traditional military missions.[71] Throughout the 32 years of the New Order regime, the ABRI acted as the backbone of Suharto's authoritarian rule.

The seemingly resilient New Order regime abruptly collapsed in the midst of economic crisis and ensuing social unrest in 1997 and 1998.[72] Since first launching its democratic regime transition, Indonesia faced enormous political, social, and economic reform tasks: recovering from the 1997 financial crisis, containing interethnic and interreligious violence, and building a stable democratic political institution. Still, the most significant mission for the new democracy in Indonesia was to disengage the ABRI from civilian politics and reorganize the military organization to become a professional and politically neutral entity. This section examines the ways in which severe domestic threats and weak civilian leadership hampered the democratization process and the complete withdrawal of the military from politics in Indonesia, covering the period from Suharto's fall to the Megawati presidency.

Economic Crisis and Suharto's Fall

Until 1997, Suharto's New Order regime seemed to be robust as he successfully managed political stability and sustained economic growth of more than 7 percent on average throughout the three decades of his authoritarian rule. However, an unexpected economic crisis hit the country and forced all the major domestic political actors, including the ABRI, to turn against the president. The end of the Suharto's New Order started with the financial crisis that began in Thailand and soon spread to the Philippines, South Korea, and Indonesia in 1997. Within a few months of the financial crisis, the value of the Indonesian rupia plummeted from 2,500 per U.S. dollar to around 10,000, the stock market plunged from over 700 to nearly 300, and inflation soared into double digits.[73] Immediately after the financial crisis hit Indonesia, the International Monetary Fund (IMF) and the World Bank offered a package to save the country's economy. The financial crisis brought a swift destabilizing impact to the authoritarian regime and succeeding democratic leadership.

The IMF and the Suharto government reached an agreement for structural reforms for the economy as a precondition for the rescue package, but the agreement was not properly implemented, which only exacerbated the situation.[74] The poor management of the economy stemmed primarily from the corruption of Suharto's family and cronies. For example, going against the IMF's prescribed economic reforms, Suharto's youngest son Hutomo Mandala Putra (or Tommy Suharto) monopolized the national car project, his oldest daughter Siti Hardiyanti Rukmana announced her intention to build an expensive triple-decker road, and Mohammad Hassan—one of Suharto's cronies—took back the plywood industry.[75] At the age of 76, Suharto seemed to be quite isolated from everyday politics. At the height of the economic crisis, he was primarily interested in ensuring the interests of his inner circle. The widespread political corruption in his government put him in a politically difficult situation as he continued identifying himself as the "father of development" who was supposed to bring economic development to the country. Indonesian people had been willing to tolerate the oppressive rule only as long as the economy continued thriving under Suharto's leadership.[76] Once the economy fell into such deep trouble, Suharto could no longer claim legitimacy for his authoritarian rule.

The economic crisis quickly swelled to a nationwide political crisis in early 1998, as college students organized massive anti-Suharto demonstrations. Initially, students' demonstrations were small in size and centered on economic issues such as inflation and unemployment; however, they rapidly evolved into radicalized and violent political movements as ordinary citizenry joined. On several occasions, demonstrations turned into riots when lower-class people felt emboldened, damaging property and killing more than 1,000 people in Jakarta alone.[77] The riot in Jakarta targeted the ethnic Chinese community, which comprised approximately 4 percent of the population but controlled up to 70 percent of the Indonesian economy.[78] Violent protests put the already flagging economy into an even deeper crisis due to a large-scale capital flight after attacks on ethnic Chinese.

In the midst of the economic crisis and violent demonstrations, the People's Representative Council unanimously reelected Suharto as the president on March 10, 1998. However, by this time, Suharto himself found he could not carry on his presidency, and three former vice presidents pleaded with him to resign and yield the power to Vice President Bacharuddin Jusuf Habibie. Worse yet, Suharto could not form a new cabinet because, among the 45 people who were nominated for positions in his government, only three accepted the president's offer. On May 20, 1998, Suharto met with General Wiranto, the army chief of staff and defense minister, to notify him that he would resign.[79] General Wiranto guaranteed that the ABRI would protect and honor Suharto after his resignation. On the next day, Suharto stepped down and turned his presidency over to Vice President Habibie, thereby ending the three-decade-long authoritarian rule and bringing about democratic regime transition in Indonesia.

Habibie's Interim Government

Suharto's fall and the subsequent power transition occurred so abruptly and spontaneously that Habibie's transitional government was not prepared to carry out extensive political and economic reform. The interim Habibie government had to deal with numerous challenging problems, such as the severe economic crisis, violent demonstrations, interethnic and interreligious clashes, and separatist movements in Aceh, Papua, and East Timor.

Still, the ABRI remained the most powerful and best-organized political institution vis-à-vis its civilian counterparts in post-Suharto Indonesia. In this respect, it is worth considering why the ABRI did not attempt any military coup despite the fact that Indonesia suffered from numerous security challenges and dismal civilian leadership in the post-Suharto years.

To account for the ABRI's relatively passive role in the regime transition period, it is important to revisit the Suharto–ABRI relationship in the 1980s and 1990s, during which Suharto used his political skills to offset the military's political dominance. Although the ABRI became the key partner of Suharto's New Order and filled prominent positions in the government, its political power and institutional autonomy significantly diminished during the latter half of Suharto's rule, when Suharto took several measures to reduce his dependence on the ABRI. Suharto formed a political coalition with various groups such as the Islamic groups, economic technocrats, and his own palace clique, including his family. Consequently, the number of active military officers in Suharto's cabinet declined during the last decade of his rule.[80] The ABRI's political influence further shrank after Suharto dismissed General Leonardus Benyamin Murdani, who wielded great power and charismatic leadership as armed forces commander (1983–1988) and minister of defense and security (1988–1993). Suharto went on to strengthen his grip on the army by reshuffling large numbers of senior officers and appointing General Feisal Tanjung, a man personally loyal to the president, as armed forces commander. Personal ties and political loyalty were the key criteria of promotions and assignments in the ABRI for the final years of the Suharto presidency.[81]

In addition to its diminished influence during the final years of the Suharto regime, the ABRI was still far from developing into a cohesive and professionalized institution. The lack of organizational unity stemmed primarily from its guerrilla warfare experience against the Dutch colonial forces in the 1940s. During the war for independence, guerrilla forces were organized as independent units under the leadership of local commanders rather than a hierarchical and centralized command structure. Such horizontal ordering of the ABRI continued until the Suharto era as a form of territorial command structure, as explained in Chapter Three. Moreover, Suharto's manipulation of the Islamic groups created a schism along religious lines in the ABRI: the so-called red-and-white faction was led by General Wiranto and represented the nationalist and secular segments while the green faction was led by Suharto's son-in-law Lieutenant General Prabowo Subianto and endorsed modernist Muslims. Suharto consciously manipulated the factional struggles so that no consensus would emerge within the army leadership.[82] The lack of cohesion and strong leadership in the ABRI prevented army officers from dominating the political transition of 1998. However, a more direct reason for the absence of a coup in post-Suharto Indonesian politics was the fact that the ABRI enraged the Indonesian people by killing four university students who participated in anti-Suharto demonstrations. Thus, when Suharto's administration fell, ABRI was at its lowest point in terms of officers' self-esteem and public image.

Due to its disgraced profile among the people during the first stage of the democratic regime transition, the ABRI embarked on a bold plan to reformulate itself as a cohesive and professional institution. In 1999, the ABRI proposed 14 points of reform objectives, including—among others— separation of the police from the armed forces, complete withdrawal from civilian political affairs, separation from the Golkar Party, political neutrality during elections, and exclusive dedication to its external security mission.[83] During the course of the reforms, the ABRI aimed to bolster its much-tainted image among the general public and ultimately be cherished as the defender of the interest of the people. In this context, the ABRI tried to maintain a low profile in the democratization process and tried to remain politically neutral.

Although the ABRI was not strong enough to dominate post-Suharto politics and expressly desired to be a politically neutral and professionalized body, weak and disorganized civilian leadership impeded the establishment of a democratic political institution and firm civilian control over the armed forces. For example, the 1999 parliamentary elections revealed how far Indonesia's political spectrum had fragmented. More than 100 parties were formed before the election, 48 of which were eligible to participate in the election. Of these 48 parties, 19 were based on or had close ties with Islamic organizations, three with Christian groups, nine with socialist-oriented bands, and 17 with *Pancasila* ideology (or 'Five Principles' by Sukarno).[84] In the election, no single party could gain a majority, as the popular vote divided almost evenly among five major parties: *Partai Demokrasi Indonesia-Perjuangan* (PDI-P, Indonesian Democracy Party-Struggle) won 34 percent of the vote, Golkar (*Golongan Karya*, Functional Groups) won 22 percent, *Partai Kebangkitan Bangsa* (PKB, National Awakening Party) gained 12 percent; *Partai Persatuan Pembangunan* (PPP, Development Unity Party) earned 10 percent, and *Partai Amanat Nasional* (PAN, National Message Party) gained 7 percent.[85]

Short-Lived Wahid Presidency

After 17 months of the interim Habibie presidency, Abdurrahman Wahid succeeded the leadership through the General Session of the National Assembly in October 1999. Although he was the first democratically elected leader, Wahid's presidency lasted for only 20 months before he was forced to step down and hand over the leadership to Vice President Megawati Sukarnoputri in July 2001. Wahid became politically fragile after he alienated himself from the coalition groups that brought him to the presidency. In particular, he antagonized the two largest and most influential parties in the National Assembly: the PDI-P led by vice president Megawati and the former ruling Golkar Party.[86]

An important outcome of the Wahid presidency's political instability was that it provided the ABRI with the momentum to reclaim its own political influence. Indeed, in 2001, Wahid's attempt to appoint Lt. General Agus Wirahadikusumah as army chief of staff failed when 46 army generals blocked the appointment by threatening to resign. General Wirahadikusumah was a reform-minded officer who tried to eliminate corruption while he was the Commander of the Kostrad (*Komando Cadangan Strategis Angkatan Darat*, Army Strategic Reserve Command). Although he gained popularity among junior ranking officers, he maintained uneasy relations with other senior officers due to his anticorruption measures and his endorsement of President Wahid's decision to dismiss General Wiranto from his position of Coordinating Minister of Politics and Security. Furthermore, ABRI officers played an influential role in the impeachment of Wahid, which was initiated by the People's Representative Council in May 2001. After Wahid's fall, the council elected Megawati to replace him. The ABRI's role in this power transition proved to be vital, as the military withdrew support for Wahid in order to approve Megawati.

The weakness of the civilian leadership in the post-Suharto Indonesia stemmed mainly from the disentanglement of civilian political leaders and civil society groups. Not only were civil society groups fragmented and violent, but civilian political elites also failed to garner support from the broader civil society. Civil society groups were thriving in the post-Suharto period, but they could not form a united front as a pro-democracy force as they were divided along multiple ethnic and religious lines.[87] One distinctive characteristic of Indonesia's democratization process was the power transition through the elite negotiation. Suharto had been forced to transfer power to Vice President Habibie, but his resignation occurred after an agreement with ABRI leader General Wiranto. After Habibie, Wahid's short-lived presidency was possible only due to a compromise among key political leaders. Such a power transition via elite negotiation averted any serious political crisis or power vacuum while simultaneously—and inevitably—alienating civil society groups that endorsed democratic reforms. Without the support of civil society, the civilian leadership was destined to be weak.

Domestic Security Crises and the ABRI

In addition to the fragmented civilian leadership, ongoing internal security threats provided the ABRI with enough justification to regain its political influence in post-democratization Indonesian politics. Domestic security conditions progressively deteriorated in the midst of the post-Suharto political crisis. This domestic instability came from multiple sources. The most serious disturbance came from the resurgence of Islamic political organizations and related Islamic gangs and militias. The renaissance of militant Islam in the post-Suharto period originated in Suharto's mobilization of Muslims to broaden his political support base and counterbalance the ABRI in the later years of his rule. Especially during the final decade of his rule, Suharto regularly identified himself as the defender of Islamic interests, contributing to growing political consciousness of Muslim groups in democratizing Indonesia.[88] The influence of militant Muslim organizations further expanded under the Habibie presidency as he mobilized these groups to strengthen his political support base.

The resurgence of Islamic organizations inevitably intensified interethnic and interreligious conflicts after Suharto's fall. The interethnic violence primarily targeted the ethnic Chinese community, who—as an ethnic minority in numbers—controlled most economic wealth in Indonesia. The violence was not limited to Jakarta; it quickly spread to other regions, such as the Central Sulawesi, Moluccas, and Ambon, where Christian and Muslim groups launched attacks and counterattacks, killing hundreds.[89] Governors in these regions declared a truce, but this did not prevent a resurgence of violence. Meanwhile, the police seemed unable or unwilling to stop such interethnic violence.[90]

Another source of domestic insecurity came from separatist movements in several provinces, such as Papua (or Irian Jaya), East Timor, and Aceh, which threatened the state's territorial integrity. All of these regions had been dealing with decades-old independence movements. The separatist movement in Aceh, which had its roots in the Darul Islam rebellion in the 1950s, resurfaced in the late 1980s when Acehnese militias who had been trained in Libya formed the *Gerakan Aceh Merdeka* (GAM, Free Aceh Movement) and resumed the separatist movement. Although the Suharto government was able to contain Acehnese separatism in the early 1990s, the post-Suharto instability provided the GAM with another opportunity to launch pro-independence guerrilla warfare.[91] Meanwhile, Papua militias, which were less serious of a threat than those in Aceh, also formed the *Organisasi Papua Merdeka* (OPM, Free Papua Organization) to wage independence-oriented guerrilla warfare.[92] Finally, East Timor formed an independent government in 2002 after three decades of independence struggles. In sum, the political instability in post-Suharto Indonesia strengthened several separatist militia groups, thereby enabling them to resume intensified clashes with the ABRI and the regional police force.

A direct effect of the worsening domestic security threats was the ABRI's renewed political clout in newly democratized Indonesian politics. In the midst of multiple security threats from separatist movements and interethnic violence, President Megawati felt she had no choice but to bring the armed forces into politics, encouraging army officers to take any steps necessary to contain the regional disturbances and not to worry about their human rights abuses. Megawati amended the constitution to restrict retroactive legislation, exonerating army officers of past human rights abuses.[93] Furthermore, she redirected her commandership to Army Chief of Staff General Endriartondono Sutarto, who brought several ABRI officers who played influential roles in Suharto's New Order regime into the government. Hundreds of active and retired officers audaciously proposed a bill that would allow the ABRI leadership to take any military action without reporting to the president for one day. Consequently, Megawati could strengthen her presidency by establishing close ties with the ABRI, but it ultimately resulted in boosting army officers' presence and influence in politics, thereby weakening civilian control over the military.

ABRI has made no coup attempt or takeover of political power in Indonesia—at least, not during the most recent decade of democratic efforts. However, this does not necessarily mean that Indonesia's democratization process has been smooth and complete with military officers' disengagement from politics. Democratically elected leaders' control over the armed forces as a crucial component of democratic consolidation is far from complete in Indonesia, as formerly weakened army officers have regained their prerogatives in a newly democratized government. The resurgence of ABRI officers' political influence in the past few years has stemmed from predominantly two reasons. First, the newly elected political leaders—Habibie, Wahid, and Megawati—could neither exert strong political leadership nor strengthen democratic institutions. The lack of strong civilian leadership was primarily a result of the extremely fragmented political parties and civil society groups along religious and ethnic cleavages. Second, the weak civilian leadership has had to deal with increasing multiple security threats—from interethnic and interreligious violence to separatist militia movements in several regions. In the midst of heightening domestic security threats, the once-constrained ABRI obtained an opportunity to regain its political influence in a newly democratized Indonesia.

Conclusions

This chapter has examined the democratization process in four Asian countries and the military's withdrawal from politics as its crucial component. Although democratization resulted in a decline in the armed forces' political role in general, the processes and degrees of the military's disengagement from politics have differed from one country to another. South Korea and Taiwan experienced a stable and complete democratic regime transition with democratically elected civilian leaders controlling politically influential officers whereas armed forces in the Philippines and Indonesia wielded strong influence in the direction and extent of the democratization.

As the comparative study in this chapter reveals, three main structural conditions have shaped different modes of the military's political disengagement. The first factor that shaped officers' political roles was the security threats in domestic or international realms during the regime transition. Favorable security environments facilitated the armed forces' withdrawal from politics, while heightening threats rendered the military politically powerful. Second, the strength of civilian leadership directly affected the way in which the new democratic leaders dealt with politicized officers. A strong civilian leadership facilitated strong civilian control of the military in post-democratization politics, while weak and divided civilians failed to claim supremacy over the military even after the regime transition. The final significant factor was the military's organizational character, especially the presence or absence of competing factions in the army. Factions within the military made civilian control more difficult, whereas a unified and professionalized army led to firm civilian control.

Rather than relying upon the predominant literature of democratization, which takes a process- or choice-oriented approach,[94] this chapter focused on identifying key structural causes that contributed to making different modes of the military's political disengagement. Changing security environments in the 1980s and 1990s set the basic parameters that precipitated the reevaluation of the armed forces' domestic political roles. In most Asian countries with decades-long authoritarian rule, the governing body and people entered into a tacit social contract: People were willing to submit their political freedom as long as autocratic leaders could provide important public goods such as national security, domestic tranquility, and economic success. However, changing international environments in the 1980s led domestic audiences to reevaluate the authoritarian regime and armed forces' roles in it.

This chapter has highlighted variations in security threats and their influence on the military's depoliticization process among the countries surveyed. South Korea and Taiwan benefited from favorable internal and external security conditions during the regime transition period. South Korea in the 1980s witnessed significant decreases in external threats as the inter-Korean military balance came to favor the South through the reinvigoration of its security alliance with the United States. The decreasing security challenges surrounding the Korean peninsula in turn weakened the Chun regime's justification of extending the military dictatorial rule. Meanwhile, Taiwan's liberalization began as a way to overcome the domestic legitimacy crisis of the Chiang regime that came from its diplomatic derecognition in the early 1970s, ultimately forcing the KMT regime to give up its strategy of a military counterattack on mainland China. The Chiang regime adopted liberalization as a way to strengthen the political support base among ethnic Taiwanese. At the same time, generational changes across the Taiwan Strait contributed to decreasing military tension between the two Chinese governments. In particular, Deng Xiao-ping's reforms and the expansion of economic interdependence in the 1980s and 1990s significantly reduced the utility of military confrontation. These changing environments in turn strengthened Lee Teng-hui's political position against politically influential officers. On the other hand, the armed forces in the Philippines and Indonesia gained opportunities to reclaim their prerogatives in the post-democratization political scene, as these countries faced deteriorating domestic security conditions. The democratization process in the Philippines, for example, was encumbered with rising armed insurgencies by the communists and Muslims in the 1980s. The rising insurgency operations enabled the AFP to become a dominant political force in the feeble Aquino government. Similarly, the ABRI—once committed to self-imposed reforms immediately after Suharto's fall—quickly regained its political authority due to threats of national disintegration coming from interethnic, interreligious, and separatist movements.

Given the security threats, dynamic interactions among major domestic actors—civilian leadership, the military, and civil society—fashioned more complex aspects of the democratization process and civil–military interactions as its key components. First of all, the strength of the civilian leadership played a key role in shaping routes to democratization and how civilian leaders claimed their supremacy over the army. More specifically, civilian leadership's ability to curb armed forces' political influence was possible only when the civilians successfully mobilized support from pro-democracy civil society groups and institutionalized democratic norms and practices, as was the case in South Korea and Taiwan. In South Korea, the Kim Young-sam government was able to depoliticize army officers and purge the former coup perpetrators by allying itself with pro-democracy civil society groups that strongly endorsed far-reaching democratic reforms. Similarly, Taiwan's Lee Teng-hui was strong enough to control the speed and direction of the democratic transition primarily due to the one-party dominant system under the KMT. However, the weak civilian leadership in the Philippines and Indonesia could not claim authority over the armed forces. The weakness of the Philippines' Aquino government was attributable to its alienation from the People's Movement that forced Marcos' downfall while old conservative families took control of the new democracy. Similarly, post-democratization Indonesia also suffered from extremely weak and fragmented leadership emerging from sociopolitical cleavages along ethnic and religious differences.

Finally, the comparison of democratic transitions has further shown that democratic consolidation depends on whether the civilian leadership is willing or able to eliminate factions and reorganize the armed forces into a cohesive organization. The newly elected president in South Korea focused his policy priority on purging *Hanahoe* officers from the army hierarchy and reorganizing the military as a cohesive organ, thereby restraining the armed forces' resistance to the civilian leadership. As a result, no sign of civil–military friction or the possibility of a military coup has since emerged in South Korea. Taiwan's experience reveals the same insights. Lee Teng-hui consolidated his grip over the armed forces by eliminating General Hau's political clout in post-democratization Taiwan. Meanwhile, democratization in the Philippines has been far from being consolidated, and civilian leaders' control of the AFP remains incomplete as constant rumors of coups d'état linger even after two decades of democratic efforts. Aquino's failure to institutionalize democratic control of the AFP stemmed largely from her unwillingness or inability to remove factions and implement wide-ranging reform. In Indonesia, the ABRI has not developed into a cohesive institution mainly for the same reason: fragmentation of civilian politics. In the Philippines and Indonesia, one of the major tasks for civilian leaders is to reorganize the armed forces as a cohesive institution with an effective hierarchical order.

Notes

1. Victor Cha, "Security and Democracy in South Korean Development," in *Korea's Democratization*, ed. Samuel Kim (London: Cambridge University Press, 2003), 205.
2. For more information about the pro-democracy movements in Gwangju, see Sang-yong Jung, ed., *Gwangju Minju Hangjaeng (The People's Struggle for Democracy in Gwangju)* (Seoul: Dolbege, 1990); Hanguk Hyondaesa Saryo Yonguso, *Gwangju 5-wol Hangjaeng Saryojip (Complete Collection of the Historical Materials on the May People's Uprising in Gwangju)* (Seoul: Pulbit, 1990).
3. World Bank, *World Tables 1993* (Washington D.C.: World Bank, 1994).
4. Seong-yi Yoon, "Democratization in South Korea: Social Movements and Their Political Opportunity Structures," *Asian Perspective* 21 (1997), 156–8.
5. B. C. Koh, "The 1985 Parliamentary Election in South Korea," *Asian Survey* 25 (1985), 883–97; also see C. I. Eugene Kim, "South Korea in 1985: An Eventual Year Amidst Uncertainty," *Asian Survey* 26 (1986), 67–71.
6. Won-ki Hwang, "Developmental Dictatorship and Democratization in South Korea: The State and Society in Transformation, 1987–1997," (PhD diss., Brown University, 2006), 75–92.
7. Ji-hun Cho, *80-Nyondae Huban Cheongyeon Haksaengundong (The Youth and Student Movements of the late-1980s)* (Seoul: Hyungsung-sa, 1989), 16.
8. Young-whan Kihl, *Transforming Korean Politics: Democracy, Reform, and Culture* (New York: M.E. Sharpe, 2005), 83–4.
9. Samuel P. Huntington, *The Third Wave: Democratization in the Late Twentieth Century* (Norman: University of Oklahoma Press, 1991), 124.
10. Sung-joo Han, "South Korea in 1987: The Politics of Democratization," *Asian Survey* 28 (1988), 52–6; also see Bret L. Billet, "South Korea at the Crossroads: An Evolving Democracy or Authoritarianism Revisited?" *Asian Survey* 30 (1990).
11. Carl J. Saxer, "Generals and Presidents: Establishing Civilian and Democratic Control in South Korea," *Armed Forces and Society* 30 (2004), 388.
12. See Terence Roehrig, *The Prosecution of Former Military Leaders in Newly Democratic Nations: The Cases of Argentina, Greece, and South Korea* (London: McFarland & Company, 2002), 161–6.
13. Aurel Croissant, "Riding the Tiger: Civilian Control and the Military in Democratizing Korea," *Armed Forces and Society* 30 (2004), 366.

14 For more detailed information about Roh's *Nordpolitik*, see Byung-joon Ahn, "South Korea's International Relations: Quest for Security, Prosperity, and Unification," *The Asian Update* (New York: Asia Society, 1991); Byung-joon Ahn, "South Korean-Soviet Relations: Contemporary Issues and Prospects," *Asian Survey* 31 (1991); Young-whan Kihl, "South Korea's Foreign Relations: Diplomatic Activism and Policy Dilemma," in *Korea Briefing*, ed. Donald N. Clark (New York: Asia Society, 1991); Hong Liu, "The Sino-South Korean Normalization: A Triangular Explanation," *Asian Survey* 33 (1991).

15 Another reason for the radical groups' weakening was the fall of communist states in Eastern Europe. As former socialist countries jettisoned their ideology and adopted liberal democracy and market economy, the radical Marxist or North Korea's Juche ideology also lost its popularity in Korean society. For the decline of the Minjung movement, see Gi-wook Shin, "Marxism, Anti-Americanism, and Democracy in South Korea: An Examination of Nationalist Intellectual Discourse," *Positions: East Asian Cultures Critique* 3 (1995).

16 For moderation of civil society groups in South Korea, see Sun-hyuk Kim, *The Politics of Democratization in Korea: The Role of Civil Society* (Pittsburgh: University of Pittsburgh Press, 2000); Sun-hyuk Kim, "Civil Society in Democratizing Korea," in *Korea's Democratization*, ed. Samuel Kim (London: Cambridge University Press, 2003); Jae-chul Lee, "Deepening and Improving Democracy: Association in South Korea," (PhD diss., University of Missouri at Columbia, 2005).

17 Hong-nack Kim, "The 1988 Parliamentary Election in South Korea," *Asian Survey* 29 (1989).

18 Jin Park, "Political Change in South Korea: The Challenge of the Conservative Alliance," *Asian Survey* 30 (1990).

19 Hong-young Lee, "South Korea in 1992: A Turning Point in Democratization," *Asian Survey* 33 (1992), 35–6.

20 *Hanguk Ilbo (Korean Daily Newspaper)*, December 22, 1992.

21 In the 1992 National Assembly election, the ruling DLP won 116 seats, Kim Dae-jung's DP 75, Chung Ju-young's UPP 24 seats. The UPP represented the conservative elements in Korea and was close to the ruling DLP in its ideological orientation. For the 1992 National Assembly election results, see Foreign Broadcast Information Service, *Daily Report, East Asia*, March 26, 1992, 22–3.

22 Saxer, 2004, 393.

23 Sanghyun Kim, "South Korea's Kim Young Sam Government: Political Agendas," *Asian Survey* 36 (1996), 512.

24 The key members of the *Hanahoe* who conspired the 1979 coup included Kim Bok-dong, Chong Ho-yong, Choi Song-taek, Kwon Ik-hyon, Son Yong-kil, Roh Chong-ki, Park Gap-yong, Nam-Chung-su. All of these members monopolized key positions in the army and the intelligence agencies during the Chun and Roh regimes. See, Eui-sop Song, "Documentary Hanahoe," *Chugan Hanguk (Weekly Korea)*, June 1, 1993, 29.

25 John Kie-chiang Oh, *Korean Politics: The Quest for Democratization and Development* (Ithaca: Cornell University Press, 1999), 133–4.

26 *Hanguk Ilbo*, August 13, 1993.

27 Doh-chull Shin, *Mass Politics and Culture in Democratizing Korea* (Oxford: Oxford University Press, 1999), 200.

28 Some of the representative civil society groups included the Korean Confederation of Trade Unions (KCTU, in 1995), Citizens' Coalition for Economic Justice (CCEJ, in 1989), Korean Foundation for Environmental Movement (KFEM, in 1993), and People's Solidarity for Participatory Democracy (PSPD, in 1994). For the discussion of civil society's change in the period, see Su-hoon Lee, "Transitional Politics of Korea, 1987–1992: Activation of Civil Society," *Pacific Affairs* 66 (1993); Sun-hyuk Kim, "Civil Society in South Korea," *Journal of North East Asian Studies* 15 (1996); Sun-hyuk Kim, "State and Civil Society in South Korea's Democratic Consolidation: Is the Battle Really Over?" *Asian Survey* 37 (1997).

29 Some of the exemplary works on civil–military relations in one-party states are, David J. Betz, *Civil–Military Relations in Russia and Eastern Europe* (New York: RoutledgeCurzon, 2004); Roman Kolkowicz, *The Soviet Military and the Communist Party* (Princeton: Princeton University Press, 1967); Zoltan D. Barany, *Soldiers and Politics in Eastern Europe, 1945–1990: The Case of Hungary* (New York: St. Martin's Press, 1993); Jonathan R. Adelman, ed., *Communist Armies in Politics* (Boulder: Westview Press, 1982); Roman Kolkowicz and Andrzej Korbonski, eds, *Soldiers, Peasants, and Bureaucrats* (London: George Allen & Unwin, 1982).

30 An exception is M. Taylor Fravel, "Towards Civilian Supremacy: Civil–Military Relations in Taiwan's Democratization," *Armed Forces and Society* 29 (2002).

31 For Deng Xiao-ping's approach to Taiwan in the 1970s and 1980s, see Hung-mao Tien, ed., *Mainland China, Taiwan, the U.S. Policy* (Cambridge: Oelgeschlager, Gunn and Hain, 1983); King-yuh Chang, *A Framework for China's Unification* (Taipei: Kwang Hwa, 1986); Robert G. Sutter, *Chinese Foreign Policy: Developments after Mao* (New York: Praeger, 1986).

32 Hung-mao Tien, "Social Change and Political Development in Taiwan," in *Taiwan in a Time of Transition*, ed. Harvey Feldman, Michael Y. M. Kau, and Ilpyong J. Kim (New York: Paragon House, 1988), 6.
33 Chiao-chiao Hsieh, *Strategy for Survival: The Foreign Policy and External Relations of the Republic of China on Taiwan, 1949–1979* (London: The Sherwood Press, 1985), 233.
34 Yun Fan, "Taiwan: No Civil Society, No Democracy," in *Civil Society and Political Change in Asia: Expanding and Contracting Democratic Space*, ed. Muthiah Alagappa (Stanford: Stanford University Press, 2004), 165.
35 For tangwai's role in Taiwan's democratization, see Fan, 2004; Yun-han Chu, "Social Protests and Political Democratization in Taiwan," in *The Other Taiwan: 1945 to the Present*, ed. Murray A. Rubinstein (New York: M. E. Sharpe, 1994); Teresa Wright, "Student Mobilization in Taiwan: Civil Society and Its Discontents," *Asian Survey* 39 (1999).
36 Fan, *Civil Society and Political Change in Asia*, 167.
37 Shelley Rigger, *Politics in Taiwan: Voting for Democracy* (New York: Routledge, 1999), 126.
38 Murray A. Rubinstein, "Taiwan's Socioeconomic Modernization," in *Taiwan: A New History*, ed. Murray A. Rubinstein (New York: M. E. Sharpe, 1999), 446.
39 See Tsu-cheng Chou, "Electoral Competition and the Development of Opposition in Taiwan," *The Annals* 20 (1992); John F. Copper, "The Role of Minor Political Parties in Taiwan," *World Affairs* 155 (1993); Teh-fu Hwang, "Electoral Competition and Democratic Transition in the Republic of China," *Issues and Studies* 27 (1991); Yu-ming Shaw, ed., *Building Democracy in the Republic of China* (Taipei: The Asia and World Institute, 1984).
40 Rigger, *Politics in Taiwan*, 121–2.
41 For General Hau's political role during democratization, see Yun-han Chu, *Crafting Democracy in Taiwan* (Taipei: Institute for National Policy Research, 1992); Fravel, 2002.
42 Hung-mao Tien and Tun-jen Cheng, "Crafting Democratic Institutions in Taiwan," *The China Journal* 37 (1997), 5–6.
43 Fravel, 2002, 67.
44 James D. Seymour, "Taiwan in 1988: No More Bandits," *Asian Survey* 29 (1989), 61.
45 Discrepancies between percentage of popular vote share and percentage of seats come from the so-called "SVMM elections" (single, nontransferable voting in multimember districts). For the SVMM's influence on

Taiwanese elections during democratization, see Rigger, 1999, 103–77; Jaushieh Joseph Wu, *Taiwan's Democratization: Forces Behind the New Momentum* (New York: Oxford University Press, 1995), 73–85.

46 See Muthiah Alagappa, "Introduction: Presidential Election, Democratization, and Cross-Strait Relations," in *Taiwan's Presidential Politics: Democratization and Cross-Strait Relations in the 21st Century*, ed. Muthiah Alagappa (New York: M. E. Sharpe, 2001), 30–8; Xiaobo Hu and Gang Lin, "The PRC View of Taiwan under Lee Teng-hui," in *Sayonara to the Lee Teng-hui Era: Politics in Taiwan, 1988–2000*, ed. Wei-chin Lee and T. Y. Wang (New York: University Press of America, 2003), 277–97.

47 Fravel, 2002, 63.

48 Tien and Cheng, 1997, 9–11.

49 Fravel, 2002, 68.

50 For detailed analysis of the 1996 presidential election, see Eric P. Moon, "Single Non-transferable Vote Methods in Taiwan in 1996: Effects of an Electoral System," *Asian Survey* 37 (1997), 652–68; Tun-jen Cheng, "Taiwan in 1996: From Euphoria to Melodrama," *Asian Survey* 37 (1997), 43–51.

51 For detailed analysis of the 2000 presidential election results and implications, see Yu-shan Wu, "Taiwan in 2000: Managing the Aftershocks from Power Transfer," *Asian Survey* 41 (2001), 40–8; T. Y. Wang, "Cross-Strait Relations after the 2000 Election in Taiwan: Changing Tactics in a New Reality," *Asian Survey* 41 (2001), 716–36.

52 G. Sidney Silliman, "The Philippines in 1983: Authoritarianism Beleaguered," *Asian Survey* 24 (1984), 154.

53 Cardinal Sin persuaded Aquino to join the opposition forces and accept a joint ticket with Salvador Laurel for the 1986 presidential election. Robert L. Youngblood, *Marcos against the Church: Economic Development and Political Repression in the Philippines* (Ithaca: Cornell University Press, 1990), 200.

54 Herbert S. Malin, "The Philippines in 1984: Grappling with Crisis," *Asian Survey* 25 (1985), 203.

55 Bernardo M. Villegas, "The Philippines in 1986: Democratic Reconstruction in the Post-Marcos Era," *Asian Survey* 27 (1987), 196.

56 For more information on the 1986 election frauds, see *Far Eastern Economic Review* (January 30, 1986), 12; Romeo Manlapaz, *The Mathematics of Deception: A Study of the 1986 Presidential Election Tallies* (Quezon City: Third World Studies Center, University of the Philippines, 1986); Jennifer Conroy Franco, *Elections and Democratization in the Philippines* (New York: Routledge, 2001), 173–81.

57 Mark R. Thomson, *The Anti-Marcos Struggle: Personalistic Rule and Democratic Transition in the Philippines* (New Haven: Yale University Press, 1995), 142.
58 See, Petronilo Bn. Daroy, "On the Eve of Dictatorship and Revolution," in *Dictatorship and Revolution: Roots of People's Power*, ed. Aurora Javate de Dios (Manila: Conspectus, 1988), 1–125.
59 Carl H. Lande, The Political Crisis," in *Crisis in the Philippines: The Marcos Era and Beyond*, ed. John Bresnan (Princeton: Princeton University Press, 1986), 143.
60 Cecilio T. Arillo, *Breakaway: The Inside Story of the Four-Day Revolution in the Philippines, February 22–25, 1986* (Manila: CTA, 1986), 117.
61 David J. Steinberg, *The Philippines: A Singular and a Plural Place*, 2nd edn (Boulder: Westview Press, 1990), 148; Walden Bello, "Aquino's Elite Pluralism: Initial Reflections," *Third World Quarterly* 8 (1986), 1020; Kyung-kyo Seo, "Military Involvement in Politics and the Prospects for Democracy: Thailand, the Philippines, and South Korea in Comparative Perspective," (PhD diss., Southern Illinois University at Carbondale, 1993), 236.
62 Renato S. Velasco, "Philippine Democracy: Promise and Performance," in *Democratization in Southeast and East Asia*, ed. Anek Laothamatas (New York: St. Martin's Press, 1997), 94.
63 John T. Sidel, *Capital, Coercion, and Crime: Bossism in the Philippines* (Stanford: Stanford University Press, 1999), 73–8.
64 Felipe B. Miranda and Ruben F. Ciron, "Development and the Military in the Philippines: Military Perceptions in a Time of Continuing Crisis," in *Soldiers and Stability in Southeast Asia*, ed. J. Soedjati Djiwandono and Yong Mun Cheong (Singapore: Institute of Southeast Asian Studies, 1988), 163–211.
65 Carolina G. Hernandez, "The Philippines in 1987: Challenges of Redemocratization," *Asian Survey* 28 (1988), 236; Alex Bello Brillantes, "Insurgency and Peace Policies of the Aquino Government," *PSSC Social Science Information* (April–September, 1987), 3–9.
66 Carolina G. Hernandez, "The Philippines in 1988: Reaching out to Peace and Economic Recovery," *Asian Survey* 29 (1989), 159.
67 Some of the left-leaning members in the administration included, among others, Labor Minister Aqusto Sanchez, Local Government Minister Aquilino Pimentel, and Executive Secretary Joker P. Arroyo. Gretchen Casper, *Fragile Democracies: The Legacies of Authoritarian Rule* (Pittsburgh: University of Pittsburgh Press, 1995), 142.
68 Thomson, *The Anti-Marcos Struggle*, 169.
69 Casper, *Fragile Democracies*, 143.

70 The December 1989 coup attempt, for example, severely damaged the economy by shattering the credibility of the Aquino government among the Filipinos and international business communities. For the 1989 coup's effect on the Philippine economy, see David G. Timberman, "The Philippines in 1990: On Shaky Ground," *Asian Survey* 31 (1991), 158–61.

71 Annette Clear, "Politics: From Endurance to Evolution," in *Indonesia: The Great Transition*, ed. John Bresnan (Lanham: Rowman & Littlefield, 2005), 46–147.

72 Even though the 1997 financial crisis was the direct cause of Suharto's fall, organized opposition forces had been built up since the early 1990s. See, Kastorius Sinaga, "Number of Local NGO's Mushrooming," *Jakarta Post*, November 2, 1993; Philip Eldridge, *Non-Government Organizations and Democratic Participation in Indonesia* (Kuala Lumpur: Oxford University Press, 1995); Edward Aspinall, *Student Dissident in Indonesia in the 1980s* (Clayton, Victoria: Centre of Southeast Asian Studies, 1993); Edward Aspinall, "Indonesia: Civil Society and Democratic Breakthrough," in *Civil Society and Political Change in Asia: Expanding and Contracting Democratic Space*, ed. Muthiah Alagappa (Stanford: Stanford University Press, 2004).

73 Judith Bird, "Indonesia in 1997: The Tinderbox Year," *Asian Survey* 38 (1998), 175.

74 For the IMF's economic package deal with Indonesia, see Central Banking, *Reforming the IMF: Lessons from Indonesia* (http://www.centralbanking.co.uk/publications/pdf/Hanke.pdf); Hall Hill, *The Indonesian Economy in Crisis: Causes, Consequences, and Lessons* (Singapore: Institute of Southeast Asia Studies, 1999).

75 R. William Liddle, "Indonesia's Unexpected Failure of Leadership," in *The Politics of Post-Suharto Indonesia*, Adam Schwarz and Jonathan Paris (New York: Council on Foreign Relations Press, 1999), 17–18.

76 Clear, *Indonesia*, 153.

77 Violent riots were quite frequent throughout the 1990s even before the 1997 economic crisis began. Elizabeth Fuller Collins, "Indonesia: A Violent Culture?" *Asian Survey* 42 (2002); Lowell Dittmer, "The Legacy of Violence in Indonesia," *Asian Survey* 42 (2002); Susan Berfield and Dewi Loveard, "Ten Days that Shook Indonesia," *Asiaweek*, July 21, 1998.

78 Adam Schwarz, "Introduction: The Politics of Post-Suharto Indonesia," in Schwarz and Paris, eds, 1999, 2.

79 Judith Bird, "Indonesia in 1998: The Pot Boils Over," *Asian Survey* 39 (1999), 29.

80 Michael R. J. Vatikiotis, *Indonesian Politics Under Suharto* (London: Routledge, 1993), 25.
81 Angel Rabasa and John Haseman, *The Military and Democracy in Indonesia: Challenges, Politics, and Power* (RAND: National Security Research Division, 2002), 38.
82 For detailed information about factions within the ABRI, see, Takashi Shiraishi, "The Indonesian Military in Politics," in Schwarz and Paris, eds, 1999, 76–82.
83 Jusuf Wanandi, "Challenge of the TNI and Its Role in Indonesia's Future," in *Governance in Indonesia: Challenges Facing the Megawati Presidency*, ed. Hadi Soesastro, Anthony L. Smith, and Han Mui Ling (Singapore: Institute of Southeast Asian Studies, 2003), pp. 94–5.
84 For detailed information about those 48 political parties, see Kathleen E. Woodward, "Violent Masses, Elites, and Democratization: The Indonesian Case," (PhD diss., The Ohio State University, 2002), 340–2.
85 See, National Democratic Institute for International Affairs, *The 1999 Presidential Election, MPR General Session and Post-Election Development in Indonesia* (Washington D.C.: National Democratic Institute, November 28, 1999), 39; R. William Liddle, "Indonesia in 1999: Democracy Restored," *Asian Survey* 40 (2000), 32–9.
86 Rabasa and Haseman, *The Military and Democracy in Indonesia*, 42.
87 For the civil society's role in the post-Suharto Indonesia, see Edward Aspinall, "Indonesia: Transformation of Civil Society and Democratic Breakthrough," in Alagappa, ed., 2004, 61–95; Edward Aspinall, *Opposing Suharto: Compromise, Resistance and Regime Change in Indonesia* (Stanford: Stanford University Press, 2005); Robert Hefner, *Civil Islam: Muslims and Democratization in Indonesia* (Princeton: Princeton University Press, 2000).
88 Rabasa and Haseman, *The Military and Democracy in Indonesia*, 84.
89 John McBeth and Oren Murphy, "Bloodbath," *Far Eastern Economic Review*, July 6, 2000, 20–2.
90 R. William Liddle, "Indonesia in 2000: A Shaky Start for Democracy," *Asian Survey* 41 (2001), 215.
91 International Crisis Group, "Ending Repression in Irian Jaya," (September, 2001), available at <http://www.crisisweb.org>.
92 Human Rights Watch, "Violence and Political Impasse in Papua," (July, 2001), available at <http://www.hrw.org>.
93 Clear, *Indonesia*, 179.
94 See, for example, Juan Linz, *Crisis, Breakdown and Reequilibration* (Baltimore: Johns Hopkins University Press, 1978); Gullermo O'Donnell,

Philippe Schmitter, and Laurence Whitehead, eds, *Transitions from Authoritarian Rule: Prospects for Democracy* (Baltimore: Johns Hopkins University Press, 1986); Adam Przeworski, *Democracy and the Market: Political and Economic Reforms in Eastern Europe and Latin America* (New York: Cambridge University Press, 1991).

CHAPTER FIVE

The Military and Democratic Consolidation

The three previous chapters have examined the rise and fall of the military's domestic political role in four Asian countries from the 1940s through the 1990s. The first historical stage (1940s–1950s) was the military's political role during the early years of the state-building process, in which security threat environments shaped the armed forces' organizational characteristics, doctrines, and political roles. The second stage (1960s–1970s) moved on to discuss how a confluence of structural conditions—namely, external/internal threats, strength of the civilian leadership, and the unity of the military—resulted in different manifestations of the military's political role: the military's political control via coups d'état and military dictatorship in South Korea and Indonesia on the one hand, and officers' participation in the domestic governing process under the civilian authoritarian supervision in Taiwan and the Philippines on the other. The third historical stage (1980s–1990s) accounted for different modes of officers' withdrawal from politics during democratization: complete depoliticization of the military and subordination to the democratically elected civilian leadership in South Korea and Taiwan, and the officers' political influence both during and after the regime transition in the Philippines and Indonesia.

The current chapter analyzes the military's domestic political role in the post-democratization era and its implications for democratic consolidation in the four Asian countries. Although the four states have undergone democratic transitions during the past two decades, the so-called "praetorian problem" remains a vital concern that civilian leaders in these countries need to overcome.[1] Based on the theoretical standpoint from Chapter One and empirical findings in the subsequent empirical chapters, this chapter identifies the current status of the military's political role in the four countries and dissects major structural barriers to the democratic control over the armed forces.

Similar to the previous three chapters, this chapter is composed of four sections. The first section explains the role of the Korean army in the democratic consolidation era. Although the possibility of another military coup and a return to military dictatorship is quite a remote possibility in South Korea, the country must still cope with certain challenges in order to secure stable civilian control of the military, including the North Korean threat and the problem of institutionalizing democratic norms and practices. The second section analyzes the Taiwanese case, where a stable democratic regime transition does not necessarily guarantee the military's subordination to the civilian leadership due to problems such as the identity issue among Taiwanese people, the country's relationship with mainland China in terms of the island's independence, and the ailing civilian leadership. However, against these backdrops, Taiwan and South Korea have been more successful in institutionalizing stable civilian control of the armed forces than the next two cases.

The third and fourth sections examine the Philippines and Indonesia, in which army officers still play significant roles in domestic politics even after two decades of democratic experimentation. The two countries have to cope with politicized armed forces, which create more daunting challenges to the newly elected civilian leaders. Both countries face greater probabilities that the military may regain political influence in the foreseeable future, primarily due to internal security threats, weak civilian leadership, and the lack of organizational unity and professionalism in the military. Overall, it is apparent that consolidated democracy with strong civilian control of the military is feasible when countries can accomplish the following three conditions under control: successful maneuvering of security challenges, establishment of strong civilian leadership, and reorganization of the military as a cohesive body with no factional struggles.

To evaluate the current state of civil–military relations in the four Asian countries, this chapter employs two major categories of civilian control of the military: Civilian Control Indicators (CCI) and Challenges to Civilian Control (CCC). The CCI uses five specific indicators: (1) the military's loyalty to democratic leadership, (2) the military's political neutrality, (3) military presence in key governmental positions, (4) defined security missions, and (5) the military's participation in policy-making process. The CCC aims to identify structural impediments to civilian control of the military: (1) security challenges, (2) challenges to civilian leadership, (3) the military's organizational unity, and (4) the role of civil society. This chapter applies these specific indicators across the cases for a structured-focused analysis to evaluate the current status of civil–military relations with comparative perspectives.

I. South Korea

The democratization process that civil society groups initiated brought an end to the three-decade-long military dictatorship and installed a democratic government in South Korea. Although democratization in the country began from below with demonstrations by students and labor unions in the mid-1980s, subsequent regime change continued with negotiations at the elite level. This so-called transplacement mode of transition brought slow but stable and far-reaching democratization. As Samuel P. Huntington suggests, democratization through negotiations in the transplacement mode is less prone to violence and therefore most suitable for democratic consolidation.[2] Furthermore, the stable regime transition culminated in the Kim Young-sam government's restructuring of the armed forces toward a politically neutral and professionalized organization in the 1990s.

After two decades of democratic reforms, South Korea is now considered a consolidated democracy. As detailed in Chapter Four, the Kim presidency (1993–1997) set the course for democratic consolidation by carrying out extensive political institutional and electoral reforms. As noted, the most crucial aspect of consolidation was military reform. President Kim successfully disbanded the clandestine *Hanahoe* (one mind) faction in the army, thereby removing politicized officers while subsequently building up unified and professionalized armed forces. The democratic transition concluded when the opposition leader and long-time pro-democracy activist, Kim Dae-jung, became president in 1998. The top brass, who had openly warned against the possibility of Kim Dae-jung's becoming president in the 1988 election, now readily expressed their allegiance to the new president.

The question remains whether the democratic consolidation in South Korea will proceed further and whether civilian control over the armed forces will become a given reality. Although the military's direct appropriation of political power is highly unlikely, several structural impediments to democratic deepening still exist in South Korea, such as the increasing security challenges from North Korea, the restructuring of the security alliance with the United States, the rising social costs of economic restructuring in the aftermath of the 1997 financial crisis, and the weak, divided, and corrupt civilian politics. Table 5.1 presents specific indicators of the current civil–military relations in South Korea.

As Table 5.1 indicates, major indicators of civilian control over the armed forces demonstrate that the military's political participation is minimal in post-democratization South Korea. When Kim Dae-jung became the first president from the opposition party in the 1997 presidential election, the army leadership pronounced its loyalty to him. Five years later, President Roh Moo-hyun also secured the military's allegiance. The military's political neutrality during the power succession processes bore significant implications for the institutionalization of civilian control over the military in that both presidents came from the far left side of the ideological spectrum in the eyes of the conservatives and the military leadership that had strong anticommunist ethos. This indicates that the military's loyalty to the democratically elected leaders was now firmly established. In addition, the military has not intervened in the election processes since the inception of democratization, but instead maintained political neutrality. It has become clear that civil–military relations in South Korea have established institutional and constitutional control over military officers, but not based on the president's personal charisma or the military's ideological predilection.

Although active military officers do not participate in political affairs, retired officers still hold several positions in the executive and legislative branches and maintain influence in the policy-making process. In the executive branch, approximately 9.7 percent of the cabinet officials have military backgrounds, whereas retired officers occupy 2.7 percent in the National Assembly.[3] These retired officers in various government positions have close personal connections with the army leadership and often represent the institutional interests of the military in the policy-making process. Furthermore, the top brass in the army influences foreign and security policy-making, given the presence of the constant threat from North Korea and civilian leaders' lack of knowledge of and experience with national security affairs.

Civilian control over the military does not emerge as a noticeable political issue in South Korea, yet two major structural barriers still remain for civilian leaders to consolidate a stable democratic control mechanism: (1) security challenges from North Korea and (2) the weakness of civilian leadership (ideological and regional cleavages, corruption, and the loss of public support).

As discussed in the previous chapter, South Korea benefited more from favorable security environments during its democratic regime transition and military reform (1986–1997) than during any other period of history. During the 1980s, the military balance between the two Koreas turned to favor South Korea. In addition, the end of the Cold War and the ensuing détente surrounding the Korean peninsula provided South Korea with an opportunity to expand its political and economic relationship with former communist states—including the Soviet Union, Eastern Europe, and mainland China—without losing U.S. security commitments. The favorable security conditions during this period eliminated the military's justification for political involvement and empowered civil society and pro-democracy groups.

However, during the Kim Dae-jung presidency (1998–2002), two contrasting security situations developed. On the one hand, the Kim government's

Sunshine policy toward North Korea seemed to bring reconciliation between the two Koreas. The Sunshine policy signified a refutation of war or major military conflicts as a means of national reunification. The policy initiative was based on the assumption that the sudden collapse of North Korea would not be desirable for either of the two Koreas or neighboring countries; therefore, engaging the North was necessary for preventing war. The Kim government's policy separated political–military issues from economic cooperation and focused on economic aid to poverty-stricken North Korea. The economic engagement would eventually reduce political–military tensions, and the two Koreas would steadily move toward peaceful reunification.[4] The policy culminated in the summit meeting between Kim Dae-jung and North Korean leader Kim Jong-il in Pyongyang, which produced the North-South Joint Declaration in June 2000, including the roadmap to Korean reunification, reunion of separated families, and expansion of economic, social, and cultural exchanges between the two Koreas.[5] The summit meeting concluded with Kim Jong-il's promise that he would visit Seoul in the near future.

However, the Sunshine policy and the North-South summit meeting failed to further create a peace-building mechanism in the Korean peninsula. Indeed, several obstacles to developing peaceful relations between the two regimes still remain. First and foremost, the Sunshine policy failed to build consensus among domestic audiences in South Korea; rather, the policy became a source of political–ideological polarization of the society. The Grand National Party (GNP)—the opposition conservative party—heavily criticized the Kim government's northern policy for its unilaterally conciliatory attitude and lack of reciprocity. Several belligerent moves by North Korea reinforced the opposition GNP's criticism. In the first year of the Kim presidency, various incidents occurred involving North Korean spy submarines' infiltration into the South. To make matters worse, North Korea test-fired a multistage, long-range rocket missile, called *Daepodong* 1, across the northern islands of Japan, with debris reaching close to Alaska.[6] In the following year, North Korean patrol boats crossed the Northern Limit Line of the West Sea, a U.N.-demarcated borderline, causing an exchange of fire by the armed forces of the South and the North. During the incident, a North Korean battleship was destroyed while five others were severely damaged.[7]

North Korea's hostile behavior further strengthened the political voice and influence of the opposition GNP and the conservative groups in South Korea. The opposition GNP's political strength grew further after it won a majority of seats in the 2000 National Assembly elections, while the ruling

Millennium Democratic Party (MDP) lost its majority status by winning only 35 percent of the total vote and 115 of the 273 seats.[8] The election resulted in the so-called *yosoyadae* (ruling minority and opposition majority), a situation whereby the opposition GNP took offense to the Kim government's northern policy by mobilizing the anti-North Korean and anticommunist ethos among the people.

As the Kim government was trying to muddle through its relationship with an unpredictable North Korea, the George W. Bush administration's North Korea policy dealt a heavy blow to President Kim's Sunshine policy. The Bush administration charged that North Korea had violated the 1994 Agreed Framework and secretly continued a nuclear project.[9] In turn, North Korea perceived growing threats from the Bush administration's tougher policy, as Bush's January 2002 State of the Union address included North Korea—along with Iran and Iraq—as a member of the "axis of evil" that was endangering international security and promoting global terrorism.[10] The Bush administration's tough stance on North Korea accelerated Kim Jong-il's nuclear development program. In January 2003, North Korea declared that it would withdraw from the Nuclear Non-proliferation Treaty (NPT) and, in the following month, reactivated its nuclear reactor. In 2005, North Korea declared that it had successfully enriched enough uranium to make nuclear weapons; one year later, it conducted a nuclear test to become a new member of the Nuclear Weapon States (NWS).

In the midst of confrontations between the United States and North Korea, Kim Dae-jung found himself in a diplomatic gridlock. If he sided with Bush, it would isolate the North and precipitate a North–South confrontation, nullifying the Sunshine policy. If the South voted for North Korea, it would infuriate the United States, which had been South Korea's long-time ally and the only country that could provide security from North Korea's attack. In this situation, Kim Dae-jung tried to negotiate with both sides: keeping the Sunshine policy alive and alleviating Bush's hostility toward North Korea. When President Kim visited Washington D.C. in 2001 for a summit meeting with President Bush, he urged Bush to resume direct talks with North Korea, to which Bush responded negatively due to the North's "lack of transparency."[11] In other words, Kim's visit produced no positive results, as North Korea continued pursuing nuclear technology and the United States continued its unwillingness to negotiate with the rogue state.

Meanwhile, on South Korea's domestic political front, the Bush administration's hostility toward North Korea contributed to reinforcing anti-Americanism among the general public. Many South Koreans believed that Bush's North Korean policy destabilized the security of the Korean peninsula.

In a public opinion survey conducted in 2002, a majority of Koreans believed that the United States was more dangerous for Korean security than North Korea itself.[12] Anti-Americanism was further intensified when two Korean middle school girls were killed by an American armored vehicle on duty during a military exercise. The two soldiers responsible for the accident were subsequently acquitted by an American military court.[13]

The presidential election in December 2002 occurred at the height of anti-American demonstrations in South Korea. Roh Moo-hyun, a human rights lawyer and labor movement activist during democratization, was elected by mobilizing the anti-American sentiment—along with a progressive ideology—among the younger generations, garnering 49.9 percent of the popular vote.[14] President Roh widened diplomatic rifts with the United States. The cracks in security alliance with the United States put heavier security burdens on South Korea. The United States announced its plan to relocate its troops stationed in the DMZ further south and left open the possibility of withdrawing its troops completely from South Korea.[15] Although the top brass in the Korean army did not directly challenge the decision-making authority of the civilian leadership, they began to express their concerns about the foreign and security policy directions. The North Korean issue and difficulties within the U.S.-ROK alliance burdened the civilian leadership, and civil–military discrepancies have appeared in security policy-conceptions in recent years.

Security challenges have indeed put civilian leadership in a difficult situation; meanwhile, several other factors on the domestic political front have limited the strength of civilian leadership. The biggest challenge for the past and current civilian governance has been how to overcome ideological and regional polarization of the country. In its early period of democratization, the Kim Young-sam presidency was able to incorporate diverse economic and ideological elements in society by forming the grand conservative alliance, as discussed in the previous chapter. President Kim solved the praetorian problem by forming the alliance with the conservative ruling Democratic Justice Party (DJP), which represented the conservatives including active and retired generals. As a result, although Kim Young-sam had for decades courted pro-democracy activists, his government eventually endorsed conservative elements. The ensuing presidents—namely, Kim Dae-jung and Roh Moo-hyun—represented moderate and progressive elements of society and actively pursued engagement policy with North Korea. Consequently, political–ideological cleavages in South Korea revolve around foreign and security policies, especially policy toward North Korea, making it difficult for the government to mediate citizens' polarizing views on North Korea and the reunification issue.

Another challenge to the strength of civilian leadership comes from political cleavages along regional identities. The democratic regime transition was dictated by the "three Kims," which included the former presidents Kim Young-sam and Kim Dae-jung and opposition leader Kim Jong-pil. These three Kims mobilized the decades-long regional animosity between *Honam* (southwestern region of Korea) and *Youngnam* (southeastern region of Korea) in order to rise to power. All the post-democratization elections were determined by candidates' regional identities, thereby dividing the country into two political camps and significantly weakening presidents' ability to garner nationwide support. Although the three Kims retired from politics, regional cleavages still dictate major aspects of power struggles in South Korea.[16]

Added to these structural constraints on presidents' leadership, incessant corruption charges surrounding presidents have further weakened their moral grounds. The Kim Young-sam presidency was tainted by several corruption charges against Kim's close aides. For example, Kim Young-sam's closest advisor, Hong In-gil, was charged for his involvement in a loan scandal associated with Hanbo Steel Company. In another case, the President's second son, Kim Hyun-chul, was convicted of receiving bribes from *Chaebols*.[17] The direct effect of such corruption scandals in the Kim Young-sam government produced a significant decline of the public's support for the president. When he began his job in 1993, he had the approval of more than 90 percent of the public; his presidency ended with meager 10 percent approval rate.[18] The next Kim Dae-jung presidency followed the same path. A Nobel Peace Prize winner and pro-democracy leader for decades, Kim Dae-jung's moral cause was also lost in numerous corruption scandals involving two of his three sons and several close aides.[19] Most tragically, the most recent former president Roh Moo-hyun (2003–2008) committed suicide during the investigation of corruption scandals involving his family and close assistants. Political corruption can seriously undermine the strength of civilian leadership and the public's belief of democratic values and norms, which in turn negatively affect civilian control of the military in new democracies.

Despite these structural barriers to civilian control of the military, the South Korean case nevertheless promises the best prospects for stable civilian control of the military among the four Asian countries under study. In other words, stable civilian control is buttressed by the presence of active and influential civil society as well as the unified and professionalized army organization. The military's political neutrality—even in the strained security situation and continuing corruption charges—may serve as testimony to the military's near-complete depoliticization in South Korea. Future civil–military relations in the country will be shaped by the structural opportunities and constraints previously presented herein.

II. Taiwan

Taiwan's three-decade-long liberal reforms (1970s–1990s) and subsequent democratization (1990s–current) have transformed the country from a one-party dictatorship to a multi-party democracy. Taiwanese liberalization and democratization represent an ideal case of the "transformation" mode of regime transition, in which elites' political compromises carried out the democratization process.[20] Although the transformation mode was slow and steady, democratic reforms in Taiwan continued under the strong political leadership of Chiang Ching-kuo (1975–1988) and Lee Teng-hui (1988–2000). The elite-initiated political reforms brought about political stability, with no major disruptions during the regime transition.

However, this does not necessarily mean that the Taiwanese army simply shifted its loyalty from Chiang and his KMT party to a new constitution and the democratically elected civilian leadership, particularly given that the new leadership was of Taiwanese ethnic background. During the democratic reforms in the early 1990s, the Lee regime had to adopt several policies to alleviate the conservatives' and the military's potential threats to the regime. For example, immediately after assuming the presidency, Lee granted massive promotions to the military leadership. In addition, the president appointed General Hau Pei-tsun as defense minister in 1989 and as premier in the following year to moderate the conservative forces in both the KMT and the army.[21]

However, against this backdrop, Taiwan's political and military reforms benefited from favorable structural conditions in the early years of liberalization and subsequent democratization. Mainland China's conciliatory attitude toward Taiwan created a favorable security situation that in turn facilitated democratic reforms and the military's disengagement from politics. Since Deng Xiao-ping's rise to power in 1979, the PRC has made constant efforts to expand social and economic exchanges within Taiwan. With the easing of security challenges from the mainland, the KMT government disbanded the Taiwan Garrison Command (TGC), which had enabled the military to monitor civilian society, thus ending the Taiwanese army's internal policing missions in 1992. Furthermore, the expansion of economic and social exchanges between the two political entities made coercive and physically violent pressures an unfeasible strategy in dealing with each other.

On the domestic political front, the Lee government successfully strengthened its political power base by building a consensus around democratic reforms with the National Affairs Conference (NAC) in the early 1990s, as discussed in the previous chapter. Furthermore, the KMT's success in presidential and legislative elections provided the Lee leadership with strength and stability throughout his presidential tenure. Meanwhile, the Taiwanese army developed into a cohesive and professionalized institution, thereby precipitating army officers' depoliticization. In sum, a combination of favorable security situations, strong presidential leadership, and a professionalized army gave rise to stable democratization without major backfires from the military.

Taiwan became a consolidated democracy with the inauguration of the Chen Shui-bian presidency. In the 2000 presidential election, Chen—the leader of the opposition Democratic Progressive Party (DPP)—won the presidency by defeating Lien Chan of the ruling KMT and James Soong, an independent candidate. However, the election was very close. Chen won the presidency with just 39.3 percent of the popular vote, while Soong registered 36.8 percent and Lian gained 23.1 percent.[22] Chen's victory was a milestone in Taiwan's political development in that it brought to an end five decades of KMT rule. The DPP started from the *tangwai* as a grassroots organization by ethnic Taiwanese and endorsed political freedom and Taiwan's independence from the mainland. In this respect, from the very beginning the DPP has pursued radically different domestic and foreign policy packages than the KMT regime implemented.

After two decades of democratic reforms, the current state of civil –military relations in Taiwan signifies stable civilian control and military officers' political neutrality, as summarized in Table 5.2.[23]

Two of the democratically elected presidents—Lee and Chen, both of whom are ethnic Taiwanese—secured the armed forces' loyalty to their leadership and the constitution, which became a significant indicator of Taiwan's democracy in that the army leadership was still represented by ethnic Chinese and supported radically different foreign policy strategies from the civilian leadership. The two presidents endorsed Taiwan's independence from the mainland whereas the army leadership championed the "one China" policy and reunification.[24] Even with such differences in terms of national identity and security policy, the army leadership has not officially contested the civilian leaders' authority.

Table 5.2 Post-Democratization Civil–Military Relations in Taiwan

Indicators	Status
Civilian Control Indicators	
Military's loyalty to democratic leadership	• Official expression of loyalty to the constitution and democratically elected leadership—Lee Teng-hui (1996–2000), Chen Shui-bian (2000–2008), and Ma Ying-jeou (2008–)
Military's political neutrality	• Military closely tied with the KMT; minimal influence in elections
Military presence in key governmental positions	• No active military personnel in civilian government (several retired officers in security-related positions)
Defined security missions	• Complete withdrawal from internal security mission; focus on threats from the mainland
Military's participation in the policy-making process	• The military's influence focused on foreign and security policy-making but minimal in domestic policies
Challenges to Civilian Control	
Security challenges	• Externally, threats from the mainland/independence issue; domestically, ethnic identity issues
Challenges to civilian leadership	• Ethnic cleavages between Taiwanese and mainlanders; corruption charges
Military's organizational unity	• Highly cohesive, professionalized military
Role of civil society	• Strong but ideologically moderate civil groups

However, army officers have exerted influence in domestic political and security-related policy-making process during and after democratization. Retired generals occupied leadership positions in various security-related institutions, such as the Ministry of National Defense, the National Security Council, and the National Security Bureau, throughout the 1990s. In addition, President Lee appointed several active and retired generals as "special presidential advisors" or "strategic advisors" as a way of securing control over army leadership.[25] Although the army officers' presence in civilian administration was quite pervasive during the 1990s, their political influence has since significantly decreased.

Still the most difficult task of the military's depoliticization was how to separate the Taiwanese army from the ruling KMT party. The KMT regime tightened its control over the armed forces by introducing a political commissar system right after retreating to Taiwan. The commissar system enabled the KMT to penetrate deeply into the army organization and conduct ideological indoctrination throughout the rule of Chiang Kai-shek and his son Ching-kuo, as discussed in Chapter Three. Moreover, the officers' penetration into the party hierarchy was pervasive, holding positions in key governmental bodies including the Central Standing Committee and other central and local administrative institutions. Because of the party–army interpenetration, separating the two bodies proved to be the most difficult task during the democratic reforms of the 1990s. Although the KMT formally disengaged from the military and the military attained institutional autonomy, informal interpenetrations persist due to unofficial and personal connections between the two institutions.

What will Taiwanese civil–military relations be like in the near future? What factors will promote or obstruct democratic consolidation and civilian control over the military? Three major factors are likely to shape the future of civil–military relations in Taiwan: (1) security challenges from the mainland and the issue of Taiwanese independence; (2) weakening civilian leadership due to ethnic cleavages and corruption; and (3) party–army relations, as summarized in Table 5.2.

The greatest challenge to Taiwan's democratic consolidation and the strong civilian hold of the military organization come from the cross-Taiwan Strait relations, which have been badly strained during the past two decades. Taiwanese democratization and military reforms benefited from favorable security relations with the mainland during the 1980s and 1990s. The PRC's policy toward Formosa Island changed from tense hostility (1950s–1970s) to one of the "Peace Offensive" and mutual accommodation (1980s–1990s).[26] Détente accompanied growing economic interdependence and social and personal exchanges as the mainland broadened its domestic economic reforms.

However, the decade of mutual accommodation turned into mutual hostility and military intimidation when, in the summer of 1995, President Lee visited his *alma mater*, Cornell University, and the PRC test-fired missiles, carrying out a massive-scale military exercise in the Taiwan Strait in protest. From Beijing's perspective, Lee's visit to the United States was a clear violation of the 1972 Shanghai Joint Communiqué signed by the Chinese Communist Party and the United States recognizing the "one China" policy. When the Communiqué was pronounced, Chiang Ching-kuo welcomed the "one China" formula and publicly opposed Taiwan's independence. President Lee also followed Chiang's mainland policy during the early years of his presidency by objecting to the idea of Taiwan's independence.

However, in the mid-1990s, Lee abruptly changed his position. He announced that the Republic of China was a sovereign state and made diplomatic trips to several countries.[27] The Lee government openly adopted the "two-state doctrine." Feeling betrayed, the People's Liberation Army (PLA) launched missile tests and military exercises in the waters near Taiwan. Furthermore, President Lee's shift in foreign policy position increased tensions between the PRC and the Clinton administration.

The installation of the Chen Shui-bian presidency made the situation worse by increasing tensions across the Taiwan Strait. For the mainland government, Chen was the last presidential candidate that it wanted elected to the presidency in the 2000 elections.[28] Immediately before the 2000 presidential election, the PRC declared in a white paper that it would embark on military attacks if any one of three conditions occurred. The white paper detailed what came to be known as the "three ifs," declaring that the PRC would resort to military means if Taiwan (1) declared independence, (2) were invaded and occupied by foreign countries, or (3) indefinitely refused to conduct negotiations on the issue of unification.[29] Although the PRC's direct military attack on Taiwan remains implausible, continuing tensions across the Strait create a troubling security dilemma between the two Chinese governments.

Chen's foreign policy position has created serious tensions in the domestic political front as well. The Chen regime's pro-independence stance and the mobilization of ethnic identity issues for domestic political purposes have widened political cleavages and could weaken its leadership strength in the long run.[30] Identity issues are closely related to both the foreign policy controversy over the independence/reunification issue and Taiwan's relationship with the mainland. For example, in the 2004 presidential elections, the incumbent Chen secured his second presidential term by mobilizing anti-China sentiments and the notion of Taiwanese nationalism.[31] Political elites' mobilization of identity and independence issues further exacerbated the political cleavages based on ethnic communities.[32] Moreover, the DPP's control of the government significantly constricted the possibility of diplomatic negotiations with the mainland authority.

The future of civil–military relations in Taiwan will be shaped by three major structural forces. First, cross-Taiwan Strait relations will influence the military's political role in the near future. Confrontational relations with the mainland may give senior officers a bigger political voice as discrepancies rise between civilian leadership and the military over how to negotiate with the PRC. Second, civilian control of the military in Taiwan will also depend on how civilian leadership can overcome sociopolitical cleavages along ethnic lines. Civilian leadership will find it increasingly difficult to control army officers if civilians intensify ethnic cleavages for their own political purposes. Finally, the future of civil–military relations in Taiwan will depend on establishing institutional autonomy and defining the separation between the KMT party and the military.

III. The Philippines

Democratization in the Philippines began in 1986 with the overthrow of the authoritarian Marcos regime and the installation of the democratically elected Aquino regime. The so-called People Power was so overwhelming that president Marcos and his military forces could not control the pro-democracy movement. The People Power was also influential enough to bring spillover effects to other Asian countries' democratization movements, including South Korea, Pakistan, and Burma.

Although the People Power provided important momentum for the downfall of the authoritarianism, it was the Armed Forces of the Philippines (AFP) that played a decisive role in the Marcos ouster and subsequent democratization. As such, the AFP presumed that it would maintain a powerful role in the democratically elected Aquino government. Different factions within the AFP—either Marcos loyalists or the Reformed Armed Forces of the Philippines Movement (RAM), or both—staged no fewer than nine major coup attempts during the Aquino presidency to regain political domination. The nascent democratic regime was severely incapacitated by the fragmented but violent political forces: the Marcos loyalists and pre-martial law oligarchs on the far-right, and the Communist Party of the Philippines (CPP) and the National Democratic Front (NDF) on the extreme left. In such a fragmented political climate, the Aquino regime failed to mobilize the People Power for her democratic reforms. Furthermore, the growing insurgency movements by the New People's Army (NPA), the CPP's armed organ, and the Muslim Moro National Liberation Front (MNLF) provided the AFP with opportunities to regain its political influence in the Aquino government.[33]

The AFP's threat to the regime significantly decreased once Fidel Ramos, retired general and defense minister in the Aquino regime, became president in 1992. President Ramos successfully secured the AFP's loyalty, but only after bringing many of the top military brass into his government. As a result, the armed forces—both active and retired officers—continue to play an influential role in politics even after two decades of democratic experiments. This section surveys the military's political role in the post-democratization period—from the Ramos presidency (1992–1997) to the Arroyo presidency (2001–2010)—and identifies major barriers to the democratic control over the AFP as well as prospects for democratic consolidation in the Philippines.

The current status of civilian control over the AFP is weak and shaky at best, as officers still exert substantial influence in everyday civilian politics. Even after two decades of democratization, civilian leaders have failed to secure army officers' political neutrality and allegiance to the constitution and democratically elected leadership.

As Table 5.3 illustrates, Philippine society has put forth multiple challenges that civilian leaders must overcome to institutionalize democratic control over the AFP. The most serious challenge is domestic security threats from the communist NPA's armed insurgencies, Muslims' MNLF/MILF secessionist movements, and several other terrorist groups engaged in bombings and kidnappings of Filipinos and foreign tourists for ransom.

The communist insurgency movements reached their peak during the mid- to late 1980s, in the midst of political turmoil and continuing economic crisis. During the Aquino presidency in the late 1980s, the NPA forces spread their armed uprisings throughout the archipelago when the peace negotiations between the government and the CPP representatives failed, as discussed in the previous chapter. Meanwhile, communist forces expanded their influence in the Aquino government as well as with ordinary citizens, with more than ten million people reportedly joining the communist party's regional organization.

However, the communist and Muslim insurgency movements significantly decreased after Ramos rose to the presidency in 1992. Several factors contributed to the weakening of the CPP and NPA's influence in the early 1990s.

Table 5.3 Post-Democratization Civil–Military Relations in the Philippines

Indicators	Status
Civilian Control Indicators	
Military's loyalty to democratic leadership	• Lack of loyalty to the constitution and democratically elected leadership (constant rumors of and/or real coup attempts by the AFP)
Military's political neutrality	• Officers' personal ties with civilian politicians mobilized soldiers to influence elections
Military presence in key governmental positions	• No active military personnel in the government; several retired officers in key governmental positions and the legislative branch
Defined security missions	• Continued internal security and policing missions (due to major threats from communists and Muslims)
Military's participation in the policy-making process	• AFP's influence in internal security and counterinsurgency programs
Challenges to Civilian Control	
Security challenges	• Increasing domestic threats from the CPP/NPA and the MNLF/MILF (armed conflicts with the insurgents; frequent terrorist bombings and kidnappings)
Challenges to civilian leadership	• Weak civilian leadership (corruption; cronyism; civil society's withdrawal of support for presidents)
Military's organizational unity	• Lack of institutional unity and professionalism (factional struggle within the AFP)
Role of civil society	• Strong, but minimal influence in governmental policy-making (dominated by cartelized elites); strong civil society, a burden to government

First, the decline of communist armed insurgents was related to the broader international context of the demise of communist regimes worldwide with the end of the Cold War. Second, the communist insurgents suffered from internal struggles among different factions over leadership and differences in ideology and logistics. The split in the CPP/NPA throughout the 1990s related to the issues of insurgency strategy and leadership. CPP founder Jose Mara Sison remained faithful to the Maoist-style armed struggle, while the moderates preferred expanding its influence by using legal and electoral means.[34] Finally, the much improved economic conditions under the Ramos presidency strengthened the moderate factions' voice within the CPP and NPA. At the same time, steady economic growth weakened the CPP's influence among the Filipinos. Political stability under the Ramos presidency brought about fast economic growth and low inflation rates.[35]

Upon assuming the presidency in 1992, Ramos formed the National Unification Commission (NUC) to initiate a peace process. The NUC brought together various insurgency groups, including the RAM rebels, the National Democratic Front (NDF), and the Muslim secessionist leaders. At the NUC conference, Ramos launched his peace initiative by releasing most of the rebel leaders—including 65 communist leaders, 68 RAM rebel soldiers, and several other dissident leaders in 1992.[36] However, the peace process did not progress further, primarily due to the factional struggles within the insurgency groups. Factional infightings significantly diminished the rebels' influence while factional struggles and the lack of unified leadership made the peace negotiation process much more complicated. The communist umbrella organization NDF suffered from factional struggles between the Maoist line led by Sison and the Manila Rizal Committee, which pursued moderate approaches. The situation was similar within the Muslim secessionist movements, as the MNLF, led by Nur Misuari, was split into several factional lines with different insurgency strategies. For example, a Muslim group led by Abu Sayyaf opposed the MNLF's peace negotiations with the Ramos government and pursued a more violent strategy, kidnapping foreigners and Christians as well as carrying out bombings. In 1994, the Abu Sayyaf group kidnapped more than 70 Christians and bombed an airplane of the Philippine Airlines.[37] Meanwhile, another Muslim fragment, Muslim Islamic Liberation Front (MILF), also focused on armed struggles in the Philippines.

After five years of a long peace negotiation process, the Ramos government and the MNLF reached a peace agreement in 1996 that also precipitated peace negotiations with the MILF and the communist NDF.[38] With the peace agreement, the MNLF insurgents were integrated into the regular AFP in 1997 and Misuari became an important political supporter for President Ramos. The six years of the Ramos presidency (1992–1997) were a uniquely stable regime that secured civilian leaders' control over the AFP, reduced domestic security threats from communist and Muslim insurgents, and achieved stable economic growth.

However, political stability and economic growth did not outlive the Ramos presidency. The vulnerable Philippine economy was hardest hit by the Asian financial crisis of 1997, which began in Bangkok but quickly spread to other Asian countries, including Indonesia, Malaysia, and South Korea. The economic difficulties and changes of civilian leadership provided insurgency groups with a renewed momentum to expand their armed struggles. In these circumstances, officers in the AFP began to regain their political influence in the Joseph Estrada presidency (1998–2001) and the Arroyo presidency (2001–current). Deteriorating domestic security situations caused by the revival of insurgency movements in the most recent decade have been closely related with the weak and corrupt civilian leadership.

In the 1998 presidential election, former movie star Joseph Estrada won the presidency, garnering 40 percent of the total popular vote among 11 presidential candidates—the largest electoral victory in the history of Philippine presidential elections.[39] The Estrada presidency was radically different from its predecessor in terms of political ideology and leadership style. Estrada rose to the presidency with the slogan *Erap para sa mahirap* (Erap is for the poor).[40] His campaign pledged to narrow the grave inequality gap between the rich and poor.

Although the populist slogan was extremely effective during the election, Filipinos' support for Estrada quickly evaporated due to rampant corruption and the president's favoritism to his cronies. For example, the "liberalization" of the airline industries focused on giving benefits to Philippine Airlines, a company controlled by his close friend Lucio Tan. The same story repeated itself in banking industry reforms, which gave preferential benefits to the president's friend George Go. During the years of the Estrada presidency, approximately 90 percent of companies in the country were owned by the top 20 stockholders, who were often connected with one another through family ties.[41] In the three years of his presidency, Estrada faced constant rumors of corruption and political scandals as well as rumors of an impending military coup d'état.

The Senate impeached the president on January 20, 2001, after Ilocos Sur Governor Luis "Chavit" Singson's revelation that he had paid bribes to the president. The disclosure of bribery inflamed mass demonstrations led by the then-Vice President Gloria Macapagal-Arroyo (who resigned from the

Estrada cabinet), two former presidents (Aquino and Ramos), and civil society groups that included the Catholic Church and the business community.[42] Similar to the 1986 situation in which the People Power and a segment of the AFP overthrew the Marcos dictatorship, the military played a decisive role in Estrada's resignation. On January 19, at the height of the anti-Estrada demonstration, Armed Forces Chief of Staff General Angelo T. Reyes formally declared the AFP's withdrawal of support for the president. The next day, Estrada stepped down and departed the Malacanang Presidential Palace.

After the impeachment, Vice President Arroyo assumed the fourth presidency and was reelected in the 2004 presidential election, winning 40 percent of total vote.[43] However, the new president was no better than her predecessor. Other presidential candidates charged President Arroyo with election fraud and filed a formal lawsuit for a recount of the votes. The allegations led to a serious political crisis in 2004, in which former President Aquino and civil society groups organized another People Power movement to impeach President Arroyo. Although the impeachment did not take place, the Arroyo regime was paralyzed by its lack of legitimacy.

In recent years, degenerating domestic security conditions along with the reappearance of insurgency movements and the failing civilian leadership have provided the AFP with opportunities to regain its political power. During the past decade, numerous retired officers have been appointed to key governmental positions or entered the legislative body by winning popular votes. More seriously, constant rumors of military coup have surfaced; for example, in 2003, a group of 300 AFP officers staged a coup demanding the resignation of President Arroyo, Defense Secretary General Reyes, and AFP intelligence Chief Brigadier General Victor Corpus. This "Oakwood coup" attempt ended with no major physical violence, and the coup leaders were arrested. Three years later, in 2006, a group of AFP officers led by Brigadier General Danilo Lim and Marine Colonel Ariel Querubin planned another coup to overthrow the corrupt civilian authority.[44] The coup attempt did not materialize because President Arroyo declared a state of emergency and co-opted senior AFP officers to secure the military's loyalty to her. Even after these aborted coup attempts, constant rumors of coups have ensued in everyday politics.

Twenty years of democratic regime transition in the Philippines failed to achieve democratic consolidation. Indeed, the country still suffers from the constant possibility of military coups d'état. Most damagingly, increasing domestic security threats in the coming years will make civilian control over the AFP much more difficult. Weak and corrupt civilian leadership will provide the AFP with an ongoing opportunity to overthrow civilian government via a coup d'état, in which a military reform in the Philippines will become a remote possibility. These three structural barriers—worsening domestic security threats, failing civilian leadership, and factionalized AFP—preclude any possibility of attaining democratic control over the AFP and stable democratic governance in the Philippines in the foreseeable future.

IV. Indonesia

Democratic regime transition in Indonesia began with the sudden downfall of the authoritarian Suharto regime in the middle of the Asian financial crisis in 1997 and subsequent violent demonstrations. The regime transition was so unpredictable and unprepared that the post-Suharto political situation was extremely volatile. Furthermore, the democratization process was tainted by numerous instances of interethnic and interreligious violence throughout the archipelago and independence movements in East Timor, Aceh, and Papua. In light of such pervasive violence and degenerating domestic security conditions, the *Angkatan Bersenjata Republik Indonesia* (ABRI, Armed Forces of the Republic of Indonesia) regained its political influence in the post-democratization era, as discussed in the previous chapter.

After a decade of democratic reforms, the ABRI still exercises a significant amount of influence in domestic political and economic affairs. As Table 5.4 shows, the democratically elected leadership has not yet secured the ABRI's loyalty to the regime or to the newly written constitution. On the contrary, ABRI officers openly express their own political views and sometimes overwhelm the decision-making power of the civilian leadership. The impeachment of President Abdurrahman Wahid in 2001 was a result of the ABRI's withdrawal of support for the president.[45] The ABRI exercised its prerogative power in the impeachment process when Wahid challenged the People's Consultative Assembly's decision to remove him from the presidency due to his corruption and mishandling of violent conflicts. When President Wahid sought to declare a state of emergency, the army leadership publicly opposed it by threatening to intervene in politics.[46] The impeachment was partly a reaction from the ABRI against the Wahid government's attempt to make military reforms, including the dismissal of General Wiranto from his leadership in the army and the appointment of the reform-minded officers in key positions.

Table 5.4 Post-Democratization Civil–Military Relations in Indonesia

Indicators	Status
Civilian Control Indicators	
Military's loyalty to democratic leadership	• Lack of ABRI's loyalty to the constitution and democratically elected leaders
Military's political neutrality	• ABRI officers openly express their political views; frequent civil–military conflict in internal security policy issues; maintains dwifungsi doctrine
Military presence in key governmental positions	• Officers actively engaged in central and local administrative positions; ABRI officers automatically guaranteed seats in the Parliament
Defined security missions	• Focus on domestic security missions; suppression of secessionist movements; widespread involvement in local economic affairs
Military's participation in the policy-making process	• Active and retired officers actively participate in several nonsecurity policy-making activities
Challenges to Civilian Control	
Security challenges	• Threats to the national disintegration; regional secessionist movements (East Timor, Aceh, Papua); interethnic and interreligious conflicts; terrorism
Challenges to civilian leadership	• Weak civilian leadership (fragmentation of political parties)
Military's organizational unity	• Lack of institutional unity and professionalism; factions in the army
Role of civil society	• Violence-prone civil society groups; aggravated political fragmentation

Once it conducted self-imposed reforms in the late 1990s, the ABRI regained its political influence in the power transition process from Wahid to Megawati Sukarnoputri, daughter of the founding father and former President Sukarno and vice president in the Wahid government. President Megawati learned from Wahid's impeachment that marginalizing the ABRI in important political decisions could backfire; thus, she brought several retired ABRI officers into key positions in her cabinet. For instance, as coordinating minister of political and security affairs, she appointed Susilo Bambang Yudhoyono, who had played a key role in resisting Wahid's declaration of a state of emergency in 2001. As minister of home affairs, Megawati hired Hari Sabarno, who had been decisive in mobilizing military and police factions in the legislative body to support her.[47] Consequently, ABRI officers regained their political influence not only in the Megawati cabinet, but also in local administrative positions.

Although the Megawati presidency brought some level of political stability, it was possible at the expense of democratic values and practices in Indonesian politics. Under Megawati's presidency, several former officials under the Suharto regime came back to regain their influence in post-democratization politics. Megawati appointed Bambang Kesowo as cabinet secretary and state secretariat, which had been the main instrument for executive power under the Suharto leadership. She also named Feisal Tamin as minister of administrative reform; Feisal had served in the Ministry of Home Affairs under Suharto. Furthermore, Megawati reestablished a State Information Agency charged with controlling the mass media.[48] The Megawati government seemed to revert back to Suharto's New Order era by appointing numerous retired and active ABRI officers and Suharto's close acquaintances to key positions in the cabinet.

As noted, the Indonesian case presents the most difficult scenario of challenges to democratization and democratic consolidation in which civilian leaders establish firm control over the armed forces and restructure the organization into a professionalized and politically neutral body. The biggest challenge to institutionalizing democracy and civilian control over the army is the degenerating domestic security conditions in the aftermath of the authoritarian Suharto's fall. The most daunting challenge to Indonesia has always been the problem of achieving strong and centralized nation-building. With more than 1,000 inhabited islands, more than 300 ethnic groups, and several different religions, central governments in Jakarta have struggled with separatist movements throughout the archipelago. National disintegration has further increased due to the Dutch colonial power's divide-and-rule policies. Sukarno's eradication of parliamentary democracy and the installation of authoritarian Guided Democracy in the late 1950s aimed to overcome possible national disintegration by the Muslim separatist movements in the outer islands. Suharto's New Order subsequently effectively mobilized ABRI forces to suppress any separatist movements with heavy-handed tactics. Suharto could sustain the territorial unity by using both sticks and carrots: suppressing any independence movements while providing social and economic benefits to those unruly provinces.

However, the fall of Suharto's New Order regime and the onset of a grave economic crisis provided several regions with the momentum to reassert independence. The first region that gained independence was East Timor. Under increasing international pressure, the central government gave East Timorese a referendum, in which 78.5 percent of the voters opposed the government's offer of political autonomy and instead preferred total independence. The independence was achieved as U.N. troops were dispatched to control the territory. Unfortunately, in this process, thousands of East Timorese were killed by the pro-Indonesia militias that were trained and equipped by the ABRI.[49]

The independence of East Timor brought three significant effects to the domestic politics of Indonesia. First, president Wahid's decision to give independence to the East Timorese enraged ABRI officers who had strongly espoused the territorial integrity of the state from the beginning of the republic. The president's decision was made without consulting army leadership, which became one of the major reasons that ABRI leadership withdrew its support from the president and sided with Megawati. Second, the East Timorese independence sent a clear signal to other regions that had been pursuing independence such as Aceh and Papua (or Irian Jaya), making internal security conditions much more unstable. Finally, degenerating security conditions provided the ABRI with the opportunity to regain its political influence. President Megawati formed a strategic alliance with the ABRI to secure her political position as well as cope with the pro-independence movements throughout the outer islands.

The ABRI's influence in politics further expanded when Yudhoyono, a retired ABRI officer, succeeded Megawati through the first direct presidential election in 2004, garnering 60.6 percent of the votes compared to the incumbent's 39.4 percent. Two rounds of voting took place in the 2004 presidential election. Initially, five presidential candidates were on the ballot: (1) Partai Demokrat's Yudhoyono winning 33.6 percent; (2) PDI-P's Megawati, 26.6 percent; (3) Golkar's Wiranto, 22.2 percent; (4) Amien Rais of the Partai Amanat Nasional (PAN, National Mandate Party), 14.7 percent; and (5) the incumbent vice president Hamah Haz, 3 percent.[50] As no candidate garnered an absolute majority, a runoff election was held between Yudhoyono and Megawati, in which the former won the majority vote. Under Yudhoyono's leadership, a number of retired ABRI officers held positions in the government, including the home affairs minister. Meanwhile, several of the old Suharto-era politicians and government officials returned to fill important positions in the current government.[51]

Several circumstances contributed to bringing numerous active and retired officers as well as Suharto's cronies into post-democratization Indonesian politics. First, as previously discussed, the degenerating domestic security conditions empowered the ABRI to reassert its political authority. Second, all the presidents after Suharto's fall found it difficult to mobilize support from pro-democracy civil society groups. Three decades of Suharto's dictatorial rule had effectively precluded any possibility that influential civil society groups would emerge to challenge the authoritarian rule. Instead, pro-governmental groups such as the Golkar Party and military organizations dominated the societal arena. Moreover, civil society groups in the post-democratization era pose a heavy burden for civilian leadership as they are divided along ethnic and religious cleavages, consequently producing conflicts and violence.[52] Therefore, civil society groups are not a source of strong civilian leadership, but rather a source of political liability.

Finally, but equally important, political parties—like civil society groups—have become fragmented along ethnic and religious fault lines so that no single president can secure a majority in the legislative body. In the 1999 parliamentary election—the first democratic election since 1955—48 political parties competed; 21 parties won at least one of the 462 seats.[53] President Wahid's ruling PKB gained only 11 percent of the parliamentary seats. The 2004 parliamentary election also showed extreme fragmentation of political parties, as 11 parties took at least 2 percent of the parliamentary seats. President Yudhoyono's *Partai Demokrat* (Democratic Party) won only 7.5 percent of the total popular votes.[54] In such extreme fragmentation of political parties, it is almost impossible to form a stable coalition government. In this situation, the ABRI is perceived by civilian leaders as the most attractive and effective coalition partner to govern the society.

In sum, democratization in Indonesia, along with the Philippines, represents the most difficult case for democratic consolidation and stable civilian control over the armed forces. Extremely precarious internal security conditions have provided the ABRI with justification for its continued role in civilian political affairs. In domestic politics, the fragmented political structure weakens civilian leaders' power vis-à-vis the military leadership. Meanwhile, incapacitated civilian leaders find the ABRI to be a strategic partner for governing the country. Due to these circumstances, the ABRI will continue to exert its political influence, making the institutionalization of democratic control of the military in Indonesia unlikely in the near future.

Conclusions

This chapter has addressed the civil–military dynamics in the four countries under study following their democratic regime transitions. Furthermore, in light of the theoretical arguments and empirical findings discussed in the previous chapters, this chapter presented prospects for the military's political role in the near future. Currently, South Korea and Taiwan demonstrate stable and firm civilian control over the armed forces and further democratic consolidation, whereas the Philippines and Indonesia suffer from a lack of civilian control of the military, making post-democratization politics complicated.

In the four cases under study, one major barrier to establishing firm civilian control of the military is—as the theory posited herein suggests—challenging security threat environments. For the South Korean and Taiwanese cases, favorable security conditions in the early years of democratization facilitated far-reaching democratic reforms, including the army's depoliticization. However, democratization in the Philippines and Indonesia was tarnished by mounting internal conflicts and violence—namely, the communist insurgents and Muslim separatist movements in the Philippines and interethnic/religious conflicts and separatist movements in Indonesia. In the latter two cases, intimidating domestic threats provided politicized officers with justifications for regaining their political influence.

Although South Korea and Taiwan benefited from favorable security environments during the early years of democratization, the ensuing security challenges now pose a significant hurdle for civilian leaders seeking to maintain control over the army. Externally, South Korea faces threats from North Korea, a regime that suffers from a devastated economy and isolation from the international community but is willing to continue a nuclear brinkmanship. Meanwhile, Taiwan's current and future security conditions are even more unpredictable due to President Chen Shui-bian's mobilization of Taiwanese ethnic identity and independence issues for his political purposes. Although the KMT's Ma Ying-jeou diminished tensions across the Taiwan Strait, the relationship between the two Chinese governments will continue to be a major source of instability and possible military confrontation in the future. Civilian control of the military in the two cases will depend upon how these countries deal with international security challenges. Meanwhile, internal threats in the Philippines and Indonesia pose even more direct and grave challenges to civilian leaders' control of the politicized officers. In the Philippines, domestic insurgency movements make civilian control of the military increasingly difficult, as it focuses on internal security and nonmilitary missions. Similarly, ABRI's internal security roles and nonmilitary missions enable it to assume more active positions in political, administrative, and economic affairs in Indonesia.

These security threats set the general patterns of the military's political influence; however, two major domestic factors—strength of civilian leadership and the military's organizational character—determine a more specific aspect of civil–military relations. In terms of the strength of civilian leadership, all four countries continue to struggle to build democratic institutions and norms to replace old authoritarian regimes. South Korea and Taiwan have demonstrated a more stable and institutionalized democratic leadership, while the other two cases are still struggling with the lack of workable democratic governance. The strength of civilian leadership directly influences the civilian leaders' ability to control army officers. Extremely weak civilian leadership in the post-democratization Philippines and Indonesia makes it difficult to attain the military's obedience.

At the same time, the unity of the military organization impinges on army officers' political orientation. Unified and professionalized armed forces promote army officers' depoliticization and political neutrality, making civilian control easier. Otherwise, civilian elites find it difficult to control a factionalized military, and officers' struggles often precipitate political participation. Armed forces in South Korea and Taiwan developed into a unified and professionalized body during the early years of democratization, which in turn led to the army's political neutrality. In contrast, armed forces in the Philippines and Indonesia have suffered from a lack of the military's organizational unity and professionalism, making civilian leaders difficult to control to this day.

The empirical evidence suggests that future civil–military relations in the four countries will be shaped by major structural preconditions, such as security threats, the strength of civilian leadership, and the unity of the armed forces. Considering these structural compositions, South Korea and Taiwan are more likely to secure democratic consolidation and control over the armed forces whereas Indonesia and the Philippines will continue to struggle with constructing viable democratic regimes and controlling politically assertive officers.

Notes

1 Samuel P. Huntington, *The Third Wave: Democratization in the Late Twentieth Century* (Norman: University of Oklahoma Press, 1991), 231–53.
2 Ibid., 276.
3 Carl J. Saxer, "Generals and Presidents: Establishing Civilian and Democratic Control in South Korea," *Armed Forces and Society* 30 (2004), 366.
4 Office of the President, Republic of Korea, *Government of the People: Selected Speeches of President Kim Dae-jung*, vols. 1–2 (Seoul: ROK Government). For more detailed analysis of the Kim Dae-jung government's Sunshine policy, see Chung-in Moon and David Steinberg, eds., *Kim Dae Jung Government and Sunshine Policy* (Seoul: Yonsei University Press, 1999); Chung-in Moon, "The Kim Dae Jung Government's Peace Policy toward North Korea," *Asian Perspective* 25 (2001).
5 *Korea Unification Bulletin* 2 (2000), 1; Chung-in Moon, "The Sunshine Policy and the Korean Summit: Assessments and Prospects," *East Asian Review* 12 (2000), 22–9.
6 Yong-Chool Ha, "South Korea in 2000: A Summit and the Search for New Institutional Identity," *Asian Survey* 41 (2001), 138.
7 Young-kwan Yoon, "South Korea in 1999: Overcoming Cold War Legacies," *Asian Survey* 40 (2000), 165.
8 Young-whan Kihl, *Transforming Korean Politics: Democracy, Reform, and Culture* (New York: M. E. Sharpe, 2005), 16.
9 In the 1994 Agreed Framework, North Korea pledged to freeze its nuclear development program and accept the IAEA inspection. In return, North Korea would receive crude oil and new light-water reactors from the United States until 2003. See, Derek McDougall, *The International Politics of the New Asia Pacific* (Boulder: Lynne Rienner Publishers, 1997), 141–7; C. S. Eliot Kang, "North Korea's International Relations: The Successful Failure?" in *The International Relations of Northeast Asia*, ed. Samuel S. Kim (Lanham: Rowman & Littlefield Publishers, 2004), 287–92.
10 The White House, *2002 State of the Union Address*, January 29, 2002, (web: http://www.state.gov/r/pa/ei/wh/rem/7672.htm).
11 David Sanger, "Bush Tells Seoul Talks with North Won't Resume Now," *New York Times*, March 8, 2001.
12 Victor D. Cha, "Shaping Change and Cultivating Ideas in the US-ROK Alliance," in *The Future of America's Alliances in Northeast Asia*, ed.

Michael H. Armacost and Daniel I. Okimoto (Stanford: Asia-Pacific Research Center, 2004), 136–7.
13 Hong-young Lee, "South Korea in 2002: Multiple Political Dramas," *Asian Survey* 43 (2003), 74.
14 For the 2002 Presidential Election results, see Republic of Korea, *National Election Commission* (web: http://www.nec.go.kr)
15 Anna Fifield, "US to Delay Troop Cuts in S Korea," *Financial Times*, October 5, 2004.
16 Kisuk Cho, "Regionalism in Korean Elections and Democratization: An Empirical Analysis," *Asian Perspective* 22 (1998); David C. Kang, "Regional Politics and Democratic Consolidation in Korea," in *Korea's Democratization*, ed. Samuel S. Kim (New York: Cambridge University Press, 2003), 161–80; Eunjung Choi, "*Economic Voting vs. Cleavage Voting in the United States, Korea, and Taiwan*," (paper presented at the Annual Meeting of the Midwest Political Science Association, April 2005).
17 Chung-in Moon and Jongryn Mo, "The Kim Young-Sam Government: Its Legacies and Prospects for Governance in South Korea," in *Democratization and Globalization in Korea: Assessments and Prospects*, ed. Chung-in Moon and Jongryn Mo (Seoul: Yonsei University Press, 1999), 402; B. C. Koh, "South Korea in 1996: Internal Strains and External Challenges," *Asian Survey* 37 (1997), 6.
18 Doh C. Shin, *Mass Politics and Culture in Democratizing Korea* (New York: Cambridge University Press, 1999), xxxi.
19 Kihl, *Transforming Korean Politics*, 282–3.
20 Huntington, *The Third Wave*, 113.
21 Hung-mao Tien and Yun-han Chu, 'Taiwan's Domestic Political Reforms: Institutional Change and Power Realignment," in *Taiwan in the Asia-Pacific in the 1990s*, ed. Gary Klintworth (St. Leonards: Allen & Unwin, 1994), 14.
22 Yu-shan Wu, "Taiwan in 2000: Managing the Aftershocks from Power Transfer," *Asian Survey* 41 (2001), 41–3.
23 For more detailed description of the Taiwanese civil–military relations in the post-democratization era, see M. Taylor Fravel, "Towards Civilian Supremacy: Civil–Military Relations in Taiwan's Democratization," *Armed Forces and Society* 29 (2002), 63–75.
24 John Fuh-sheng Hsieh, "National Identity and Taiwan's Mainland China Policy," *Journal of Contemporary China* 13 (2004); Yun-han Chu, "Taiwan's National Identity Politics and the Prospect of Cross-Strait Relations," *Asian Survey* 44 (2004).
25 Fravel, 2002, 66.

26 Cal Clark, "Taiwan's 2004 Presidential Election: The End of Chen Shui-bian's 'Strategic Ambiguity' on Cross-Strait Relations," *East Asia* 21 (2004), 26.
27 Xiaobo Hu and Gang Lin, "The PRC View of Taiwan under Lee Teng-hui," in *Sayonara to the Lee Teng-hui Era: Politics in Taiwan, 1988–2000*, ed. Wei-chin Lee and T. Y. Wang (Lanham: University Press of America, 2003), 278.
28 T. Y. Wang, "Cross-Strait Relations after the 2000 Election in Taiwan," *Asian Survey* 41 (2001), 716.
29 Taiwan Affairs Office, "The One-China Principle and the Taiwan Issue," *People's Daily Online*, February 21, 2000, at http://www.peopledaily.com.cn/; another available source is the Embassy of the PRC in the United States, at http://wwww.china-embassy.org/eng/7114.html.
30 For the ethnic identity's influence in the Taiwanese electoral politics in recent years, see John Fuh-Sheng Hsieh, "National Identity and Taiwan's Mainland China Policy," *Journal of Contemporary China* 13 (2004); Joseph Y. S. Cheng and Camoes C. K. Tam, "The Taiwan Presidential Election and Its Implications for Cross-Strait Relations: A Political Cleavage Perspective," *Asian Affairs* 32 (2005); Deborah A. Brown, ed., *Taiwan's 2000 Presidential Election: Implication for Taiwan's Politics, Security, Economy, and Relations with the Mainland* (New York: Center for Asian Studies, St. John's University, 2001); Shelley Rigger, *From Opposition to Power: Taiwan's Democratic Progressive Party* (Boulder: Lynne Rienner, 2001); Marie Taciana and Leila Fernandez Stembridge, eds., *China Today: Economic Reforms, Social Conflict, and Collective Identities* (London: RoutledgeCurzon, 2003); Yun-han Chu, *Crafting Democracy in Taiwan* (Taipei: Institute for National Policy Research, 1992).
31 Steve Chan, "Taiwan 2004: Electoral Contests and Political Stasis," *Asian Survey* 45 (2005), 55.
32 Cheng and Tam, 2005, 20.
33 Rosanne Rutten, "Revolutionary Specialists, Strongmen, and the State: Post-Movement Careers of CCP-NPA Cadres in a Philippine Province, 1990s-2001," *South East Asia Research* 9 (2001); Mark R. Thomson, "The Decline of Philippine Communism: A Review Essay," *South East Asia Research* 6 (1998); Nathan Gilbert Quimpo, "Options in the Pursuit of a Just, Comprehensive, and Stable Peace in the Southern Philippines," *Asian Survey* 41 (2001); Nathan Gilbert Quimpo, "Back to War in Mindanao: The Weaknesses of a Power-based Approach in Conflict Resolution," *Philippine Political Science Journal* 21 (2000); Jacques Bertrand, "Peace

and Conflict in the Southern Philippines: Why the 1996 Peace Agreement is Fragile," *Pacific Affairs* 73 (2000).
34 For the CPP's internal divisions, see John McBeth, "Internal Contradictions: Support for Communists Wanes as Party Splits," *Far Eastern Economic Review* 26, (August, 1993); Patricio N. Abinales, ed., *The Revolution Falters: The Left in the Philippine Politics after 1986* (Ithaca: Cornell University Press, 1996); Joel Rocamora, *Breaking Through: The Struggle within the Communist Party of the Philippines* (Manila: Anvil Press, 1994); Kathleen Weekley, *The Communist Party of the Philippines 1968–1993: A Story of Its Theory and Practice* (Quezon City: University of the Philippines Press, 2001).
35 Carolina Hernandez, "The Philippines in 1996: A House Finally in Order?" *Asian Survey* 37 (1997), 209–10.
36 Alex B. Brillantes, Jr., "The Philippines in 1992: Ready for Take Off?" *Asian Survey* 33 (1993), 226–7.
37 Jeffrey Riedinger, "The Philippines in 1994: Renew Growth and Contested Reforms," *Asian Survey* 35 (1995), 211.
38 Amando Doronila, "The MNLF Joins Mainstream Politics," *Philippine Daily Inquirer* (July 19, 1996), 9.
39 Claro Cortes, "*New President in the Philippines*," <web: http:www.abcnews.com/sections/world/DailyNews/philippines980529.html/>.
40 Gabriella R. Montinola, "The Philippines in 1998: Opportunity and Crisis," *Asian Survey* 39 (1999), 67.
41 David C. Kang, *Crony Capitalism: Corruption and Development in South Korea and the Philippines* (New York: Cambridge University Press, 2002), 175–80.
42 Mel C. Labrador, "The Philippines in 2000: In Search of a Silver Lining," *Asian Survey* 41 (2001), 224.
43 Temario C. Rivera, "The Philippines in 2004: New Mandate, Daunting Problems," *Asian Survey* 45 (2005), 127.
44 A. Lin Neumann, "Philippines: Military on the Move," *Asia Times,* February 28, 2006.
45 Aleksius Jemadu, "Democratisation and the Dilemma of Nation-building in Post-Suharto Indonesia: The Case of Aceh," *Asian Ethnicity* 5 (2004), 325.
46 Michael S. Malley, "Indonesia in 2001: Restoring Stability in Jakarta," *Asian Survey* 42 (2002), 125.
47 Ibid., 126.
48 "Information Minister Ponders New Ways to Rein in Media," *Jakarta Post,* December 29, 2001.

49 For more detailed information about the independence process in East Timor, see Ann Marie Murphy, "Indonesia and Globalization," *Asian Perspective* 23 (1999), 229–59; R. William Liddle, "Indonesia in 1999: Democracy Restored," *Asian Survey* 40 (2000), 39–40.
50 R. William Liddle and Saiful Mujani, "Indonesia in 2004: The Rise of Susilo Bambang Yudhoyono," *Asian Survey* 45 (2005), 119–21.
51 Baladas Ghoshal, "Democratic Transition and Political Development in Post-Soeharto Indonesia," *Contemporary Southeast Asia* 26 (2004), 514.
52 For the discussion of civil society's role in Indonesian politics, see Elizabeth Fuller Collins, "Indonesia: A Violent Culture?" *Asian Survey* 42 (2002); Edward Aspinall, *Opposing Suharto: Compromise, Resistance, and Regime Change in Indonesia* (Stanford: Stanford University Press, 2005); Edward Aspinall, "Indonesia: Transformation of Civil Society and Democratic Breakthrough," in *Civil Society and Political Change in Asia: Expanding and Contracting Democratic Space*, ed. Muthiah Alagappa (Stanford: Stanford University Press, 2004).
53 Liddle, 2000, 32.
54 Liddle and Mujani, 2005, 120.

CHAPTER SIX

Conclusion

The main theme of this book has been the rise and fall of the military's domestic political roles in four Asian countries—South Korea, Taiwan, the Philippines, and Indonesia—from the state-building period (1940s–1950s) through the recent decades of democratization and consolidation (1980s–current). In a broader sense, this book sought to explain overall political development and decay at different historical stages as well as the military's roles in it. The chapters in this book divided the historical stages into four distinct junctures of civil–military interactions: (1) state-building and the military (1940s–1950s); (2) political decay and the rise of the military's political power (1960s–1970s); (3) democratization and the military's depoliticization (1980s–1990s); and (4) the post-democratization military (1990s–current).

The main thesis of this book is that the military as an institution is an integral part of a country's governing structure and, therefore, army officers' participation in politics shapes the nature and direction of political life—either positively or negatively. The political role of the armed forces is, in turn, influenced by the specific contexts of internal and external security threats that the country faces. This is the case due to the fact that the military is first and foremost a security institution that directly responds to various internal and external security challenges that a country faces. The empirical chapters of this book have convincingly demonstrated that changes in a country's security conditions also bring changes in the military's organizational structures, doctrinal characters, officers' poise of self-defined missions, and ultimately officers' political roles. Furthermore, given the structural condition of security threats, two main conditions in domestic politics—namely, the strength of civilian leadership and the military's organizational unity/professionalism—serve to manifest a more specific and nuanced aspect of the military's political role.

This conclusion focuses on summarizing the main theoretical propositions and empirical evidence from previous empirical chapters and discussing the implications that the study of the four East Asian cases revealed. Theoretically, it succinctly demonstrates the inherent limitations of existing theoretical frameworks on civil–military relations, especially the institutional theory and Michael Desch's structural theory. Empirically, it provides an encompassing view of the dynamics of the armed forces' roles in civilian governance in the past, current, and future political stages of those Asian countries under study. This book concludes with a discussion of major empirical and policy lessons that the experiences of these cases reveal.

Theory and Empirical Findings

The structural theory discussed herein suggests that high security threats in the domestic or international arena generate a structural condition for the military to be politically influential, whereas low security threats run counter to its political influence. The first effect of growing security threats is the expansion of the military organization. Moreover, a high level of threats gives civilian leaders structural incentives to become more authoritarian and take coercive measures to rule society as general security threats in many cases coincide with threats to regime survival. In this situation, civilian leaders mobilize armed forces into politics to cope with security challenges to both the regime and the state. As a result, one notable outcome of high security threats is the expansion and strengthening of the state apparatus that monopolizes the means of physical violence (i.e., the military and the police). By the same logic, then, low security threats also force a reevaluation of the military's role in politics. In this condition, civilian leaders' attempts to bring army officers into politics generally meet strong resistance from domestic audiences. When security threats are low, civil society groups' pressure against authoritarian regimes and the military becomes increasingly influential.

Although security threats set the basic tendencies of the military's political influence, a more detailed aspect of civil–military relations is determined by intervening variables at the domestic level. The first intervening variable at the domestic level is the cohesiveness of the military organization. A unified military institution is conducive to stable civilian control and promotes military professionalism and institutional autonomy, whereas a factionalized army is detrimental to professionalism and officers' political neutrality. The second intervening variable is the strength of civilian leadership. Strong civilian leadership overall generally translates into strong civilian control of the military, while weak and divided leadership breeds the armed forces' intervention in politics. The final intervening variable is the strength of civil society. A strong and ideologically moderate civil society contributes to strong civilian control of the military. On the contrary, civil society groups

Table 6.1 Security Threats and the Military's Domestic Influence, Summary of Results

	High External Threats	Low External Threats
High Internal Threats	S. Korea in 1950–1960s Taiwan in 1940s–1960s *Strong Military Presence* *(Q1)*	Philippines in 1970–1990s Indonesia in 1940–1990s *Strong Military Presence* *(Q2)*
Low Internal Threats	S. Korea in 1970s Taiwan in 1970s *Strong Military Presence* *(Q3)*	Philippines in 1940–1960s S. Korea in 1980–1990s Taiwan in 1980–1990s *Strong Civilian Control* *(Q4)*

Table 6.2 Specific Manifestations of the Military's Engagement, Summary of Results

	Civilian Leadership	Civil Society	Military Unity	Military's Political Role
S. Korea				
1950s	Strong	Weak	Divided	Strong under Civilian
1960s	Weak	Weak	Divided	Coup d'état
1980–1990s	Strong	Strong	Unified	Politically Neutral
Taiwan				
1940–1960s	Strong	Weak	Unified	Strong under Civilian
1970s	Strong	Weak	Unified	Strong under Civilian
1980–1990s	Strong	Strong	Unified	Politically Neutral
Philippines				
1960s	Strong	Weak	Unified	Politically Neutral
1970s	Weak	Weak	Divided	Strong under Civilian
1980–1990s	Weak	Strong	Divided	Coup d'état
Indonesia				
1940s–1965	Weak	Weak	Divided	Strong under Civilian
1965–1998	Strong	Weak	Divided	Coup d'état
1998–current	Weak	Strong	Divided	Strong under Civilian

that advocate a radical ideology or adopt a strategy of physical violence make civilian control of the armed forces more difficult.

The four empirical chapters conducted a structured-focused comparative analysis of civil–military relations in four Asian countries by dividing them into four historical stages. Overall, the empirical evidence strongly supports the theoretical propositions, as summarized in Tables 6.1 and 6.2.

As Table 6.1 indicates, the armed forces wielded strong political influence in the structural conditions of Q1 (High External/High Internal), Q2 (Low External/High Internal), and Q3 (High External/Low Internal). Only in the structural condition of Q4 (Low External/Low Internal) was civilian control of the military stable and firm. Moreover, further specific features of civil–military relations were determined by three major domestic variables, as summarized in Table 6.2. Overall, these findings directly refute Michael Desch's theoretical propositions discussed in the Introduction of this book.

South Korea

During the last six decades, civil–military relations in South Korea have evolved over three distinct periods: (1) the rise of the politically influential military during state-building (1950s), (2) politicized officers' domination of civilian politics (1960s–1980s), and (3) their withdrawal from politics and subordination to democratically elected civilian leadership (1990s–current). In the first phase, extreme internal and external security threats during the state-building period brought about the expansion of the army organization. In particular, the Korean War (1950–1953) had tremendous impacts on the armed forces and their political roles. The war resulted in the vast expansion of the army, with almost 700,000 soldiers consuming more than 50 percent of all governmental spending. In addition, the war left the democratically elected President Rhee Syngman as an almost omnipotent figure in Korean politics. During and after the war, President Rhee increased his political power by amending the constitution to become president-for-life. On numerous occasions, he mobilized army officers into politics to suppress any political opposition. In addition, he purposefully aggravated factional struggles within the army as a way of controlling politicized officers. Overall, extreme security threats in South Korea's state-building period brought about an increasingly authoritarian civilian leadership, expansion of the military organization, and politicization of army officers by the authoritarian civilian leadership.

Becoming a politically influential body under President Rhee Syngman's rule, senior army officers played a decisive role in Rhee's downfall. President Rhee was forced out in the middle of the April 19th Student Revolution in 1960, which erupted as a demonstration against the Rhee regime's authoritarian repression, corruption, and fraud in the 1960 presidential election. The Rhee government declared martial law and brought in heavily armed military forces to put down the demonstration. However, the police and the military did not follow the President's order and instead forced him to step down.

With the ouster of Rhee Syngman, South Korea restored democracy with a parliamentary political system under the leadership of Prime Minister Chang Myon. Yet the new regime was too weak and incompetent to deal with the multiple problems that had intensified under the Rhee government, such as economic corrosion, factional struggles within the ruling circle, and impatient and often violent student protesters. The Chang regime faced gridlock between two political extremes: radicalized college students and pro-communist groups on the left versus conservative anticommunist forces including senior army officers on the right. Restored political freedom provided pro-communist groups with opportunities to expand their influence in society, worsening domestic security conditions. The Korean army also continued to suffer from factional struggles fostered by Rhee's exploitation of factional competition. When the Rhee regime collapsed, a group of junior officers led by Park Jung-hee attempted to cleanse old and corrupt senior officers by organizing a "purification" campaign within the military.

When the Chang government failed to provide political order, Park Jung-hee and his followers carried out a military coup on May 16, 1961. General Park consolidated his dictatorial rule in the subsequent years by declaring the *Yushin* (revitalization) constitution in October 1972, abolishing the National Assembly, and outlawing any type of political activity. The *Yushin* was justified when security conditions became grave due to North Korea's armed infiltrations into the South. Likewise, the installation of a military-dictatorial rule in South Korea was a combination of three structural conditions: the failure of civilian leadership, a factionalized military, and a radicalized civil society that exacerbated poor security conditions.

The military's withdrawal from politics during democratization was precipitated by improving security conditions in Korea in the 1980s. Previously, the military's dictatorial rule had been justified by the presence of constant threats from a hostile North Korea. However, beginning in the 1980s, the military balance between the two Koreas turned in favor of the South, thereby making anxiety about North Korea an unconvincing justification for dictatorship. Moreover, the end of the Cold War and South Korea's diplomatic ties with former communist countries during the democratization process drastically improved the country's security conditions.

The changing security environments empowered pro-democracy political elites and civil society groups vis-à-vis the military. Although democratization in Korea started from the radical *Minjung* (people) movements from below, the subsequent democratic transition was followed by elite compromise, which led to a stable regime transition. At the same time, civil society's support for democratic reform was vital to the democratically elected leaders' military reform, as was the case in the Kim Young-sam presidency (1993–1997). President Kim mobilized civil society's support for disbanding the *Hanahoe* (one mind) faction in the military and purging politically influential senior officers, including two former presidents—namely, Chun Doo-hwan and Roh Tae-woo. Meanwhile, the existence of a cohesive and professional army encouraged stronger civilian control of the military during and after democratization. The concurrence of three major structural conditions contributed to South Korea's successful military depoliticization: favorable security environments, strong civilian leadership supported by civil society, and the unified and professionalized army.

Taiwan

The Kuomintang (KMT) government also faced multiple domestic and international security challenges from the beginning of its formation in the 1910s. During its stay on mainland China, the KMT had to fight influential provincial warlords and the Japanese invasion in the 1920s and 1930s as well as wage a long battle with the Chinese Communist Party (CCP) and its revolutionary army. When World War II ended, the KMT and the CCP entered into an even more intense civil war (1945–1949), until the former lost and retreated to Taiwan in 1949. In these security challenges, army officers played important political, administrative, and economic roles in the KMT government from the earliest days of the Republic.

The KMT regime had to cope with even more daunting domestic and international security challenges after its retreat to Taiwan. Domestically, KMT forces provoked a deterioration of internal security conditions by adopting heavy-handed tactics against the native Taiwanese, leading to the violent February 28th Uprising in 1947. This incident aggravated tensions between Chinese mainlanders and ethnic Taiwanese, becoming a major source of domestic instability. Meanwhile, more daunting security challenges came from the CCP, which wanted to conclude the civil war and achieve complete unification of the territory. Throughout the 1950s and 1960s, the People's Liberation Army (PLA) posed grave threats to the KMT in Taiwan. At the same time, the KMT government also wanted to continue the civil war in order to retake the mainland territory. The nationalist government used considerable domestic resources for military buildup, installing military bases with 100,000 troops on the islands of Quemoy and Matsu as well as carrying out bombing raids and guerrilla warfare in the southern part of the mainland.

In such a perilous security condition, all the political powers were concentrated in one man: Generalissimo Chiang Kai-shek. In the early years of the KMT on the mainland, Chiang secured his political power within the party by mobilizing army officers' support. He established the Whampoa Military Academy in the 1920s and expanded his connections with senior army officers. After the retreat to Taiwan, the army assumed a more prominent political role, especially as security challenges continued to grow. The KMT regime declared martial law in 1949 and created the Taiwan Garrison Command in the following year, which gave the military the right to intervene in social and political affairs. Similar to the South Korean case, domestic and international security challenges for the KMT regime resulted in the organizational expansion of the Taiwanese army and its political role. Meanwhile, security threats created an autocratic regime in Taiwan, concentrating political powers within Chiang Kai-shek's hands.

However, in contrast to the South Korean case, the Taiwanese army never attempted to overthrow the civilian leadership, although army officers' penetration in the civilian political arena was almost omnipresent. The first structural condition that precluded the military's political domination was the strength of civilian leadership by Chiang Kai-shek and his son Chiang Ching-kuo. Strong civilian leadership came from Chiang's successful reforms of the KMT party and the army. In the area of party reform, he focused on removing age-old factions and establishing a highly centralized and ideologically indoctrinated organization. In the area of military reform, he focused on eliminating factional competitions and strengthening the party's control over the army by introducing a political commissar (or warfare) system.

The changing security environments surrounding Taiwan enhanced political liberalization during the 1970s and 1980s. Changes in international relations during the 1970s resulted in the diplomatic isolation of the KMT regime, whereas the PRC became an increasingly influential actor. Ironically, these changes had two contrasting effects: (1) the KMT was forced to give up its military means for dealing with the PRC and (2) the KMT encouraged political liberalization as a way of solving the legitimacy crisis both domestically and internationally. Chiang Ching-kuo's political reforms focused on "Taiwanizing" the KMT party and the army. From the early 1970s, ethnic Taiwanese began to fill important positions in the party, including the Central Standing Committee. They also began occupying higher-ranking positions in the military.

The two decades of Taiwanization under Chiang's leadership precluded any succession problem during the power transition from Chiang to Lee Teng-hui, an ethnic Taiwanese. However, the biggest challenge facing Taiwan's democratization was to reform KMT party–army relations. Prior to democratization, the KMT became deeply engaged in military affairs with the political commissar system, while senior army officers held prominent positions in the party, including the Central Standing Committee. Lee curbed senior officers' influence with his adept political skills, appointing General Hau Pei-tsun as premier and simultaneously mobilizing political support from the opposition Democratic Progressive Party and civil society groups. Lee conducted military reforms without facing any backfire from army leadership because the Taiwanese army had developed into a cohesive and professionalized body long before democratic reform began. In short, the military's withdrawal from politics during democratization in Taiwan was facilitated by the aforementioned three major structural conditions: lessening internal and external security threats, strong civilian leadership, and the unified and professionalized Taiwanese army.

The Philippines

In 1946, the Philippines achieved sovereign statehood after years of American tutelage. The Philippines began its republic with a democratic political regime and a politically neutral military. From the 1940s until the late 1960s, the Philippines did not face any serious security challenges primarily due to its geographic isolation from the Asian continent and the security commitment from the United States. During this period, democratically elected presidents firmly controlled the Armed Forces of the Philippines (AFP), which was small in size and politically neutral.

However, by the late 1960s, two domestic insurgency movements became influential enough to pose threats to the Ferdinand Marcos government: the Communist Party of the Philippines (CPP) and its New People's Army (NPA), which aimed to overthrow the regime and establish a communist government, as well as the Muslim Moro National Liberation Front (MNLF), which fought to create an independent Muslim state in Mindanao. Rising domestic insurgency movements provided President Marcos with justification for the declaration of martial law in 1972. Marcos soon extended his presidential tenure beyond the constitutional limit and centralized political power within his hands. At the same time, mounting security threats led to the expansion of the AFP and its political role. AFP officers assumed important political, administrative, judicial, and economic positions in the

Marcos regime. During the 1970s, rising internal security challenges stirred the expansion of the AFP organization, an increasingly authoritarian civilian leadership, and army officers' deep penetration into civilian political affairs.

Although the Marcos government did not face any coup attempts throughout the years of martial law, his personalistic control over army officers seriously damaged professionalism and aggravated factional struggles in the AFP. Officers who either came from Ilocos or were personally connected to the president or his wife were promoted to the highest positions in the AFP hierarchy, receiving enormous benefits and monopolizing key commandership positions. Meanwhile, officers who were non-Ilocos or unclear in their loyalty to the president were assigned to areas outside Metro Manila, where they engaged in dangerous counterinsurgency warfare with the communist NPA and the Muslim MNLF. A group of junior officers outside Marcos' inner circle formed a clandestine fraternity, Reform the Armed Forces of the Philippines Movement (RAM).

RAM officers, led by General Fidel Ramos and General Juan Ponce Enrile, played a decisive role in ending the Marcos dictatorship and instituting a democratic regime. When both Marcos and Corazon Aquino declared victory in the inconclusive 1986 presidential election, RAM members revolted against Marcos and sided with Aquino. Although the "People Power" rally created the momentum for democratization, it was the AFP that enabled the democratic regime transition. Because of their prominent role in Marcos' ouster, RAM officers became influential in the Aquino government.

As the first democratically elected president since 1965, President Corazon Aquino tried to enact a number of important reforms: purging Marcos loyalists in both the government and the AFP, rebuilding a democratic institution with a new constitution, and recovering from severe economic crisis. Yet she did not succeed in any of these tasks due to her weak and inefficient leadership stemming from extreme political fragmentation. Still, the leadership crisis in the Aquino government centered on disagreements with the AFP over the counterinsurgency programs regarding the NPA and the MNLF. The AFP insisted on rough measures against the rebels, while the Aquino government preferred peaceful means. Aquino incited the AFP by releasing political prisoners, including the CPP leader Jose Maria Sison, and initiating a ceasefire and peace talks with the CPP and the MNLF. Negotiations between the government and the National Democratic Front (NDF), an umbrella organization of underground leftist groups, resulted in a 60-day truce effective December 10, 1986, although the truce agreement did not last long due to a discrepancy on key issues. The NDF demanded a voice in the Aquino government and the integration of NPA militias into the AFP organization. Similarly, the Aquino government's peace talks with the Moro secessionists also failed when the MNLF demanded the autonomy of Mindanao and the integration of its army into the AFP organization. Security conditions significantly deteriorated after Aquino government's peace efforts with the insurgents ended in failure, and the NPA and the MNLF expanded their armed uprisings in the late 1980s.

It was not long before segments of the AFP withdrew their support for Aquino. RAM members or Marcos loyalists staged numerous coup attempts within the first four years of the Aquino presidency. These recurring coup attempts forced the Aquino government to accept most of the AFP officers' demands, increasing the military budget by 60 percent and accepting the AFP's counterinsurgency plan.

Civilian control over the AFP became stabilized only after Fidel Ramos was elected president in 1992. As a former chief of staff with strong support from Philippine Military Academy (PMA) graduates, Ramos curbed the RAM's influence in domestic politics. However, his control over the AFP was secured by bringing in several senior AFP officers to his government. Although the Philippines did not return to military rule, its democratization process was tainted by numerous coup attempts and handicapped by a weak civilian leadership.

Indonesia

Finally, Indonesia also had to cope with extreme domestic security threats from the beginning of its independence in 1949. After engaging in five years of independence war with Dutch forces, Indonesia started as a parliamentary democracy with multiple parties, although this parliamentary democracy did not last long given its inability to deal with multifaceted security challenges from ethnic and religious conflicts as well as threats of territorial disintegration. One of the major security threats was the Darul Islam uprisings, aimed at creating an Islamic Republic in Indonesia and later spreading to other regions, such as Aceh and South Sulawesi.

Faced with the possibility of national disintegration, President Achmad Sukarno abolished the parliamentary system and declared "Guided Democracy" in 1957, concentrating political authority within the president. He further declared martial law and brought the Republic of Indonesia Armed Forces (*Angkatan Bersenjata Republik Indonesia;* ABRI) into politics, enabling them to play key administrative and economic roles. In this situation, the ABRI, led by General Abdul Haris Nasution, declared the "Middle Way" doctrine that justified ABRI's political participation as an equal partner alongside civilian leadership. Likewise, the state-building period witnessed growing internal threats, which resulted in the installation of authoritarian "Guided Democracy" and the expansion of ABRI's political influence.

President Sukarno's Guided Democracy successfully contained major internal security threats by declaring martial law and bringing ABRI officers into politics. Under Guided Democracy, the ABRI exercised strong political power so that President Sukarno felt threatened by politically influential officers. He formed a political coalition with the Indonesian Communist Party (*Partai Kommunis Indonesia*, PKI) to curb ABRI's political dominance in his government. The Sukarno–PKI coalition made several important political decisions that intensified the ABRI's concern for national security. First, the "Crush Malaysia" campaign (i.e., *Konfrontasi*) created diplomatic disputes with major Western powers, including the United States and Britain. Second, the PKI-initiated land reform (*aski sepihak*, unilateral action) raised violent conflicts between PKI-led peasants and regional landlords aligned with regional military units. Third, the Sukarno regime's foreign policy isolated itself from major Western powers, which in turn caused an economic crisis in the early 1960s. Finally, the Sukarno–PKI coalition lifted martial law in 1963 and planned to downsize the ABRI and its budget.

When generals in the ABRI were plotting a coup d'état to topple Sukarno, a group of pro-PKI officers launched a preemptive coup in 1965, killing most of the highest-ranking officers. During this situation, Major General Haji Mohammad Suharto contained the coup forces and best controlled the political crisis. The ABRI took over political power from President Sukarno and put him under house arrest. Suharto declared a "New Order," in which the ABRI played an extensive role in Indonesian politics until 1998. In sum, the ABRI coup and establishment of military dictatorial rule in Indonesia were outcomes of the convergence of three major factors: civilian leadership's failure to provide political and security order, influential but violent civil society, and the ABRI's *dwifungsi* (dual function) doctrine.

Suharto's New Order regime (1968–1998) abruptly ended in the middle of an economic crisis and ensuing social unrest, during which time Vice President B. J. Habibie succeeded the presidency. The power transition was so unexpected that the Habibie leadership was not prepared to carry out political and economic reforms. Various problems that had remained dormant under the New Order began to surface, forcing the new government to deal with violent demonstrations, interethnic and interreligious clashes, and separatist insurgency movements in Aceh, Papua, and East Timor. The democratically elected leaders, plagued by weak leadership, failed to control these crises.

Multiple internal security threats provided the ABRI with an opportunity to regain political influence. Immediately following Suharto's fall, the ABRI was accused of corruption and human rights abuses during the authoritarian rule. In this adverse milieu, the ABRI leadership attempted to reformulate the institution as a cohesive and professionalized body and limit its political role in the early years of democratization. Before long, however, the ABRI began to reclaim its political influence, particularly when President Abdurrahman Wahid—the successor to Habibie—was forced to step down after less than two years into his presidency. The ABRI withdrew its support for Wahid due to the differences between the president and the military leadership in dealing with the domestic insurgency movements in the outer islands.

The ABRI recovered its political influence under the Megawati presidency (2001–present). President Megawati Sukarnoputri found the ABRI to be an attractive political ally when facing political, economic, and security problems. The president lacked support from political parties and civil society groups, which were highly fragmented along ethnic and religious cleavages. Therefore, she brought ABRI leadership to her government to compensate for her political weakness. The ABRI's voice has become even bigger as the new democratic regime has faced increasing intercommunal violence, separatist movements, and terrorist threats in recent years.

Security Threats and the Future of the Military's Political Role

What do the four countries' historical trajectories say about the future prospect of civil–military relations? In light of the theoretical arguments and empirical analyses put forth regarding the first three historical stages, the final empirical study illustrated the current status and future prospects of civil–military relations. Among the four empirical cases, South Korea represents the most stable civilian control of the military in the post-democratization period, followed by Taiwan. In contrast, the Philippines and Indonesia have highly unstable civil–military relations, as army officers wield enormous political influence in the post-democratization political scene.

After two decades of democratic reforms, South Korea is now entitled to be called a consolidated democracy. The most crucial part of democratic reform was rebuilding the military into a professionalized and politically neutral body by disbanding the clandestine *Hanahoe* (one mind) faction.

Three major structural conditions in South Korea reinforce stable civilian control of the military in the post-democratization era: (1) favorable security conditions, (2) strong civilian leadership backed by civil society groups, and (3) a cohesive and professionalized army. Meanwhile, challenges for civil–military relations in the near future will come from the highly unpredictable North Korea, whose instability has the potential to create serious political and security crises in the Korean peninsula and the surrounding region. This situation will be detrimental to civilian control of the military in South Korea especially as the national security policies—its policy toward the North—are highly politicized. The civilian leadership in South Korea has been ideologically polarized in dealing with North Korea: Conservatives prefer tough measures on North Korea's nuclear development, whereas progressives want to continue the engagement (Sunshine) policy.

Taiwan successfully reached democratic consolidation when the Taiwanese army withdrew its influence from the KMT party and central and provincial governments in the 1990s. The key to military reform was the split of the institutional interpenetration between the KMT party and the army as well as the redirection of the army's allegiance away from the KMT and toward the constitution and democratically elected civilian leadership. However, unlike the South Korean case, Taiwan will face barriers to institutionalizing democratic control of the military. A major complexity in Taiwanese civil–military relations comes from two fundamental structural constraints. The first is the weakening civilian leadership stemming from ethnic cleavages between Chinese mainlanders and ethnic Taiwanese. The second is growing security threats from the mainland government revolving around the Taiwanese independence issue. These two conditions are intertwined, as the ethnic cleavages manifest along the issue of Taiwan's relationship with the mainland regime. Similar to the South Korean case, the politicization and polarization of national security policies—especially cross-Strait relations—will also politicize the Taiwanese armed forces.

In the case of the Philippines, the AFP continues to wield enormous political power even after two decades of democratic government. Civilian leaders in the Philippines have failed to secure army officers' political neutrality and allegiance to the government and constitution. Several coup attempts have been made against current President Gloria Macapagal-Arroyo (2001–2010). Prospects for civilian control of the military in the Philippines are even more pessimistic in all structural conditions. First, growing internal security threats by communist insurgents and Muslim separatist movements provide the AFP with opportunities to expand its political clout. Second, civilian leadership suffers from corruption, cronyism, and the failure to build workable democratic institutions. Finally, the AFP remains divided into factions based on schooling and regional backgrounds, further complicating civilian control over and monitoring of the military.

Indonesia also features quite a pessimistic scenario for future civil–military relations. The ABRI, which once conducted self-imposed institutional reforms, reclaimed its political authority during the impeachment of President Wahid in 2001. Like the Philippines, Indonesia faces many structural barriers in establishing civilian control of the military. First, post-democratization Indonesia has been plagued by growing internal security threats arising from interethnic and interreligious violence, secessionist movements in Aceh and Papua, and terrorist bombings by extremist Muslim organizations. Second, civilian leaders find it hard to reach political consensus due to extremely fragmented political parties and civil society groups. Finally, the ABRI still lacks organizational unity and an effective command structure, which makes civilian control extremely ineffective. It is quite surprising that the ABRI have made no coup attempts since Suharto's fall. One evident reason is that presidents—especially Megawati and Yudhoyono—either guaranteed the military's institutional prerogatives or their personal connection with the military leadership (especially Yudhoyono's case).

Lessons from the Evidence

The study of military politics in four Asian countries reveals important empirical and policy lessons to the future trajectory of civil–military relations and the democratic deepening in these countries. As previously mentioned, civilian control of the military is an integral part of democratic governance—particularly in newly democratized countries as the military often poses the biggest challenges to the regime transition and democratic consolidation. Based on the empirical evidence from the four Asian countries discussed herein, this book concludes by mentioning three important lessons.

First, severe domestic and/or international security challenges make civilian control extremely difficult. As discussed in the theoretical discussion, rising security threats result in the military's organizational and role expansion. In this respect, civilian leaders in South Korea and Taiwan are in a better position to enforce strong control over the armed forces, as the main threats come from outside—i.e., North Korea and mainland China. On the other hand, security conditions in the Philippines and Indonesia preclude civilian strength vis-à-vis military officers. Militaries in the latter two cases conduct essentially nonmilitary missions, including local and provincial administrative duties, managerial roles in major industries, and policing missions for domestic order. These nonmilitary activities will undoubtedly expand the military's corporate interest by creating patron–client relations between local/provincial politicians and military officers and garnering the military's revenues from the management of industries. It is imperative that, for the purpose of the military's depoliticization, civilian leadership in the Philippines and Indonesia substantially increase defense spending to reduce the military's economic activities. Policies such as increases in defense spending, weapons modernization, and better pay for officers may reduce the military's entrenchment of corporate interest.

Second, experiences from the four Asian cases reveal the fact that both performance success and failure of military-dominant regimes bring about democratic regime transition while only successful authoritarian regimes engender stable regime change. Authoritarian regimes in South Korea and Taiwan brought phenomenal economic development to their countries, which in turn led to urbanization, higher education, a large middle class, and consequently pro-democracy voices.[1] On the other hand, dictatorial regimes in the Philippines and Indonesia carried out only mediocre performance in their economies and continue to struggle with fragile economies; civilian regimes in these countries are no better than their predecessors. The economic development and domestic security conditions go hand in hand: Economic crisis heightens insurgency movements, which in turn amplify the economic crisis. In this respect, stable civilian control of the military will be possible when the civilian leadership succeeds in managing both economic development and domestic security.

Finally, democratic transitions in the four cases portray important lessons on the focal point of the military reform in the post-democratization stage as well as its impact on democratic consolidation. Experiences in these Asian countries illustrate that stable civilian control of the military is possible only when the new democratic leadership is willing/able to reorganize the military as a unified and cohesive institution. Normally, a military organization under authoritarianism suffers from a lack of institutional unity; as a result, factional struggles among different groups of officer corps continue to exist in the post-democratization setting mainly because of the authoritarian leader's divide-and-rule tactics. Factions in the pre-democratization military are generally created among soldiers who share similar backgrounds, such as shared hometowns, military schooling and alumnus systems, ethnic and religious identities, and economic classes. Factionalized militaries are far more difficult for a new civilian leadership to control for two major reasons: the problem of monitoring and sanctioning as well as military factions' appetite/aspiration for domination of the civilian political arena.[2] Ultimately, in the factionalized military, officers' allegiance goes to their factional leaders, not their civilian masters; at the same time, civilian leaders find it difficult to monitor/sanction these secret factions.

The contrast among the four cases—South Korea and Taiwan on the one hand, and the Philippines and Indonesia on the other hand—succinctly illustrates this point. The armed forces in the first two cases have been reorganized into a cohesive and professionalized institution: the South Korean case under the Kim Young-sam administration in the 1990s and Taiwan under Chiang Kai-shek/Ching-kuo's reorganization and indoctrination of the Taiwanese army. However, militaries in the Philippines and Indonesia still lack organizational cohesion. In this aspect, the AFP presents the most difficult case for the military reform, as numerous factions frequently challenge the authority of civilian leadership through coup attempts. The military reorganization plan that focuses on removing inter-factional struggles must entail provision of various benefits to the military—increases in pay and welfare benefits, introduction of advanced weapons, merit-based promotion system, and so on—to minimize both officers' grievances and resistance to the reform initiatives.

Notes

1 Adam Przeworski et al., *Democracy and Development* (New York: Cambridge University Press, 2000); also see Zoltan D. Barany, *Building Democratic Armies: Lessons from Africa, Asia, Europe, and the Americas* (Princeton: Princeton University Press, forthcoming).
2 Jongseok Woo, "Crafting Democratic Control of the Military in South Korea and the Philippines," (paper presented at the Southwest Political Science Association Conference, Denver, CO, April 8–11, 2009); also see Deborah D. Avant, *Political Institutions and Military Change: Lessons from Peripheral Wars* (Ithaca: Cornell University Press, 1994); Peter Feaver, "Crisis as Shirking: An Agency Theory Explanation of the Souring of American Civil–Military Relations." *Armed Forces and Society* 24 (1998), 407–34.

Bibliography

Abinales, Patricio N, ed. *The Revolution Falters: The Left in the Philippine Politics after 1986*. Ithaca: Cornell University Press, 1996.

Abinales, Patricio N., and Donna J. Amoroso. *State and Society in the Philippines*. Lanham: Rowman & Littlefield, 2005.

Abrahamsson, Bengt. *Military Professionalization and Political Power*. Beverly Hills: Sage Publications, 1972.

Abueva, Jose V. "Filipino Democracy and the American Legacy." *Annals of the American Academy of Political and Social Science* 428 (1976): 114–33.

Adelman, Jonathan R. ed. *Communist Armies in Politics*. Boulder: Westview Press, 1982.

Ahn, Byung-joon. "South Korea's International Relations: Quest for Security, Prosperity, and Unification." *The Asian Update*. New York: Asia Society, 1991.

— "South Korean-Soviet Relations: Contemporary Issues and Prospects." *Asian Survey* 31 (1991): 816–25.

Alagappa, Muthiah. "Introduction: Presidential Election, Democratization, and Cross-Strait Relations." In *Taiwan's Presidential Politics: Democratization and Cross-Strait Relations in the Twenty-First Century*, edited by Muthiah Alagappa. New York: M.E. Sharpe, 2001.

Alagappa, Muthiah, ed. *Coercion and Governance: The Declining Political Role of the Military in Asia*. Stanford: Stanford University Press, 2001.

— *Military Professionalism in Asia: Conceptual and Empirical Perspectives*. Honolulu: East-West Center, 2001.

Allison, John M. "Indonesia: The Year of the Pragmatists." *Asian Survey* 9 (1969): 130–7.

Andreski, Stanislav. *Military Organization and Society*. London: Routledge, 1968.

Arillo, Cecilio T. *Breakaway: The Inside Story of the Four-Day Revolution in the Philippines, February 22–25, 1986*. Manila: CTA, 1986.

Aspinall, Edward. *Student Dissident in Indonesia in the 1980s*. Clayton: Centre of Southeast Asian Studies, 1993.

— "Indonesia: Transformation of Civil Society and Democratic Breakthrough." In *Civil Society and Political Change in Asia: Expanding and Contracting Democratic Space*, edited by Muthiah Alagappa. Stanford: Stanford University Press, 2004.

— *Opposing Suharto: Compromise, Resistance, and Regime Change in Indonesia*. Stanford: Stanford University Press, 2005.

Avant, Deborah D. *Political Institutions and Military Change: Lessons from Peripheral Wars*. Ithaca: Cornell University Press, 1994.

Barany, Zoltan D. *Soldiers and Politics in Eastern Europe, 1945–1990: The Case of Hungary.* New York: St. Martin's Press, 1993.

— "Democratic Consolidation and the Military: The East European Experience." *Comparative Politics* 30 (1997): 21–44.

— *Democratic Breakdown and the Decline of the Russian Military.* Princeton: Princeton University Press, 2007.

Berfield, Susan, and Dewi Loveard. "Ten Days that Shook Indonesia." *Asiaweek,* July 21, 1998.

Bertrand, Jacques. "Peace and Conflict in the Southern Philippines: Why the 1996 Peace Agreement is Fragile." *Pacific Affairs* 73 (2000): 37–54.

Betz, David J. *Civil–Military Relations in Russia and Eastern Europe.* New York: RoutledgeCurzon, 2004.

Billet, Bret L. "South Korea at the Crossroads: An Evolving Democracy or Authoritarianism Revisited?" *Asian Survey* 30 (1990): 300–11.

Binder, Leonard, James S. Colman, Joseph LaPalombara, Lucian W. Pye, Sidney Verba, and Myron Weiner. *Crises and Sequences in Political Development.* Princeton: Princeton University Press, 1971.

Bird, Judith. "Indonesia in 1997: The Tinderbox Year." *Asian Survey* 38 (1998): 168–76.

— "Indonesia in 1998: The Pot Boils Over." *Asian Survey* 39 (1999): 27–37.

Born, Hans, Marina Caparini, Karl Haltiner, and Jurgen Kuhlmann, eds. *Civil–Military Relations in Europe: Learning from Crisis and Institutional Change.* New York: Routledge, 2009.

Bourchier, David, and Vedi R. Hadiz. *Indonesian Politics and Society: A Reader.* New York: RoutledgeCurzon, 2003.

Bradner, Stephen. "Korea: Experiment and Instability." *Japan Quarterly* 8 (1961): 412–20.

Briggs, Walter. "The Military Revolution in Korea: On Its Leader and Achievements." *Korean Quarterly* 5 (1963).

Brillantes, Alex Bello. "Insurgency and Peace Policies of the Aquino Government." *PSSC Social Science Information* (1987): 3–9.

— "The Philippines in 1992: Ready for Take Off?" *Asian Survey* 33 (1993): 226–7.

Brown, Deborah A, ed. *Taiwan's 2000 Presidential Election: Implication for Taiwan's Politics, Security, Economy, and Relations with the Mainland.* New York: Center for Asian Studies, St John's University, 2001.

Buendia, Rizal G. "The Secessionist Movement and the Peace Process in the Philippines and Indonesia: The Case of Mindanao and Aceh." *Asia Pacific Social Science Review* 5 (2005): 51–67.

Bullard, Monte R. *The Soldier and the Citizen: The Role of the Military in Taiwan's Development.* New York: M.E. Sharpe, 1997.

Burton, Sandra. *Impossible Dream: The Marcoses, the Aquinos, and the Unfinished Revolution.* New York: Warner Books, 1989.

Casper, Gretchen. *Fragile Democracies: The Legacies of Authoritarian Rule.* Pittsburgh: University of Pittsburgh Press, 1995.

Cavendish, Patrick. "The New China of the Kuomintang." In *Modern China's Search for Political Form,* edited by Jack Gray. London: Oxford University Press, 1969.

Celoza, Albert F. *Ferdinand Marcos and the Philippines: The Political Economy of Authoritarianism.* Westport: Praeger, 1997.

Cha, Victor. "Security and Democracy in South Korean Development." In *Korea's Democratization*, edited by Samuel Kim. London: Cambridge University Press, 2003.
— "Shaping Change and Cultivating Ideas in the US-ROK Alliance." In *The Future of America's Alliances in Northeast Asia*, edited by Michael H. Armacost and Daniel I. Okimoto. Stanford: Asia-Pacific Research Center, 2004.
Chan, Steve. "Taiwan in 2004: Electoral Contests and Political Stasis." *Asian Survey* 45 (2005): 54–8.
Chang, King-yuh. *A Framework for China's Unification*. Taipei: Kwang Hwa, 1986.
Cheng, Hsiao-shih. "The Polity and the Military: A Framework for Analyzing Civil–Military Relations in Taiwan." *Journal of Social Sciences and Philosophy* 5 (1990): 129–72.
Cheng, Joseph Y. S., and Camoes C. K. Tam. "The Taiwan Presidential Election and Its Implications for Cross-Strait Relations: A Political Cleavage Perspective." *Asian Affairs: An American Review* 32 (2005): 3–24.
Cheng, Peter P. "Taiwan in 1975: A Year of Transition." *Asian Survey* 16 (1976): 61–5.
Cheng, Tun-jen. "Taiwan in 1996: From Euphoria to Melodrama." *Asian Survey* 37 (1997):43–51.
Cho, Ji-hun. *80-Nyondae Huban Cheongyeon Haksaengundong (The Youth and Student Movements of the late-1980s)*. Seoul: Hyungsung-sa, 1989.
Cho, Kisuk. "Regionalism in Korean Elections and Democratization: An Empirical Analysis." *Asian Perspectives* 22 (1998): 135–56.
Choi, Eungjung. "Economic Voting vs. Cleavage Voting in the United States, Korea, and Taiwan." Paper presented at the annual meeting for the Midwest Political Science Association, Chicago, Illinois, April, 2005.
Choi, Jang-jip. "Democratization, Civil Society, and Civil Movements in Korea." In *Understanding Korean Civil Society*, edited by Jang-jip Choi. Seoul: Hanul Press, 1996.
Chou, Tsu-cheng. "Electoral Competition and the Development of Opposition in Taiwan." *The Annals* 20 (1992).
Chu, Yun-han. *Crafting Democracy in Taiwan*. Taipei: Institute for National Policy Research, 1992.
— "Social Protests and Political Democratization in Taiwan." In *The Other Taiwan: 1945 to the Present*, edited by Murray A. Rubinstein. New York: M.E. Sharpe, 1994.
— "Taiwan's National Identity Politics and the Prospect of Cross-Strait Relations." *East Asia* 21 (2004): 484–512.
Chung, Joseph S. "North Korea's Seven Year Plan (1961–1970): Economic Performance and Reforms." *Asian Survey* 12 (1972): 527–45.
Chung, Kyung-cho. *New Korea: New Land of the Morning Calm*. New York: Macmillan, 1962.
Clare, Kenneth G., Gerald J. Foster, R. Hannus and W. Hrabko. *Area Handbook for the Republic of Korea*. Washington D.C.: GPO, 1969.
Clark, Cal. "Taiwan's 2004 Presidential Election: The End of Chen Shui-bian's 'Strategic Ambiguity' on Cross-Strait Relations." *East Asia* 21 (2004): 25–37.
Clear, Annette. "Politics: From Endurance to Evolution." In *Indonesia: The Great Transition*, edited by John Bresnan, 46–147. Lanham: Rowman & Littlefield Publishing, 2005.

Collins, Elizabeth F. "Indonesia: A Violent Culture?" *Asian Survey* 42 (2002): 582–604.
Colton, Timothy. *Commissars, Commanders and Civilian Authority: The Structure of Soviet Military Politics.* Cambridge: Harvard University Press, 1979.
Congressional Quarterly, ed. *China: U.S. Policy Since 1945.* Washington D.C.: Congressional Quarterly Inc., 1980.
Cooper, John F. *Taiwan: Nation-State or Province?* Boulder: Westview Press, 1990.
— "The Role of Minor Political Parties in Taiwan." *World Affairs* 155 (1993): 95–108.
Cortes, Claro. "New President in the Philippines." ABC News. http://www.abcnews.com/sections/world/DailyNews/philippines980529.html/ (accessed August 20, 2005)
Cottey, Andrew, Timothy Edmunds, and Anthony Forester. "The Second Generation Problematic: Rethinking Democracy and Civil–Military Relations." *Armed Forces and Security* 29 (2002): 31–56.
Cribb, Robert. *The Indonesia Killings 1965–1966: Studies from Java and Bali.* Centre of Southeast Asian Studies: Monash Papers on Southeast Asia, 1994.
Croissant, Aurel. "Riding the Tiger: Civilian Control and the Military in Democratizing Korea." *Armed Forces and Society* 30 (2004): 357–81.
Crouch, Harold. *The Army and Politics in Indonesia*, 2nd edn. Ithaca: Cornell University Press, 1988.
Daroy, Petronilo Bn. "On the Eve of Dictatorship and Revolution." In *Dictatorship and Revolution: Roots of People's Power*, edited by Aurora Javate de Dios, Petronilo Bn Daroy, and Lorna Kalaw-Tirol, 1–125. Manila: Conspectus, 1988.
Davidson, Gary M. *A Short History of Taiwan: The Case for Independence.* Westport: Praeger, 2003.
Desch, Michael C. "Threat Environments and Military Missions," in *Civil–Military Relations and Democracy*, edited by Larry Diamond and Marc F. Plattner. Baltimore: John Hopkins University Press, 1996.
— *Civilian Control of the Military: The Changing Security Environment.* Baltimore: John Hopkins University Press, 1999.
Dickson, Bruce J. "The Lessons of Defeat: The Reorganization of the Kuomintang on Taiwan, 1950–1952." *The China Quarterly* 133 (1993): 56–84.
Dittmer, Lowell. "The Legacy of Violence in Indonesia." *Asian Survey* 42 (2002): 541–4.
Djiwandono, J. Soedjati. "The Military and National Development in Indonesia." In *Soldiers and Stability in Southeast Asia*, edited by J. Soedjati Djiwandono and Yong Mun Cheong. Singapore: Institute of Southeast Asian Studies, 1988.
Doherty, John F. *Who Controls the Philippines Economy: Some Need Not Try as Hard as Others.* Honolulu: University of Hawaii Press, 1982.
Doronila, Amando. "The MNLF Joins Mainstream Politics." *Philippine Daily Inquirer*, July 19, 1996.
Douglas, William A. "Korean Students and Politics." *Asian Survey* 3 (1963): 584–95.
Drakeley, Steven. *The History of Indonesia.* Westport: Greenwood Press, 2005.
Edmonds, Timothy, Andrew Cottey, and Anthony Forester, eds. *Civil–Military Relations in Post-Communist Europe: Reviewing the Transition.* New York: Routledge, 2005.

Eldridge, Philip. *Non-Government Organizations and Democratic Participation in Indonesia*. Kuala Lumpur: Oxford University Press, 1995.
Fan, Yun. "Taiwan: No Civil Society, No Democracy." In *Civil Society and Political Change in Asia: Expanding and Contracting Democratic Space*, edited by Muthiah Alagappa. Stanford: Stanford University Press, 2004.
Feaver, Peter. *Armed Servants: Agency, Oversight, and Civil–Military Relations*. Cambridge: Harvard University Press, 2003.
Feith, Herbert. *The Decline of Constitutional Democracy in Indonesia*. Ithaca: Cornell University Press, 1962.
— "Constitutional Democracy: How Well Did it Function?" In *Democracy in Indonesia: 1950s and 1990s*, edited by David Bourchier and John Legge. Centre for Southeast Asian Studies, Monash University, Monash Papers on Southeast Asia No. 31 (1994).
Feldman, Harvey J. "Development of US-Taiwan Relations, 1948–1987." In *Taiwan in a Time of Transition*, edited by Harvey Feldman, Michael Y. M. Kau, and Ilpyong Kim, 129–73. New York: Paragon House, 1988.
Ferdinand, Peter. "The Taiwanese Economy." In *Take-off for Taiwan*, edited by Peter Ferdinand. London: Royal Institute for International Affairs, 1996.
Fifield, Anna. "U.S. to Delay Troop Cuts in S. Korea." *Financial Times*, October 5, 2004.
Finer, Samuel E. *The Man on Horseback: The Role of the Military in Politics*. New York: Frederick A. Praeger, 1962.
Franco, Jennifer C. *Elections and Democratization in the Philippines*. New York: Routledge, 2001.
Fravel, M. Taylor. "Towards Civilian Supremacy: Civil–Military Relations in Taiwan's Democratization." *Armed Forces and Society* 29 (2002): 62–75.
Gaddis, John L. *The Cold War: A New History*. New York: The Penguin Press, 2005.
Galicia-Hernandez, Carolina. "The Extent of Civilian Control of the Military in the Philippines: 1946–1976." PhD diss., University of New York at Buffalo, 1979.
Garthoff, Raymond L. *Détente and Confrontation: American-Soviet Relations from Nixon to Reagan*. Washington D.C.: Brookings Institution, 1985.
Geertz, Clifford. "The Integrative Revolution." In *Old Societies and New States: The Quest for Modernity in Asia and Africa*, edited by Clifford Geertz. New York: Free Press, 1963.
George, Alexander, and Andrew Bennett. *Case Studies and Theory Development in Social Sciences*. Cambridge: MIT Press, 2005.
Ghoshal, Baladas. *Indonesian Politics 1955–1959: The Emergence of Guided Democracy*. New Delhi: K.P. Bagchi & Co., 1982.
— "Democratic Transition and Political Development in Post-Soharto Indonesia." *Contemporary Southeast Asia* 26 (2004): 506–29.
Giordano, Pasquale T. *Awakening to Mission: The Philippine Catholic Church, 1965–1981*. Quezon City: New Day, 1988.
Goodman, Louis W., Johanna S. R. Mendelson, and Juan Rial, eds. *The Military and Democracy: The Future of Civil–Military Relations in Latin America*. Lexington: Lexington Books, 1990.
Ha, Yong-Chool. "South Korea in 2000: A Summit and the Search for New Institutional Identity." *Asian Survey* 41 (2001): 30–9.

Haggard, Stephan. "The Political Economy of the Philippine Debt Crisis." In *Economic Crisis and Policy Choice: The Politics of Adjustment in the Third World*, edited by Joan M. Nelson. Princeton: Princeton University Press, 1990.

Han, Heung-soo, ed. *Hanguk Jeongchi Dongtae Ron (Political Behavior in Korea)*. Seoul: Orum, 1996.

Han, Sung-joo. *The Failure of Democracy in South Korea*. Berkeley: University of California Press, 1974.

— "South Korea and the United States: The Alliance Survives." *Asian Survey* 20 (1980): 1075–86.

— "South Korea in 1987: The Politics of Democratization." *Asian Survey* 28 (1988): 52–6.

Han, Yong-won. *Hanguk-eui Gunbu Jeongchi (Military Politics in Korea)*. Seoul: Daewang-sa, 1993.

— "Gunbu-eui Jedojeok Sungjang-gua Jeongchi-jeok Haengdongju-eui (The rise of the military institution and its political activism)." In *Hanguk Hyondae Jeongchiran 1* (Modern Korean Politics I), edited by Bae-ho Han. Seoul: Orum, 2000.

Hardy, Richard P. *The Philippine Bishops Speak (1968–1983)*. Quezon City: Maryknoll School of Theology, 1984.

Hedman, Eva-Lotta. "The Philippines: Not So Military, Not So Civil." In *Coercion and Governance: The Declining Political Role of the Military in Asia*, edited by Muthiah Alagappa. Stanford: Stanford University Press, 2001.

Hefner, Robert. *Civil Islam: Muslims and Democratization in Indonesia*. Princeton: Princeton University Press, 2000.

Henderson, Gregory. *Korea: The Politics of Vortex*. Cambridge: Harvard University Press, 1968.

Hernandez, Carolina G. "The Extent of Civilian Control of the Military in the Philippines, 1946–1976." PhD diss., State University of New York at Buffalo, 1979.

— "The Philippines in 1987: Challenges of Redemocratization." *Asian Survey* 28 (1988): 229–41.

— "The Philippines in 1988: Reaching out to Peace and Economic Recovery." *Asian Survey* 29 (1989): 154–64.

— "The Philippines in 1996: A House Finally in Order?" *Asian Survey* 37 (1997): 204–12.

Hill, Hall. *The Indonesia Economy in Crisis: Causes, Consequences, and Lessons*. Singapore: Institute of Southeast Asia Studies, 1999.

Hindley, Donald. "Indonesia's Confrontation with Malaysia: A Search for Motives." *Asian Survey* 4 (1964): 904–13.

Hong, Yong-pyo. *State Security and Regime Security: President Syngman Rhee and the Insecurity Dilemma in South Korea, 1953–1960*. New York: St. Martin's Press, 2000.

Hsieh, Chiao C. *Strategy for Survival: The Foreign Policy and External Relations of the Republic of China on Taiwan, 1949–1979*. London: The Sherwood Press, 1985.

Hsieh, John Fuh-sheng. "National Identity and Taiwan's Mainland China Policy." *Journal of Contemporary China* 13 (2004): 479–90.

Hu, Xiaobo, and Gang Lin. "The PRC View of Taiwan under Lee Teng-hui." In *Sayonara to the Lee Teng-hui Era: Politics in Taiwan, 1988–2000*, edited by

Wei-chin Lee and T.Y. Wang, 277–97. New York: University Press of America, 2003.
Huebner, Jon W. "The Abortive Liberation of Taiwan." *The China Quarterly* 110 (1987): 256–75.
Hunter, Wendy. *Eroding Military Influence in Brazil: Politicians against Soldiers.* Chapel Hill: University of North Carolina, 1997.
Huntington, Samuel P. *The Soldier and the State: The Theory and Politics of Civil–Military Relations.* Cambridge: Harvard University Press, 1957.
Political Order in Changing Societies. New Haven: Yale University Press, 1968.
— *The Third Wave: Democratization in the Late Twentieth Century.* Norman: University of Oklahoma Press, 1991.
— "Reforming Civil–Military Relations." In *Civil–Military Relations and Democracy*, edited by Larry Diamond and Marc Plattner. Baltimore: The John Hopkins University Press, 1996.
Hwang, Teh-fu. "Electoral Competition and Democratic Transition in the Republic of China." *Issues and Studies* 27 (1991): 97–123.
Hwang, Won-ki. *Developmental Dictatorship and Democratization in South Korea: The State and Society in Transformation, 1987–1997.* PhD diss., Brown University, 2006.
I-Cheng, Loh. *The China Yearbook, 1959–1960.* Taipei: China Publishing Company, 1959.
Janowitz, Morris. *The Professional Soldier.* New York: Free Press, 1960.
— *The Military in the Political Development of New Nations: An Essay in Comparative Analysis.* Chicago: University of Chicago Press, 1964.
Jemadu, Aleksius. "Democratization and the Dilemma of Nation-building in Post-Soharto Indonesia: The Case of Aceh." *Asian Ethnicity* 5 (2004): 315–31.
Jun, Jinseok."South Korea: Consolidating Democratic Civilian Control." In *Coercion and Governance: The Declining Political Role of the Military in Asia*, edited by Muthiah Alagappa. Stanford: Stanford University Press, 2001.
Jung, Sang-yong, ed. *Gwangju Minju Hangjaeng (The People's Struggle for Democracy in Gwangju).* Seoul: Dolbege, 1990.
Kang, C. S. Eliot. "North Korea's International Relations: The Successful Failure?" In *The International Relations of Northeast Asia*, edited by Samuel S. Kim. Lanham: Rowman & Littlefield Publishers, 2004.
Kang, David C. *Crony Capitalism: Corruption and Development in South Korea and the Philippines.* New York: Cambridge University Press, 2002.
— "Regional Politics and Democratic Consolidation in Korea." In *Korea's Democratization*, edited by Samuel S. Kim. New York: Cambridge University Press, 2003.
Kerr, George H. *Formosa Betrayed.* Boston: Houghton Mifflin, 1965.
Kessler, Richard J. "Development and the Military: Role of the Philippine Military in Development." In *Soldiers and Stability in Southeast Asia*, edited by Soedjati Djiwandono and Yong Mun Chong. Singapore: Institute of Southeast Asian Studies, 1988.
— *Rebellion and Repression in the Philippines.* New Haven: Yale University Press, 1989.
Kihl, Young-whan. "South Korea's Foreign Relations: Diplomatic Activism and Policy Dilemma." In *Korea Briefing: Toward Reunification*, edited by David R. McCann. New York: Asia Society, 1991.
— *Transforming Korean Politics: Democracy, Reform, and Culture.* New York: M.E. Sharpe, 2005.

Kim, C. I. Eugene. "South Korea in 1985: An Eventual Year Amidst Uncertainty." *Asian Survey* 26 (1986): 67–71.
Kim, Hong-nack. "The 1988 Parliamentary Election in South Korea." *Asian Survey* 29 (1989): 481–95.
Kim, Jungwon. *Divided Korea: The Politics of Development, 1945–1972*. Cambridge: Harvard University Press, 1976.
Kim, Kwang-oong. "Hanguk Min-gun Gwanryo Elite eui Ideology-wa Jeongchi (Ideology and Politics of the Civilian and Military Elites in South Korea)." *Kyegan Kyunghyang*, Spring 1998.
Kim, Sanghyun. "South Korea's Kim Young Sam Government: Political Agendas." *Asian Survey* 36 (1996): 511–22.
Kim, Sejin. *The Politics of Military Revolution in Korea*. Chapel Hill: The University of North Carolina Press, 1971.
Kim, Sun-hyuk. "State and Civil Society in South Korea's Democratic Consolidation: Is the Battle Really Over?" *Asian Survey* 37 (1997): 1135–44.
— *The Politics of Democratization in Korea: The Role of Civil Society*. Pittsburgh: University of Pittsburgh Press, 2000.
—"Civil Society in Democratizing Korea." In *Korea's Democratization*, edited by Samuel Kim. London: Cambridge University Press, 2003.
Kingsbury, Damien. *The Politics of Indonesia*. New York: Oxford University Press, 1988.
— *Power Politics and the Indonesian Military*. New York: Routledge, 2003.
Koh, B. C. "The 1985 Parliamentary Election in South Korea." *Asian Survey* 25 (1985): 883–97.
— "South Korea in 1996: Internal Strains and External Challenges." *Asian Survey* 37 (1997): 1–9.
Kolkowicz, Rowman. *The Soviet Military and the Communist Party*. Princeton: Princeton University Press, 1967.
Kolkowicz, Rowman and Adrzej Korbonski, eds. *Soldiers, Peasants, and Bureaucrats*. London: George Allen & Unwin, 1982.
Kposowa, Augustine J., and J. Craig Jenkins. "The Structural Source of Military Coups in Post Colonial Africa, 1957–1984." *American Journal of Sociology* 99 (1993): 126–63.
Kristiadi, J. "The Armed Forces." In *Indonesia: The Challenge of Change*, edited by Richard W. Baker, M. Hadi Soesastro, J. Kristiadi, and Douglas E. Ramage. New York: St. Martin's Press, 1999.
Kuhlmann, Jurgen and Jean Callaghan, eds. *Military and Society in 21st Century Europe: A Comparative Analysis*. New Brunswick: Transaction Publishers, 2001.
Labrador, Mel C. "The Philippines in 2000: In Search of a Silver Lining." *Asian Survey* 41 (2001): 221–9.
Lande, Carl H. "Political Crisis." In *Crisis in the Philippines: The Marcos Era and Beyond*, edited by Josh Bresnan. Princeton: Princeton University Press, 1986.
Lasswell, Harold. "The Garrison State." *American Journal of Sociology* 46 (1941): 455–68.
Lee, Chong-sik. "South Korea in 1980: The Emergence of a New Authoritarian Order." *Asian Survey* 21 (1981): 125–43.

Lee, Dae-kyu, Kyu-hui Hwang, and In-hyuk Kim, eds. *Bigyo Gunbu Jeongchi Gaeip-ron (Comparative Analysis of Military Intervention in Politics)*. Busan: Dong-A University Press, 2001.
Lee, Hong-young. "South Korea in 1992: A Turning Point in Democratization." *Asian Survey* 33 (1992): 32–42.
— "South Korea in 2002: Multiple Political Dramas." *Asian Survey* 43 (2003): 64–77.
Lee, Jae-chul. "Deepening and Improving Democracy: Association in South Korea." PhD diss., University of Missouri at Columbia, 2005.
Lee, Su-hoon. "Transitional Politics of Korea, 1987–1992: Activation of Civil Society." *Pacific Affairs* 66 (1993): 351–67.
Lee, Yong-ho. "The Politics of Democratic Experiment: 1948–1974." In *Korean Politics in Transition*, edited by Edward Reynolds Wright. Seattle: University of Washington Press, 1975.
Lev, Daniel S. "Indonesia in 1965: The Year of the Coup." *Asian Survey* 6 (1966): 103–10.
Liddle, R. William. "Indonesia's Unexpected Failure of Leadership." In *The Politics of Post-Suharto Indonesia*, edited by Adam Schwarz and Jonathan Paris. New York: Council on Foreign Relations Press, 1999.
— "Indonesia in 1999: Democracy Restored." *Asian Survey* 40 (2000): 32–40.
— "Indonesia in 2000: A Shaky Start for Democracy." *Asian Survey* 41 (2000): 208–20.
Liddle, R. William and Saiful Mujani. "Indonesia in 2004: The Rise of Susilo Bambang Yudhoyono." *Asian Survey* 45 (2005): 119–27.
Liddle, William R. "Indonesia's Democratic Past and Future." *Comparative Politics* 24 (1992): 443–62.
Linz, Juan. *Crisis, Breakdown and Reequilibration*. Baltimore: Johns Hopkins University Press, 1978.
Liu, Hong. "The Sino-South Korean Normalization: A Triangular Explanation." *Asian Survey* 33 (1991): 1083–94.
Lo, Ching-cheng. "Taiwan: The Remaining Challenges." In *Coercion and Governance: The Declining Political Role of the Military in Asia*, edited by Muthiah Alagappa. Stanford: Stanford University Press, 2001.
Long, Simon. *Taiwan: China's Lost Frontier*. London: Macmillan, 1991.
Lovell, John P. "The Military and Politics in Postwar Korea." In *Korean Politics in Transition*, edited by Edward Reynolds Wright, 153–99. Seattle: University of Washington Press, 1975.
Lowry, Robert. *Indonesian Defense Policy and the Indonesian Armed Forces*. Canberra: Strategic and Defence Studies Center, Australian National University, 1993.
Mackie, Jamie A. C. *Konfrontasi: the Indonesia-Malaysia Dispute, 1963–1966*. London: Oxford University Press, 1974.
Maguire, Keith. *The Rise of Modern Taiwan*. London: Ashgate, 1998.
Malin, Herbert S. "The Philippines in 1984: Grappling with Crisis." *Asian Survey* 25 (1985): 198–205.
Malley, Michael S. "Indonesia in 2001: Restoring Stability in Jakarta." *Asian Survey* 42 (2002): 124–32.

Manlapaz, Romeo. *The Mathematics of Deception: A Study of the 1986 Presidential Election Tallies.* Quezon City: Third World Studies Center, University of the Philippines, 1986.

May, Ronald J. and Viberto Selochan, eds. *The Military and Democracy in Asia and the Pacific.* New South Wales: ANU Press, 1964.

Maynard, Harold W. "The Role of the Indonesian Armed Forces." In *The Armed Forces in Contemporary Asian Societies*, edited by Edward Olson and Stephen Jurika. Boulder: Westview Press, 1986.

McBeth, John. "Internal Contradictions: Support for Communists Wanes as Party Splits." *Far Eastern Economic Review*, August 26, 1993.

McBeth, John, and Oren Murphy. "Bloodbath." *Far Eastern Economic Review*, July 6, 2000.

McDougall, Derek. *The International Politics of the New Asia Pacific.* Boulder: Lynne Rienner Publishers, 1997.

McKeown, Timothy J. "Case Studies and the Limits of the Quantitative Worldview." In *Rethinking Social Inquiry: Diverse Tools, Shared Standards*, edited by Henry Brady and David Collier. Lanham: Rowman & Littlefield, 2004.

Merrill, John. "The Cheju-do Rebellion." *Journal of Korean Politics* 2 (1980): 139–97.

Miranda, Felipe B., and Ruben F. Ciron. "Development and the Military in the Philippines: Military Perceptions in a Time of Continuing Crisis." In *Soldiers and Stability in Southeast Asia*, edited by J. Soedjati Djiwandono and Yong Mun Cheong, 163–211. Singapore: Institute of Southeast Asian Studies, 1988.

Molloy, Ivan. "Revolution in the Philippines: The Question of an Alliance between Islam and Communism." *Asian Survey* 25 (1985): 822–33.

Montinola, Gabriella R. "The Philippines in 1998: Opportunity and Crisis." *Asian Survey* 39 (1999): 64–71.

Moody, Peter R. *Political Change on Taiwan: A Study of Ruling Party Adaptability.* New York: Praeger, 1992.

Moon, Chung-in. "The Sunshine Policy and the Korean Summit: Assessments and Prospects." *East Asian Review* 12 (2000): 22–9.

Moon, Chung-in and Jongryn Mo. "The Kim Young-Sam Government: Its Legacies and Prospects for Governance in South Korea." In *Democratization and Globalization in Korea: Assessments and Prospects*, edited by Chung-in Moon and Jongryn Mo. Seoul: Yonsei University Press, 1999.

Moon, Chung-in and David Steinberg, eds., *Kim Dae Jung Government and Sunshine Policy.* Seoul: Yonsei University Press, 1999.

Moon, Eric P. "Single Non-transferable Vote Methods in Taiwan in 1996: Effects of an Electoral System." *Asian Survey* 37 (1997): 652–68.

Mortimer, Rex. *Indonesian Communism under Sukarno: Ideology and Politics, 1959–1965.* Ithaca: Cornell University Press, 1974.

Muego, Benjamin. *Spectator Society: The Philippine under Martial Rule.* Athens: Ohio University Center for International Studies, 1988.

Murphy, Ann Marie. "Indonesia and Globalization." *Asian Perspective* 23 (1999): 229–59.

National Democratic Institute for International Affairs. *The 1999 Presidential Election, MPR General Session and Post-Election Development in Indonesia.* Washington D.C.: National Democratic Institute, 1999.

Neumann, A. Lin. "Philippines: Military on the Move." *Asia Times*, February 28, 2006.
Niksch, Larry A. *Insurgency and Counterinsurgency in the Philippines*. Washington D.C.: Library of Congress, 1985.
Noble, Lela G. "The Moro National Liberation Front in the Philippines." *Pacific Affairs* 49 (1976): 405–24
— "Muslim Separatism in the Philippines, 1972–1981: The Making of a Stalemate." *Asian Survey* 21 (1981): 1097–1114.
— "Politics in the Marcos Era." In *Crisis in the Philippines: The Marcos Era and Beyond*, edited by Josh Bresnan. Princeton: Princeton University Press, 1986.
Nordlinger, Eric A. *Soldiers in Politics: Military Coups and Governments*. Englewood Cliffs: Prentice Hall Inc., 1977.
O'Donnell, Guillermo, Philippe C. Schmitter, and Laurence Whitehead, eds. *Transition from Authoritarian Rule: Southern Europe, Vol. 1*. Baltimore: The John Hopkins University Press, 1986.
Office of the President, Republic of Korea. *Government of the People: Selected Speeches of President Kim Dae-jung, vols. 1–2* (Seoul: ROK Government).
Oh, Byung-hun. "Students and Politics." In *Korean Politics in Transition*, edited by Edward Reynolds Wright, 107–52. Seattle: University of Washington Press, 1975.
Oh, Chang-hon. *Yushin Cheje-wa Hyundae Hanguk Jeongchi (Yushin and Contemporary Korean Politics)*. Seoul: Orum, 2001.
Oh, John Kie-chiang. *Korean Politics: The Quest for Democratization and Development*. Ithaca: Cornell University Press, 1999.
Oliver, Robert T. *Why War Came In Korea*. New York: Fordham University Press, 1950.
Pak, Won-sun. *Gukga Boanbup Yongu (The Study of the National Security Law) Vol. 2*. Seoul: Yoksa Bipyongsa, 1991.
Park, Jin. "Political Change in South Korea: The Challenge of the Conservative Alliance." *Asian Survey* 30 (1990): 1154–68.
Park, Jung-hee. *Uri Minjok-eui Nagal Gil (Future of our Nation)*. Seoul: Koryo, Inc., 1961.
Park, Myunglim. "Hanguk-eui Gukga Hyungsung, 1945–1948 (State-building in South Korea, 1945–1948)." *Korean Political Science Review* 29 (1995).
Peng, Ming-min. *A Taste of Freedom: Memoirs of a Formosan Independence Leader*. New York: Holt, Reinhart and Winston, 1972.
Pridham, Geoffrey, ed. *The New Mediterranean Democracies: Regime Transition in Spain, Greece and Portugal*. London: Frank Cass Ltd., 1984.
Przeworski, Adam. *Democracy and the Market: Political and Economic Reforms in Eastern Europe and Latin America*. New York: Cambridge University Press, 1991.
Quimpo, Nathan Gilbert. "Back to War in Mindanao: The Weaknesses of a Power-based Approach in Conflict Resolution." *Philippine Political Science Journal* 21 (2000): 99–126.
— "Options in the Pursuit of a Just, Comprehensive, and Stable Peace in the Southern Philippines." *Asian Survey* 41 (2001): 210–28.
Rabasa, Angel and John Haseman. *The Military and Democracy in Indonesia: Challenges, Politics, and Power*. RAND: National Security Research Division, 2002.

Reeves, David W. *The Republic of Korea*. London: Oxford University Press, 1963.
— *Golkar of Indonesia: An Alternative to the Party System*. London: Oxford University Press, 1987.
Republic of China. *The China Yearbook*. Taipei: China Publishing Company, 1979.
Republic of Korea. *Daehanminguk Seongo-sa (History of Elections in Korea)*. Seoul: Central Election Management Committee, 1964.
— "National Election Commission." Republic of Korea. http://www.nec.go.kr/ (accessed February 13, 2006).
Riedinger, Jeffrey. "The Philippines in 1994: Renewed Growth and Contested Reforms." *Asian Survey* 35 (1995): 209–17.
Rigger, Shelley. *Politics in Taiwan: Voting for Democracy*. New York: Routledge, 1999.
— *From Opposition to Power: Taiwan's Democratic Progressive Party*. Boulder: Lynne Rienner, 2001.
Rivera, Temario C. "The Philippines in 2004: New Mandate, Daunting Problems." *Asian Survey* 45 (2005): 127–33.
Robinson, Geoffrey. "Indonesia: On a New Course?" In *Coercion and Governance: The Declining Political Role of the Military in Asia*, edited by Muthiah Alagappa. Stanford: Stanford University Press, 2001.
Rocamora, Joel. *Breaking Through: The Struggle within the Communist Party of the Philippines*. Manila: Anvil Press, 1994.
Roeder, Ruldolf O. G. *The Smiling General: President Suharto of Indonesia*. Jakarta: Gunung Agung, 1969.
Roehrig, Terence. *The Prosecution of Former Military Leaders in Newly Democratic Nations: The Cases of Argentina, Greece, and South Korea*. London: McFarland & Company, 2002.
Ross, Edward W. "Taiwan's Armed Forces." In *The Armed Forces in Contemporary Asian Societies*, edited by Edward Olson and Stephen Jurika, Jr. Boulder: Westview Press, 1986.
Rubinstein, Murray A. "Taiwan's Socioeconomic Modernization." In *Taiwan: A New History*, edited by Murray A. Rubinstein. New York: M.E. Sharpe, 1999.
Rutten, Rosanne. "Revolutionary Specialists, Strongmen, and the State: Post-Movement Careers of CCP-NPA Cadres in a Philippine Province, 1990s-2001." *South East Asia Research* 9 (2001): 319–61.
Said, Salim. "Suharto's Armed Forces: Building a Power Base in New Order Indonesia, 1966–1998." *Asian Survey* 38 (1998): 535–52.
Sanger, David. "Bush Tells Seoul Talks with North Won't Resume Now." *New York Times*, March 8, 2001.
Saxer, Carl J. "Generals and Presidents: Establishing Civilian and Democratic Control in South Korea." *Armed Forces and Society* 30 (2004): 366–88.
Scalapino, Robert. "Which Route for Korea?" *Asian Survey* 2 (1961): 1–13.
Schulzinger, Robert D. *Henry Kissinger: Doctor of Diplomacy*. New York: Columbia University Press, 1989.
Schwarz, Adam. "Introduction: The Politics of Post-Suharto Indonesia." In *The Politics of Post-Suharto Indonesia*, edited by Adam Schwarz and Jonathan Paris. New York; Council on Foreign Relations Press, 1999.

Scott, Peter D. "The United States and the Overthrow of Sukarno." *Pacific Affairs* 58 (1985): 239–64.
Selochan, Viberto. "The Armed Forces of the Philippines and Political Instability." In *The Military, the State, and Development in Asia and the Pacific*, edited by Viberto Selochan. Boulder: Westview Press, 1991.
Seo, Kyung-kyo. "Military Involvement in Politics and the Prospects for Democracy: Thailand, the Philippines, and South Korea in Comparative Perspective." PhD diss., University of Southern Illinois at Carbondale, 1993.
Seymour, James D. "Taiwan in 1988: No More Bandits." *Asian Survey* 29 (1989): 54–63.
Shaw, Yu-ming, ed., *Building Democracy in the Republic of China*. Taipei: The Asia and World Institute, 1984.
Shin, Doh-chull. *Mass Politics and Culture in Democratizing Korea*. Oxford: Oxford University Press, 1999.
Shin, Gi-wook. "Marxism, Anti-Americanism, and Democracy in South Korea: An Examination of Nationalist Intellectual Discourse." *Positions: East Asian Cultures Critique* 3 (1995): 508–34.
Shiraishi, Takashi. "The Indonesian Military in Politics." In *The Politics of Post-Suharto Indonesia*, edited by Adam Schwarz and Jonathan Paris. New York: Council on Foreign Relations Press, 1999.
Sidel, John T. *Capital, Coercion, and Crime: Bossism in the Philippines*. Stanford: Stanford University Press, 1999.
Sidwell, Thomas E. *The Indonesian Military: Dwi Fungsi and Territorial Operations*. Fort Leavenworth: Foreign Military Studies Office, 1995.
Silliman, G. Sidney. "The Philippines in 1983: Authoritarianism Beleaguered." *Asian Survey* 24 (1984): 149–58.
Simons, Lewis M. *Worth Dying For*. New York: William Morrow, 1987.
Sinaga, Kastorius. "Number of Local NGO's Mushrooming." *Jakarta Post*, November 2, 1993.
Sohn, Hochul. "Hanguk Jeonjaeng-gua Ideology Ji-hyung" (The Korean War and the Ideological Terrain. *Hanguk-gua Gukje Jeongchi (Korean and International Politics)* 6 (1980): 1–27.
Song, Eui-sop. "Documentary Hanahoe." *Chugan Hanguk (Weekly Korea)*, June 1, 1993.
South Korea. *History of the Department of National Defense*. Seoul: Sungkwang-sa, 1956.
Steinberg, David J. *The Philippines; A Singular and a Plural Place*, 2nd edn. Boulder: Westview Press, 1990.
Stepan, Alfred. *Authoritarian Brazil: Origins, Policies and Future*. New Haven: Yale University Press, 1973.
— *Rethinking Military Politics: Brazil and the Southern Cone*. Princeton: Princeton University Press, 1988.
Sundhaussen, Ulf. *The Road to Power: Indonesian Military Politics, 1945–1967*. Oxford: Oxford University Press, 1982.
— "Indonesia: Past and Present Encounters with Democracy." In *Democracy in Developing Countries, Volume Three: Asia*, edited by Larry Diamond, Juan Linz, and Seymour Martin Lipset. London: Adamantine Press Limited, 1989.

Sutter, John O. "Two Faces of Konfrontasi: Crush Malaysia and the Gestapu." *Asian Survey* 6 (1966): 523–46.
Sutter, Robert G. *Chinese Foreign Policy: Developments after Mao*. New York: Praeger, 1986.
Taciana, Marie and Leila Fernandez Stembridge, eds. *China Today: Economic Reforms, Social Conflict, and Collective Identities*. London: RoutledgeCurzon Press, 2003.
Tang, Tsou. *The Embroilment over Quemoy: Mao, Chiang, and Dulles*. Salt Lake: University of Utah Press, 1959.
Tasker, Rodney. "The Hidden Hand: A Military Reform Movement Takes Hold." *Far Eastern Economic Review*, August 1, 1985.
Thomson, Mark R. *The Anti-Marcos Struggle: Personalistic Rule and Democratic Transition in the Philippines*. New Haven: Yale University Press, 1995.
— "The Decline of Philippine Communism: A Review Essay." *South East Asia Research* 6 (1998): 105–29.
Tien, Hung-mao. *Government and Politics in Kuomintang China, 1927–1937*. Stanford: Stanford University Press, 1972.
— "Social Change and Political Development in Taiwan." In *Taiwan in a Time of Transition*, edited by Harvey Feldman, Michael Y. M. Kau, and Ilpyong Kim. New York: Paragon House, 1988.
— "The Transformation of an Authoritarian Party-State: Taiwan's Developmental Experiences." *Issues and Studies* 25 (1989): 105–33.
Tien, Hung-mao, ed., *Mainland China, Taiwan, the U.S. Policy*. Cambridge: Oelgeschlager, Gunn and Hain, 1983.
Tien, Hung-mao and Tun-jen Cheng. "Crafting Democratic Institutions in Taiwan." *The China Journal* 37 (1997): 1–27.
Tien, Hung-mao and Yun-han Chu. "Taiwan's Domestic Political Reforms: Institutional Change and Power Realignment." In *Taiwan in the Asia-Pacific in the 1990s*, edited by Gary Klintworth. St. Leonards: Allen & Unwin, 1994.
Timberman, David G. "The Philippines in 1990: On Shaky Ground." *Asian Survey* 31 (1991): 153–63.
Tong, Hollington K. *Chiang Kai-shek*. Taipei: China Publishing Company, 1953.
Tsang, Steve. "Chiang Kai-shek and Kuomintang's Policy to Reconquer the Chinese Mainland, 1949–1958." In *In the Shadow of China*, edited by Steve Tsang. Honolulu: University of Hawaii Press, 1993.
Uhlin, Anders. *Indonesia and "The Third Wave of Democratization": The Indonesian Pro-Democracy Movements in a Changing World*. New York: Palgrave Macmillan, 1997.
Van der Kroef, Justus M. *The Communist Party of Indonesia*. Vancouver: University of British Columbia Press, 1965.
Vatikiotis, Michael R. J. *Indonesian Politics under Suharto*. London: Routledge, 1993.
Velasco, Renato S. "Philippine Democracy: Promise and Performance." In *Democratization in Southeast and East Asia*, edited by Anek Laothamatas. New York: St. Martin's Press, 1997.
Veremis, Thanos. *The Military in Greek Politics*. London: Hurst & Company, 1997.
Villegas, Bernardo M. "The Economic Crisis." In *Crisis in the Philippines: The Marcos Era and Beyond*, edited by John Bresnan. Princeton: Princeton University Press, 1986.

— "The Philippines in 1986: Democratic Reconstruction in the Post-Marcos Era." *Asian Survey* 27 (1987): 194–205.
Wachman, Alan M. *Taiwan: National Identity and Democratization*. New York: M.E. Sharpe, 1994.
Wanandi, Jusuf. "Challenge of the TNI and Its Role in Indonesia's Future." In *Governance in Indonesia: Challenges Facing the Megawati Presidency*, edited by Hadi Soesastro, Anthony L. Smith, and Han Mui Ling. Singapore: Institute of Southeast Asian Studies, 2003.
Wang, T. Y. "Cross-Strait Relations after the 2000 Election in Taiwan: Changing Tactics in a New Reality." *Asian Survey* 41 (2001): 716–36.
Weekley, Kathleen. *The Communist Party of the Philippines 1968–1993: A Story of Its Theory and Practice*. Quezon City: University of the Philippines Press, 2001.
Welch Jr., Claude E, ed. *Civilian Control of the Military: Theories and Cases from Developing Countries*. Albany: State University of New York Press, 1976.
Welch Jr., Claude E., and Arthur Smith. *Military Role and Military Rule: Perspectives on Civil–Military Relations*. North Scituate: Dexbury Press, 1974.
The White House. "2002 State of the Union Address, January 29, 2002." http://www.state.gov/r/pa/ei/wh/rem/7672.htm (accessed August 5, 2006).
Woo, Jongseok. "Crafting Democratic Control of the Military in South Korea and the Philippines: The Problem of Factions." Paper presented at the annual meeting for the Southwest Political Science Association, Denver, CO, April 8–11, 2009.
Woodward, Kathleen E. "Violent Masses, Elites, and Democratization: The Indonesia Case." PhD diss., Ohio State University, 2002.
World Bank, *World Tables 1993*. Washington D.C.: World Bank, 2004.
Wright, Teresa. "Student Mobilization in Taiwan: Civil Society and Its Discontents." *Asian Survey* 39 (1999): 986–1008.
Wu, Jaushieh J. *Taiwan's Democratization: Forces behind the New Momentum*. New York: Oxford University Press, 1995.
Wu, Yu-shan. "Taiwan in 2000: Managing the Aftershocks from Power Transfer." *Asian Survey* 41 (2001): 40–8.
Wurfel, David. *Filipino Politics: Development and Decay*. Ithaca: Cornell University Press, 1988.
Wynia, Gary W. *The Politics of Latin American Development*. Cambridge: Cambridge University Press, 1978.
Yahooda, Michael B. *China's Role in World Affairs*. London: Croom Helm, 1978.
Yoon, Seong-yi. "Democratization in South Korea: Social Movements and Their Political Opportunity Structures." *Asian Perspective* 21 (1997): 145–71.
Yoon, Young-Kwan. "South Korea in 1999: Overcoming Cold War Legacies." *Asian Survey* 40 (2000): 164–71.
Youngblood, Robert L. *Marcos against the Church: Economic Development and Political Repression in the Philippines*. Ithaca: Cornell University Press, 1990.

Index

Abu Sayyaf 168
Agreed Framework 157, 178n.9
Aguinaldo 126
Amien Rais 174
Angkatan Bersenjata Republik Indonesia (ABRI; Republic of Indonesia Armed Forces) 12, 49, 78–80, 95, 131–2, 133, 134–5, 136–9, 140, 141, 149n.82, 171, 172, 173–6, 193–4, 196
  birth of 47–8
  and democratization 131–7
  domestic security crises 137–9, 171, 172
  and Guided Democracy 51–3, 73–4, 192–3
  and parliamentary democracy 49–51
  and PKI 74–8, 95
  role during state-buildings 12
April 13 measure 106
April Student Revolution 65, 68, 70, 95
Aquino, Benigno 44, 83, 124
Aquino, Corazon 81, 86, 123, 125, 191
Armed Forces of the Philippines (AFP) 17, 24, 40–3, 45, 46, 54, 55, 85, 86–7, 96, 123, 124–31, 140, 141, 165–6, 167, 168–9, 170–1, 190–2, 195, 196, 198
  factional struggles within 82–3
  in Macros government 44–6
  martial law and 81–2
  political roles of 81
Aroyo, Gloria Macapagal 169, 195
aski sepihak (unilateral action) 76, 193

Bambang Kesowo 173
Barany, Zoltan D. 6, 20n.4, 20n.8, 102n.87
Bush, George W. 157

Catholic Church 83, 85, 124, 170
Central Standing Committee (CSC) 34, 89, 93, 122, 163, 189, 190
Challenges to Civilian Control (CCC) 152, 155, 162, 167, 172
Chang Myon 32, 65, 66, 67, 71, 95, 113, 187
Chen Shui-bian 104, 123, 161, 162, 164
Chiang Ching-kuo 35, 39, 87, 89, 93, 96, 97, 104, 115, 116, 117, 160, 163, 164, 189
Chiang Dynasty 117
Chiang Kai-shek 36, 38, 55, 56, 59n.33, 87–8, 91, 93, 96, 97, 114, 115, 163, 189, 198
China, People's Republic of 26, 36, 109
China Lobby 36
Chinese Communist Party (CCP) 17, 26, 33, 34, 36, 37, 38, 46, 54, 77, 87, 88, 89, 91, 92, 164, 188
Chinese mainlanders 35, 93, 121, 188, 195
Cho Bong-am 65
Chun Doo-whan 73, 104–7, 108, 109, 112, 113, 114, 140, 188
Church-Military Committee 85
Civilian Control Indicators (CCI) 152
Civilian Home Defense Force (CHDF) 46

civilian leadership 3, 6, 7, 10, 11, 14–15, 16, 17, 18, 23, 63–4, 73, 136, 137, 139, 141, 151, 152, 158, 165, 170–1, 177, 184, 186, 189, 195, 197
civil–military problematique 9
civil–military relations, structural theory of 11–15
civil war 17, 23, 24, 26, 33, 35, 36, 37, 54, 55, 71, 87, 88, 115, 118, 188
civilian factors 9
Cojuanco, Jose 127
Cold War 4, 12, 23, 24, 37, 40, 59n.26, 103, 109, 118, 154, 168, 187
Colton, Timothy 6, 20n.4, 20n.11
Commission on Elections (COMELEC) 125
Communist Party of the Philippines (CPP) 40, 41, 42, 54, 56, 85, 124, 128, 129, 165, 166, 168, 181n.34, 190, 191
Comprehensive Agrarian Reform Program (CARP) 127
Corregidor Incident 42
Corpus, Victor 170
coup d'État 1, 7, 8, 14, 16, 17, 18, 29, 31, 56, 63, 90, 94, 169, 171
  in Indonesia 47, 53, 64–73, 193
  in South Korea 29, 31, 32, 73–80, 109, 112, 113

Darul Islam 50, 77, 137, 192
Defense Security Command (DSC) 112
democratic centralism 89
democratic control 1, 8, 18, 115, 123, 141, 151, 154, 166, 171, 176, 195
Democratic Justice Party (DJP) 106, 107, 108, 110, 158
Democratic Korea Party (DKP) 106
Democratic Liberal Party (DLP) 110, 111, 143n.21
Democratic Party (DP) 65, 66, 67, 68, 69, 88, 175
Democratic Progressive Party (DPP) 35, 116, 120, 121, 122, 123, 161, 165, 190
Democratic Republican Party (DRP) 71

democratization 111, 165
Deng Xiao-ping 92, 109
depoliticization 3, 4, 15, 17, 18, 105, 118, 123, 140, 151, 160, 161, 176, 177, 183, 188, 197
Desch, Michael 9, 10, 20n.10, 22n.25
détente 109, 115, 154
developmental approach 9
disposition 9
doctrine 2, 9, 12, 47, 51, 52, 74, 75, 94, 131, 193
dwifungsi (dual function) 12, 52, 131, 193
dynamic actors 3, 11, 14, 16, 17, 140

Eastern Europe 2, 107, 143, 154
East Timor 133, 137, 138, 171, 172, 174, 182n.49, 194
Economic Stabilization Board (ESB) 90
Enrile, Juan Ponce 44, 45, 46, 81, 126, 191
Espino, Romeo C. 45, 81, 146n.56
Estrada, Joseph 169, 170

faction 30, 31, 68, 77, 83, 87, 96, 112, 121, 122, 125, 130, 134, 153, 188, 194
Feaver, Peter 9, 20n.9, 21n.19, 22n.24, 22n.30, 22n.34
February 28th Uprising 34, 35, 58n.20, 90, 188
Fei Hsi-ping 116
Feisal Tamin 173
Filipino-Chinese 84
Finer, Samuel E. 11, 20n.13, 98n.25
Formosa Island 24, 32, 39, 54, 87, 92, 163
Four Contacts 92
functional groups 51, 79

Garrison Decree 73
garrison states 10
General Political Warfare Department (GPWD) 89, 90, 93, 97
Gerakan Aceh Merdeka (GAM, Free Aceh Movement) 137, 138
Go, George 169
Golkar (Golongan Karya, Functional Group) 79, 80, 100n.50, 135, 136, 175

grand alliance 110
Grand National Party (GNP) 27, 72, 84, 90, 124, 156, 157
green faction 134
Guam Doctrine 91
guerrilla warfare 11, 40, 41, 50, 134, 138, 189
Guided Democracy 24, 47, 49, 51, 52, 53, 55, 56, 61n.70, 64, 77, 174
and ABRI 51–3, 73–4, 192–3
Gwangju 105, 113, 142n.2

Habibie, Bacharuddin Jusuf 133
Hamah Haz 174
Hanahoe (one mind) 112, 113, 114, 141, 144n.24, 153, 188, 194
Hau Pei-tsun 118, 121, 123, 160, 190
Heiho 47, 48
Henderson, Gregory 97n.5, 98n.15
Heo Jung 67
Honam 159
Honasan, Gregorio 86
Hong In-gil 159
Hong Kong 119
Hukbalahap (Huk) 40
Huntington, Samuel P. 21n.15, 21n.21, 22n.23, 68, 98n.14, 108, 111, 142n.9, 153, 178n.1, 179n.20

Ilocos 43, 82, 96, 169, 191
Indonesia 1, 2, 4, 5, 7, 8, 12, 17, 18, 23, 24, 47, 48, 49, 50, 51, 52, 53, 54, 55, 63, 64, 73, 74, 76, 77, 80, 86, 94, 95, 96, 103, 104, 123, 131, 132, 133, 134, 135, 136, 137, 138, 139, 140, 141, 151, 152, 169, 171–7, 183, 185, 192–8
Indonesian Communist Party *see* Partai Komunis Indonesia (PKI)
Indonesian Nationalist Party *see* Partai Nasional Indonesia (PNI)
institutionalist (theories/perspectives) 8, 9, 19, 56
insurgency 4, 9, 12, 26, 46, 83, 85, 124, 126, 127, 128, 131, 140, 166, 168, 169, 170, 177, 190, 194, 197
interethnic violence 137, 138
Islamic State of Indonesia 50

Japan 1, 23, 30, 33, 48, 69, 156
Japanese Imperial Army 30
Japanese invasion 33, 188
June 29 Declaration 105, 107, 109, 110
junta 1, 69, 70, 71, 72, 86, 95
jurisdiction 8

Kilusang Bagong Lipunan (KBL) 125
Kim Hyun-chul 159
Kim Il-sung 27, 31
Kim Jae-kyu 73
Kim Jin-young 112
Kim Jung-youn 66
Kim Young-sam 105, 106, 108, 110, 111, 113, 114, 153, 158, 159, 188, 198
Kissinger, Henry 91
Konfrontasi (or "Crush Malaysia" campaign) 76, 95, 193
Korea, North 1, 24, 25, 28, 30, 31, 32, 67, 69, 72, 73, 77, 95, 105, 107, 109, 153, 154, 155, 156–9, 176, 178n.4, 187, 195, 196
Korea, South 1, 24, 25, 28, 30, 31, 32, 67, 69, 72, 73, 77, 95, 105, 107, 109, 153, 154, 155, 156–9, 176, 178n.4, 187, 195, 196
constitutional amendment 28, 29, 31, 65, 106, 122
Liberal Party (LP) 32, 43, 65, 110
National Assembly 25, 26, 28, 29, 31, 34, 56n.1, 58n.22, 65, 67, 71, 72, 106, 108, 109, 110, 111, 113, 116, 117, 118, 136, 143n.21, 154, 156, 187
National Security Law 26, 57n.5, 65
presidential election 28, 29, 35, 65, 66, 68, 71, 86, 105, 106, 108, 110, 111, 113, 117, 118, 119, 122, 123, 125, 130, 146n.50,51, 153, 161, 164, 169, 170, 174, 186, 191
Second Republic 32, 67, 68, 69, 70, 113
Korean Central Intelligence Agency (KCIA) 70, 71, 73
Korean Military Academy 25, 106
Korean peninsula 24, 25, 54, 69, 72, 109, 140, 154, 156, 157, 195
Korean War (1950–1953) 17, 23, 25, 26, 27, 30, 36, 37, 54, 55, 69, 109, 186

Kostrad (Army Strategic Reserve Command) 136
Kuomintang (KMT) 26, 87, 101n.71, 114, 188

land reform 41, 76, 95, 127, 193
Lasswell, Harold 10, 22n.28
Latin America 2
Laurel, Salvador 125, 126
Lee Jong-chan 29, 30
Lee Teng-hui 94, 104, 115, 117, 141, 160, 190
Leninist party 89
liberalization 94, 104, 105, 106, 116, 123, 140, 160, 169, 189
Liberal Party (LP) 32, 43, 65, 66, 68, 110
Lim, Danilo 170
Lin Yang-kang 123

MacArthur, Douglas 40, 98n.12
Magruder, Carter 71
Magsaysay, Ramon 41
Mainland Affairs Council (MAC) 118
Mainstream 181n.38
Malacanang 126, 170
Malaysia 42, 76, 77, 95, 169
Manchurian Defense Force 30
Manila 41, 43, 82, 84, 85, 86
Mao Tse-tung 26, 36, 115
Marcos, Ferdinand 17, 40, 41, 60n.48, 101n.59, 190
Marcos, Imelda 85
martial law 17, 29, 31, 34, 39, 40, 41, 42, 43, 44, 45, 46, 51, 52, 55, 66, 72, 73, 74, 75, 77, 81, 82, 84, 85, 95, 116, 117, 124, 126, 127, 129, 165, 186, 189, 190, 191, 192, 193
Masjumi 49
Matalam Udtog 42
Matsu 37
Megawati Sukarnoputri 136, 173, 194
Middle Way doctrine 51, 52, 193
military
   civilian control of 1, 4, 8, 10, 13, 16, 18, 19, 87, 93, 97, 111, 114, 139, 152, 159, 165, 176, 177, 184, 185, 186, 188, 194, 195, 196, 197

cohesiveness 14, 15, 64, 86, 184
depoliticization of 3, 17, 118, 123, 151
institutional autonomy of 15, 109, 123, 134, 163, 165, 184
intervention in politics 2, 8, 10, 17, 18, 63, 184
political influence of 1, 16
political neutrality of 2, 29, 111, 135, 152, 153, 154, 160, 166, 177, 184, 195
professionalism 10, 15, 18, 46, 81, 82, 86, 87, 96, 123, 152, 177, 183, 184, 191
withdrawal 3, 14, 15, 18, 26, 33, 77, 81, 85, 91, 104, 107, 126, 132, 135, 139, 151, 170, 171, 186, 187, 190
Military Bases Agreement (MBA) 40
military-centric approach 9
military counterattack 37, 92, 94, 140
military dictatorship 1, 4, 6, 7, 17, 56, 63, 64, 65, 73, 94, 95, 105, 107, 109, 110, 111, 112, 113, 114, 151, 152
military domination 6, 16
military factors 9
Military Revolutionary Committee 71, 98n.21
Millennium Democratic Party (MDP) 157
Mindanao 41, 42, 129, 190, 192
Minjok Ilbo (People's Daily) 69
Minjung (people) movement 110, 114, 187
Moscow 38, 77
Murdani, Leonardus Benyamin 134
Muslim Independent Movement (MIM) 42
Muslim Islamic Liberation Front (MILF) 168
Muslim Moro National Liberation Front (MNLF) 40, 42, 46, 54, 83, 85, 124, 126, 128, 129, 166, 190, 191, 192
   peace agreement with Ramos government 168
Mutual Defense Treaty 27, 37, 38, 40, 91
Myanmar 1

Nahdlatul Ulama (NU) 49, 75, 76
Nasacom 75

Nasution, Abdul Haris 49, 50, 74, 77, 193
National Affairs Conference (NAC) 118, 161
National Coalition for a Democratic Constitution (NCDC) 106
National Consultative Assembly 78
National Democratic Front (NDF) 128, 129, 165, 168, 191
National Intelligence Coordinating Agency (NICA) 83
National Movement for Free Elections (NAMFREL) 125
National Police Commission (NPC) 46
National Security Law 26, 65
National Unification Commission (NUC) 168
New Democratic Party (NDP) 68
New Korean Democratic Party (NKDP) 106
Newly Industrialized Economies (NIEs) 90
New Order 53, 78–80, 131, 134, 138, 173, 174, 193
  end of 132–3
New Party 117, 123
New People's Army (NPA) 41, 82, 124, 166, 190
Nine-Point Unification Proposal 92
Nixon Doctrine 115
non-mainstream 121–2
Nordpolitik 109, 143n.14
Northern Limit Line 156
North-South Joint Declaration 156
Nuclear Non-Proliferation Treaty (NPT) 157
Nuclear Weapon States (NWS) 157
Nur Misuari 168

Oakwood coup 170
objective control 8
October Affair 49
One China Policy 161, 164
OPEC 80
Organisasi Papua Merdeka (OPM, Free Papua Organization) 138

Pacific War 23, 24, 30, 31, 33, 40
Pancasila (five principles) 50, 135
Park Jong-cheol 107
Park Jung-hee 29, 65, 70, 71, 72, 73, 95, 104, 112, 187
Parliament of the Streets 85
Partai Komunis Indonesia (PKI) 53, 80, 193
  and ABRI 74–8, 95
Partai Nasional Indonesia (PNI) 49, 51, 74, 75, 76
Partai Sosialis Indonesia (PSI) 51
Participation 7, 8, 14, 17, 29, 41, 52, 63, 67, 68, 80, 82, 86, 94, 103, 113, 116, 151, 152, 153, 177, 183, 193
Party for Peace and Democracy (PPD) 108, 110
Peace Offensive 163
Peng Ming-min 35, 123
People Power 165, 166, 170, 191
People's Consultative Assembly 78, 171
People's Liberation Army (PLA) 33, 36, 37, 38, 91, 164, 188
People's Representative Council 131, 133, 136
personalistic control 81, 82, 86, 96, 124, 191
Peta 47, 48
Philippine Catholic Church 124
Philippine Constabulary (PC) 43, 45, 82, 83
Philippine Military Academy (PMA) 46, 83, 86, 96, 125, 130, 192
political commissar system 87, 89, 93, 97, 115, 123, 163, 190
political development 1, 2, 3–4, 14
  Indonesia 47, 64
  Republic of China 114
  Taiwan 87, 120, 161
praetorianism 8
praetorian problem 111, 151, 158
praetorian state 6
prerogatives 4, 6, 75, 108, 111, 138, 140, 196
Presidential Security Command (PSC) 45, 82, 83

professionalism 15, 18, 46, 81, 82, 86, 87, 96, 123, 152, 177, 183, 184, 191
pull factors 9
purification campaign 70, 187
push factors 9
Pyongyang 156

Qing Dynasty 32, 58n.18, 117
quasi-civilianization 7, 71, 105, 107
quasi-military government 105, 107, 114
Quemoy 37, 38, 188

'rally around the flag' effect 10, 28
Ramos, Fidel V. 45, 81, 82, 83, 86, 96, 104, 126, 127, 130, 166, 168, 169, 170, 191, 192
Rapprochement 72, 91, 92, 115
Reagan, Ronald 105, 107
Real-Name Financial Transaction System 112
red-and-white faction 134
Reform the Armed Forces of the Philippines Movement (RAM) 46, 96, 123–4, 125, 126, 191, 192
  rise of 86–7
  support for pro-democracy forces 127–8
Republic of Korea (ROK) see Korea, South
Reunification Democratic Party (RDP) 108, 110
Reyes, Angelo T. 170
Rhee Syngman 24, 25, 26, 64, 95, 186, 187
Roh Moo-hyun 153, 158, 159
Roh Tae-woo 105, 106, 107, 109, 110, 111, 112, 113, 114, 188
ROTC 83, 96

Second Republic 32, 67, 68, 69, 70, 113
Seo Wan-su 112
Seoul 27, 66, 73, 107, 156
Seoul Olympic Games 107
separatist movements 137–8
Shanghai Joint Communiqué 91, 164
Singson, Luis "Chavit" 169

Sison, Jose Maria 41, 128, 191
Song Yo-chan 66
Southeast Asia 1, 2, 47, 76, 91
Southeast Asia Treaty Organization (SEATO) 76
Southern Europe 2
Soviet Union 24, 36, 57n.10, 59, 89, 109, 154
Stalin, Joseph 27, 36
State Affairs Council 67
State Information Agency 173
Stepan, Alfred 6, 10
structured-focused analysis 3, 152
Subianto, Prabowo 134
subordination 3, 6, 7, 14, 151, 152, 186
Suharto, Haji Mohammad 47, 131, 193
Sukarno, Achmad 24, 47, 48, 49, 50, 51, 52, 53, 55, 64, 74, 75, 76, 77, 78, 95, 131, 135, 173, 192, 193
Sunshine policy 156, 157, 195
Sun Yat-sen 38, 59, 88, 89
Sutarto, Endriartondono 138
synthetic approach 9

Taipei 33, 91, 92, 117
Taiwan (Republic of China on Taiwan) 17, 24, 54
Taiwan Garrison Command (TGC) 39, 118, 160, 189
Taiwanization 35, 93–4, 116, 117, 120, 190
Taiwan Straits 36, 37, 91, 115, 119, 140, 163, 164, 165, 176
Tan, Lucio 169
Tangwai 116, 120, 161
Tanjung, Feisal 134
Temporary Provisions 118
territorial command 74, 134
Thailand 1, 132
Three Exchanges 92
three ifs 164
three Kims 159
Three Principles of the People 89
transplacement 108, 153
Treaty of Friendship, Commerce and Navigation 91

Truman, Harry S. 36
twelve disciples 45, 81
Two State Doctrine 164

unilateral action (aski sepihak) 76, 193
United Democratic Opposition (UNIDO) 125
United Nations Command (UNC) 27
United States 24, 25, 26, 28, 30, 32, 35, 36, 37, 38, 40, 44, 69, 71, 76, 77, 78, 83, 85, 91, 95, 107, 109, 112, 115, 140, 153, 157, 158, 164, 178n.9, 190, 193
    Mutual Defense Treaty with South Korea 27
University of the Philippines 41
Untung bin Syamsuri 78

Ver, Fabian 45
Ver, Irwin 83
Ver, Rexor 83
Ver, Wyrlo 83

veto power 7, 32, 49, 114, 130
Vietnam War 72
violence, interethnic 137, 138

Wahid, Abdurrahman 136, 171, 194
Washington Post 116
West Irian 75, 76, 77
West Point 83
Whampoa Military Academy 38, 55, 59n.33, 189
Wirahadikusumah, Agus 136
Wiranto 133, 134, 136, 171, 174
World War II 1, 4, 33, 47, 48, 54, 188

Yani, Ahmad 77
Yi Ki-bung 66
Yosoyadae 110, 157
Youngnam 159
Yuan 34, 58, 88, 116, 117, 118, 121, 122, 123
Yushin (revitalization) 65, 72, 187